KINER'S KORNER

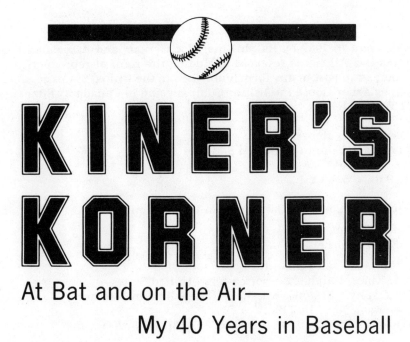

KINER'S KORNER

At Bat and on the Air— My 40 Years in Baseball

Ralph Kiner

with Joe Gergen

An Associated Features Book

ARBOR HOUSE
NEW YORK

Designed by Robert Bull
Manufactured in the United States of America

10 9 8 7 6 5 4 3 2 1

Library of Congress Cataloging-in-Publication Data

Kiner, Ralph.
  Kiner's korner.

  "An Associated Features book."
  1. Kiner, Ralph.   2. Sportcasters—United States—
Biography.   3. New York Mets (Baseball team)—History.
I. Gergen, Joe.   II. Title.
GV742.42.K56A3   1987   796.357'092'4 [B]   86–32290

ISBN: 0-87795-881-5

To my mother, Beatrice Kiner. She liked to call herself Cinderella, but it was I who attended the ball. It was her dedication and perseverance in the most difficult of times that made it possible for me to achieve my dream of becoming a major-league baseball player.

Contents

Foreword   ix

Solid Gold   1
     IN KINER'S KORNER: My Best Man   11
The Birth of a Franchise   16
     IN KINER'S KORNER: Branch Rickey   22
Casey   26
     IN KINER'S KORNER: Growing Up   32
Starting at the Bottom   37
     IN KINER'S KORNER: Choo Choo and The Beagle   48
Farewell to the Polo Grounds   52
     IN KINER'S KORNER: Breaking In   60
Shea Hey   65
     IN KINER'S KORNER: The Celebrity Game   80
A Terrific Future   85
     IN KINER'S KORNER: Small World   96
The Quiet Man   99
     IN KINER'S KORNER: Gil and Me   108
The First Championship   112
     IN KINER'S KORNER: Afterglow   125
Downfall   129
     IN KINER'S KORNER: Yogi   139
"You Gotta Believe!"   142
     IN KINER'S KORNER: Home Runs   158

The End of an Era   163

  IN KINER'S KORNER: Making the Hall of Fame   176

"Welcome to Grant's Tomb"   181

  IN KINER'S KORNER: Three for the Show   191

Mr. Baseball   195

  IN KINER'S KORNER: "Git on Your Mule, Son" 208

A Tale of Two Pitchers   212

  IN KINER'S KORNER: Love and Marriage   224

The Silver Season   228

Epilogue   236

Ralph Kiner's Major-League Record   239

Foreword

For me, it started on a golf course. That might seem like an unusual place to begin an association with a baseball team, but then, as the world was soon to discover, this was no ordinary baseball team. This was the New York Mets.

At the time, the Mets were nothing more than a collection of bats, balls, and 22 players drafted at extravagant cost from the roster of other National League teams. They had yet to lose a game, which is to say they had yet to play a game. The 1962 season would be their first.

There were many matters for officials of the expansion franchise to attend to in the winter of 1961. These included the signing of players, the renovation of a ballpark (the Polo Grounds), and the preparation of a spring training camp. Among the items on the agenda, ranking somewhere between printing tickets and designing uniforms, was the selection of three announcers for the club's radio and television broadcasts. I hadn't even thought to apply.

Broadcasting was still a relatively new occupation for me. After hitting the last of my 369 major-league home runs for the 1955 Cleveland Indians, I had accepted the position of general manager of the San Diego Padres in the Pacific Coast League.

At the time, the PCL was the strongest of the minor leagues, with enough support to consider, however briefly, the establishment of a third major league on its foundation. But in 1957, Walter O'Malley formulated plans to transfer the Dodgers from

Brooklyn to Los Angeles and Horace Stoneham's Giants were permitted to accompany them west on a second Gold Rush. Once the pride of New York, the Giants resettled in San Francisco. With the arrival of the National League teams on the West Coast for the start of the 1958 season, the PCL lapsed into decline.

The fans, once so numerous, dwindled to a precious few. Finally, it reached the point where I'd receive a phone call asking, "What time is the game today?" and feel compelled to answer, "What time can you make it?"

In 1960, on the occasion of the Pittsburgh Pirates' first pennant in 33 years, I was invited back to the town where I had enjoyed the most productive seven seasons of my career to host a local television show following each game of the World Series. That led to a radio broadcasting job with the Chicago White Sox in 1961. And that, in turn, was responsible for the assignment that would change my life.

The event was the Bing Crosby National Pro-Amateur golf tournament, which spectators and competitors alike called the Clambake, held on the Monterey Peninsula in California. I had been selected to conduct brief interviews with the pros and their celebrated partners for a national telecast. My preparation was interrupted by a telephone call from George Weiss.

Weiss has been the man behind the New York Yankees' dynasty. As general manager, he had presided over the team that won a remarkable 10 American League pennants in 12 years. Then, in the wake of the team's seven-game loss to the Pirates in the 1960 Series, he was discharged along with his handpicked manager, Casey Stengel. The Yankees decided they were too old. Weiss was 66, Stengel 70.

Among the first men to be hired by the Mets the following year was George Weiss. He was given the title of president. Naturally, he hired Stengel as manager. When Weiss reached me on the telephone in California, he was brief and business-like, as was his custom.

"Would you be interested in broadcasting the New York Mets' games?" he asked on that afternoon in January 1962.

For once, I was equally terse. "Yes," I replied.

The remainder of the conversation concerned the major sponsor of the broadcasts and its advertising agency. Weiss said officials of both organizations would be watching my performance on television the following day. With their approval, he said, the job was mine.

My nerves were particularly active the next afternoon as I stood just behind the 18th green at Pebble Beach Golf Course, exchanging small talk with touring pros as well as the movie stars and show business personalities who lent the Crosby tournament its distinctive nature. Still, the interviews were proceeding smoothly, and I felt I had created the correct impression for the jury seated 3,000 miles away in New York.

It was time for the last interview of the day. The principals were Gay Brewer, the leading professional in the tournament, and Phil Harris, a bandleader and comedian, not necessarily in that order. I was the man in the middle. It went like this:

"I'm talking to Gay Brewer, who is the leader in the clubhouse. Gay, congratulations on your fine round today."

Then, turning to Harris, a friend of long-standing and a neighbor of mine in Palm Springs, I said, "Phil, you know Gay Brewer, don't you?"

"Gay Brewer?" he said. "I thought he was a fag winemaker from Modesto."

I managed to stay on my feet for the completion of the interview, but I was certain I'd be in the market for another job in 1962 despite Harris's contention that "you're only on the air for a short time, and you've got to grab the audience's attention."

My fears were groundless. The sponsor and ad agency were both pleased with the way I had reacted to a difficult situation, reasoning that if I could handle Harris, I could handle anything that might crop up in the course of a baseball game. I was set to embark on a new career.

The years I had spent on losing teams in Pittsburgh were to serve me well those first few seasons with the Mets, when they set records for ineptitude. And it made what followed in 1969, 1973, and, especially, 1986 all the more gratifying. My quarter-century of association with the club has made me party to grinding defeat and glorious triumph, to tragedy and exultation.

The Mets have covered the full spectrum of human achievements and emotions in those 25 years, culminating with a silver anniversary season that was pure gold. I feel fortunate and proud to have been along for the ride.

Solid Gold

Official attendance at my 64th birthday party was 55,032. If you want to share such an experience with that many people, I recommend the seventh game of the World Series. That's what I did in 1986 when the Mets played the Red Sox at Shea Stadium.

Of course, that wasn't the plan. Even after 25 years as a broadcaster with the Mets, I wouldn't count on such consideration. In fact, according to the schedule worked out by the baseball commissioner's office, the 1986 World Series was to end on Oct. 26 even if it went the full seven games. My birthday is Oct. 27.

An all-day rain on the 26th, however, postponed the seventh game to the following night, enabling players and fans alike to replay the astounding sixth game for another day and presenting me with an unexpected birthday opportunity. The Mets were one victory away from a second World Championship.

Getting there hadn't been easy. Although they dominated the National League East during the regular season, taking over first place on April 23 and never relinquishing control en route to a record-equaling 108 victories, the Mets encountered major resistance in the post-season.

First, they struggled mightily to overcome the Houston As-

1

tros in a six-game NL championship series. Three of their victories required extra innings, and the sixth game, perhaps the finest and certainly the longest post-season game in major-league history, lasted 16 nerve-wracking innings. Then they fell behind the Boston Red Sox, two games to none and three games to two, in the World Series and were down to their final strike in Game Six before a rally, which had to be seen to be believed, forced a seventh game.

For those who complained that the regular season had lacked tension and drama—and the 2,762,417 fans who set a New York City major-league attendance record weren't among them—the playoffs and Series had been a revelation. And there was still one game to play, one game to decide whether everything that preceded it had been in vain.

In a year of astonishing success, the Mets began post-season play with a failure. They failed to score a run off Mike Scott and suffered a 1-0 defeat in the Astrodome. Scott had been the second pick of the Mets in the 1976 draft and had spent parts of four seasons in a New York uniform at a time when both the club and pitcher were searching for a way to win.

It was only after his second full season with the Astros that Scott made his discovery. During the winter before the 1985 season, he was taught the split-finger fastball by pitching guru Roger Craig and responded with an 18-8 record. Scott was even better in 1986, although he won the same number of games and lost 10. The man led the major leagues with 306 strikeouts and a 2.22 earned-run average and pitched a no-hitter in the division-clinching victory over the San Francisco Giants, managed by none other than Roger Craig.

After Scott yielded only five singles and struck out 14 in besting Dwight Gooden on Oct. 8, it was the opinion of the Mets that the Houston ace had added something more than the split-finger to his repertoire. Led by Gary Carter, they charged that he was doctoring the baseballs, scuffing them so that they would break sharply at the last possible instant. It was not the last time the Mets would air their complaints.

Glenn Davis's mammoth home run in the second inning provided the margin of victory. Although Gooden was touched for seven hits and walked three in seven innings, he escaped trouble on several occasions and pitched well enough to win most games. On the following night, Bob Ojeda also permitted one run and received credit for the victory when the Mets drove Nolan Ryan from the mound with a two-run burst in the fourth inning and a three-run rally in the fifth. The 5-1 triumph evened the series at one game apiece and set the stage for some theatrics at Shea Stadium.

The third game, staged in the early afternoon of Oct. 11, was only minutes old when the Astros grabbed a 4-0 lead against Ron Darling. Houston pitcher Bob Knepper appeared in complete command until the sixth inning when the Mets suddenly erupted for four runs, the last three on a home run by Darryl Strawberry. That tie didn't last a half inning as third baseman Ray Knight botched a sacrifice bunt attempt and the Astros edged ahead, 5-4, on an unearned run in the seventh inning.

The score stayed the same until the ninth when, after Wally Backman led off with a bunt single and reached second with one out, Lenny Dykstra drove a pitch by Astro relief ace Dave Smith over the right-field fence. Dykstra, who had entered the game as a pinch-hitter in the seventh inning and stayed to play center field, had hit only eight home runs during the season.

A crowd favorite in New York for his hustle and head-first style of play, Dykstra was serenaded by chants of "Len-ee, Len-ee!" as he rounded the bases and dove into a pile of teammates at home plate. "When I'm on my deathbed," said Keith Hernandez, the first baseman and unofficial captain of the Mets, "I'll be thinking, 'Len-ee, Len-ee!' "

No sooner had the shouting died than the Mets were howling again. Once again, the cause of their agony was Mike Scott. He stifled them on three singles while striking out five in a 3-1 Houston victory. When reporters entered the clubhouse after the game, Howard Johnson and Wally Backman presented a set of scuffed baseballs as evidence. Manager Dave Johnson opened a drawer in his desk to reveal still more balls scuffed in the same spot, allegedly by Scott.

Although they were to display their collection to umpire crew chief Doug Harvey and retiring National League president Chub Feeney before leaving New York, they didn't expect any action to be taken. All they knew was that the possibility of facing Scott a third time with the pennant at stake genuinely frightened them. "The idea is not to get to a seventh game," Johnson said. "I don't want to see him again."

To avoid the situation, the Mets would have to win the next

two games, the first scheduled for Monday afternoon at Shea Stadium and the second on Wednesday afternoon in the Astrodome. But first, rain intervened, postponing Game Five for a day. That game presented the best of all possible scenarios for Met fans old enough to remember when. They could rejoice in another stirring victory in extra innings and reminisce about a former championship team represented by a remarkable pitcher dressed in a strange uniform.

The date was Oct. 14. Seventeen years earlier to the day, Tommie Agee made two sensational catches to preserve a Met victory over the Baltimore Orioles in Game Three of the 1969 World Series. The second catch, with the bases loaded in the seventh inning, occurred in defense of a hard-throwing youngster named Nolan Ryan.

On Oct. 14, 1986, Agee and Ron Swoboda were invited to make the ceremonial first pitches before the game. Then Nolan Ryan walked to the mound to pitch for the Astros. Between then and now, the man had fashioned a legend. He had pitched five no-hitters, four on behalf of the California Angels and one for the Astros. He had raised the all-time major-league strikeout record to an astonishing 4,277. And now, at 39, he was trying to deny the Mets the opportunity of another World Series.

The odds certainly were against Ryan. Age wasn't the only factor. He had been bothered by elbow trouble for the first time in his career and he managed only one complete game all season. Although he had appeared as fast as ever in Game Two, he abruptly lost his velocity in the middle innings.

But the performer in Game Five was vintage Ryan. He worked nine innings, allowed two hits, walked only one batter, and struck out 12. "That's as good a game as Scott pitched," Backman said, "if not better."

Yet, it was not good enough. The first hit off Ryan was a fifth-inning homer by Strawberry which barely cleared the right-field fence and landed inches inside the foul pole. It tied the score at 1-1, and that's where it was when Ryan departed the game after nine innings, proud and undiminished. The Astros might have won in regulation had umpire Fred Brocklander not called Craig Reynolds out at first to complete an inning-ending double play in the second inning as a run crossed the plate. Replays indicated Reynolds was safe, and perhaps the run should have counted. "It very easily could have ended in nine," Ryan said. But it didn't.

It ended in the 12th when Gary Carter, battling a 1-for-17 slump, stroked a full-count pitch from Charlie Kerfeld up the middle with runners on first and second. Backman scored easily from second and Carter raised his arms in weary triumph. Then the Mets headed for the airport. They had a game the next afternoon in Houston.

Actually, it was more than a game. It was an epic. And I didn't see so much as one pitch.

In recent years, the Mets had split their broadcasting teams into radio and television. I was doing only television in 1986 and the major networks which handled the playoffs and World Series were now using their own announcers rather than employing a broadcaster from each home team, as they had done during the Mets' first two post-season trips in 1969 and 1973. I did fill in for my colleague Bob Murphy when he became ill before Game Two in Houston, but, other than that emergency radio assignment, my role was reduced to that of spectator in the biggest games of 1986.

My liberation from the broadcasting booth made me available as a last-minute replacement on a special Baseball Hall of Fame cruise aboard the Queen Elizabeth II sailing in the Caribbean. Earlier in the year, I had agreed to take the cruise on the condition the Mets did not reach the playoffs. However, another invited guest, Yogi Berra, had to decline because he was a coach on the Astros, and Arthur Richman, a Met executive who was a cruise director, had to beg off because of his duties. I was asked to fill in for a couple of days.

So, while the Mets were preparing to play Game Six in Houston, I accompanied my wife, DiAnn, on a flight to Puerto Rico, where we picked up the cruise, already in progress. It was on the QE II, in the company of fellow Hall of Famers Ernie Banks and Monte Irvin, that I heard the conclusion of the playoffs on a ship-to-shore radio signal which kept fading in and out.

As they had at the start of the series, the Mets quickly fell behind. Houston scored three runs off Ojeda in the first and, as Knepper mowed down the Mets inning after inning, it seemed their worst fears would be realized: a climactic seventh game against Mike Scott. They had managed only two hits off Knepper when Dykstra came up to bat for relief pitcher Rick Aguilera in the ninth.

In sending up the left-handed Dykstra to bat against the left-handed Knepper, Johnson was thumbing his nose at baseball's conventional wisdom. But he had done that all year, with stunning success. Dykstra made the move appear inspired when he promptly tripled to right-center field. Mookie Wilson's single drove in the Mets' first run. He advanced to second on Kevin Mitchell's groundout, then scored on a clutch double by Hernandez. Hal Lanier, the Astros' manager, replaced Knepper with Smith.

Smith, looking no steadier than he had in Game Three, walked Carter and Strawberry, loading the bases. Ray Knight's sacrifice fly to right field tied the score and sent the game into extra innings. Johnson sent Roger McDowell, his best right-handed relief pitcher, to the mound. He was superb, yielding only one hit and no runs over the next five innings.

It was the 14th when the Mets made their move, taking a 4-3 lead against Aurelio Lopez on a single by Carter, a walk to Strawberry, and Backman's one-out single. But Jesse Orosco, working his first inning of relief, was tagged for a one-out home run off the left-field foul pole by Billy Hatcher in the bottom of the inning. The game went on.

In the fifth hour and 16th inning of play, Strawberry doubled. Knight, enjoying a marvelous comeback season, asked Johnson if the manager wanted a sacrifice bunt. "Hit a drive to right field and get him in," Johnson said.

"I can do that," Knight replied. And he did, singling to right center to drive in the tie-breaking run. The Mets scored twice more, the first on a wild pitch and the second on Dykstra's single, and that was fortunate. Because the Astros rallied for two runs in the bottom of the inning and had baserunners at first and second with two out and Kevin Bass at the plate.

Two innings earlier, Hatcher had smashed an Orosco fastball. Now, with Bass about to hit, Hernandez walked down from his position at first to remind Carter. "You call any fastballs," he said, "and I'll come to the plate and we'll fight."

Carter had no intention of calling fastballs. He stayed with the slider, and Orosco bent one under Bass's bat with the count full at 3-2. The Mets had won the marathon, 7-6, and Orosco flung his glove toward the roof of the Dome. The game consumed 16 innings and 4 hours and 42 minutes, both post-season records.

We had champagne on the QE II just like they had in the visitors' clubhouse at the Astrodome. The difference was we drank ours.

I was present and accounted for at Shea Stadium for the World Series opener against the Boston Red Sox, who had survived a playoff ordeal against the California Angels. The Mets, however, seemed to be lost at sea.

The six games against the Astros, especially the last one, appeared to have drained the energy from them. They lost the first game, 1-0, just as they had done against Houston. The culprit this time was wearing a New York uniform. Tim Teuful permitted a routine grounder hit by Rich Gedman to bounce through his legs in the seventh inning. Jim Rice, who had walked and reached second on a wild pitch, scored the only run on the error. Left-hander Bruce Hurst, with relief help from ex-Met Calvin Schiraldi in the ninth, gained the victory. Ron Darling, who pitched equally as well, was saddled with the defeat.

Although the pitching matchup of the series was expected the following night, the second game was a drab affair. Neither Gooden nor Roger Clemens, the strikeout ace of the Red Sox' staff, had his best stuff. Clemens didn't last five innings. Gooden did, and that may have been a mistake. Dwight Evans's two-run homer in the fifth, after Johnson had declined to pinch-hit for Gooden with the bases loaded in the fourth, padded Boston's lead to 6-2, and the Red Sox won comfortably, 9-3.

Only once before in the history of the World Series had a team lost the first two games at home and still triumphed. Of course, that turnaround had been performed only the previous year, when the Kansas City Royals rallied to defeat the St. Louis Cardinals. To a man, the Mets said they were fully capable of such a comeback.

The manager bolstered their confidence and gave them some needed rest by canceling a workout at Fenway Park, the misshapen ballpark they had seen only once before, during an exhibition game in early September. And they responded boldly in Tuesday night's third game. Once again, Dykstra got them started, this time with a stunning leadoff home run. The

Mets raked Dennis (Oil Can) Boyd for four runs in the first inning, and the Red Sox even botched a rundown play with three of the Mets' slowest men—Hernandez, Carter, and Knight —on the bases.

Ojeda, who had been traded to the Mets from Boston for Schiraldi and Wes Gardner the previous winter, enjoyed his homecoming immensely. He pitched five-hit ball for seven innings and was credited with the 7-1 victory. Darling, the right-hander from Yale, made a homecoming of his own the following night. The Met pitcher had attended high school in the area and spent many nights in the center-field bleachers at Fenway Park. He was also superb, yielding only four hits in seven innings. Gary Carter hit a pair of homers, and Dykstra hit his second in two games, a long drive which bounced off Evans's glove and into the bullpen, in a 6-2 romp.

Through four games, the home team hadn't led even once in the Series. As a result, both Shea and Fenway had been quiet retreats. In Game Five, however, the Red Sox, with the help of shoddy Met fielding, nicked Gooden for runs in the second and third innings and the decibel count of the Series rose. Boston added two runs in the fifth, knocking out Gooden en route to a 4-2 victory which wasn't as close as the score indicated. Again, Hurst was outstanding. The Boston fans spent the final minutes of the game taunting Darryl Strawberry, who seemed thoroughly confused at bat.

While the baseball writers analyzed Gooden's decline, the Mets and Red Sox both prepared for Saturday night's sixth game at Shea by taking off on Friday. Both teams were tired, according to their managers. What happened next is something neither the Mets nor the Red Sox will ever forget. A part-time actor in daytime soap operas parachuted onto the field, uninvited, and into custody at the start of Game Six. The bizarre beginning would be topped by later developments.

Boston held a 2-0 lead in the fifth inning when a walk to Strawberry, a stolen base, singles by Knight and Mookie Wilson, and a double-play grounder enabled the Mets to tie the game. The Red Sox pushed across an unearned run in the seventh on Knight's error, but the Mets battled back again in the eighth, scoring on Carter's sacrifice fly with the bases loaded. The starting pitchers, Clemens for the Red Sox and Ojeda for the Mets, were long gone by the 10th inning.

Dave Henderson, who had saved the Red Sox from defeat in the playoffs with a two-out, two-strike home run, greeted Aguilera with a leadoff homer. Boston scored another run on a double by Wade Boggs and Marty Barrett's single, his 12th hit of the Series, making the score 5-3. When Schiraldi retired the first two batters in the bottom of the inning, the Sox were one out away from their first World Championship in 68 years.

The batter was Carter, who thrived in pressure situations. "I didn't want to make the last out," he recalled, "and have to think about it until spring training." He didn't. He singled. Kevin Mitchell, a rookie who had played several positions and hit well wherever he played, followed with a pinch-hit single. Now the batter was Knight. Schiraldi, the former Met, got two quick strikes, but Knight deposited the next pitch safely into center field, cutting the Boston lead to one run. John McNamara, the Red Sox' manager, replaced Schiraldi with veteran Bob Stanley.

Stanley worked the count on Mookie Wilson to 2-2. Then he tried to come inside with a tailing fastball. However, it was too far inside. Wilson vaulted over the pitch, and Rich Gedman, the catcher, couldn't prevent it from sailing to the backstop. The tying run scored from third and Shea Stadium shook with cheers. On a full count, Wilson hit a soft ground ball directly at first baseman Bill Buckner. The usually sure-handed veteran had been playing with two damaged ankles and had given way to a defensive replacement when the Sox led in earlier games. But this time, McNamara left him in and the ball trickled through Buckner's legs enabling Knight to score.

Somehow, the Mets had won, 6-5. In the 25-year history of the Mets, nothing had happened to equal this moment. Not the black cat that walked in front of the Cubs' bench during their critical series late in the 1969 season; not the shoe-polish incident that helped the Mets defeat the Orioles in the World Series that year; not the drive that hit the crown of the fence during the 1973 pennant race and popped into Cleon Jones's hands. Nothing could compare to the finish of Game Six of the 1986 World Series.

With both teams within one victory of a World Championship, rain the next day pushed the finale back to Monday night, Oct. 27, my birthday. I wore a new cashmere sweater, a birthday present from my wife, DiAnn, to the game that night. Once again, the Mets fell behind as Boston tagged Darling for three runs in the second inning, including back-to-back homers by Evans and Gedman.

The rainout had presented McNamara with the opportunity to bring back Hurst on three days' rest, bypassing the erratic Boyd. Hurst appeared in championship form again, breezing through five innings while allowing only one hit. Of course, the Red Sox had the ghosts of past disappointments to contend with. In their previous World Series engagement, they carried a 3-0 lead into the sixth inning of the seventh game against the Cincinnati Reds in 1975, only to lose. Hurst walked to the mound in the sixth with a 3-0 lead.

By the time he walked off, the score was tied at 3-3. Lee Mazzilli, a star in the Mets' dreariest years who had been reclaimed from the Pirates late in the season, started the rally with a pinch-hit single. A single by Wilson and a walk to Backman preceded a two-run single by Hernandez. A third run scored on Carter's pop to short right which an alert Evans turned into a force at second base.

In the seventh, Roger McDowell replaced Sid Fernandez, who had pitched a spectacular 2⅓ innings of middle relief, and retired the Sox in order. Schiraldi was McNamara's choice to succeed Hurst, and he was greeted by Knight's leadoff home run. The Mets were ahead. They scored twice more in the inning. Then Orosco came on in the eighth to strand the tying run at second base after Evans had doubled in a pair of runs.

Strawberry's home run was the key blow in a two-run eighth, and Orosco nailed down an 8-5 victory and a second World Championship for the Mets by retiring the side in the ninth. As he had in Houston, he punctuated his performance with a strikeout.

With the 116th victory of their 25th year, the Mets had fulfilled their own great expectations. And, coincidentally, they had given me a 25-carat birthday present I will remember for the rest of my life.

My Best Man

I suppose it was fitting that I heard the news at a ball-park. It was baseball that first brought us together 39 years earlier. It was baseball that was the common denominator in our lives. And it was during the telecast of a baseball game that I said goodbye to Hank Greenberg.

His death was the one sad note in a season of great joy. Not only had Greenberg been a wonderful mentor and a splendid role model but he had been my good friend since our paths crossed in spring training of 1947. He was the single greatest influence on my career and my adult life. I feel blessed to have had his counsel and to have been in his company.

Greenberg had been suffering from cancer for about a year, although I only discovered that after he passed away on Sept. 4, 1986 at his home in Beverly Hills. He was never the type to complain, and that's the way he wanted it to remain. Although we had stayed in touch by telephone throughout the winter, I was unable to see him as I always did during the Mets' two trips to Los Angeles in 1986. I was told he had become a hermit in order to work on his memoirs.

There had been rumors about his health. I was concerned, but his relatives insisted that, other than a bad back, he was well. I suspected otherwise. We were in Boston's Fenway Park to play an exhibition game against the Red Sox in what would be a sneak preview of the World Series when the truth became public.

Jay Horwitz, the Mets' director of public relations, came up to me as I got off the air in the third inning and said, "Ralph, I hope I'm not the first one to tell you this, but it just came over the wires that Hank Greenberg has died." He added that a reporter for The Associated Press wanted a reaction from me. I accommodated the man, and when I resumed my place behind the microphone, I said, "I've just heard the saddest news I could possibly have heard." And I informed the Mets' television audience of what Greenberg had meant to me and the game of baseball.

He had been one of the heroes of my youth, which was spent in Southern California. My first awareness of major-league baseball was the broadcast of the 1933 World Series between the New York Giants and the Washington Senators. By the 1934 Series, I was infatuated. That series featured the Detroit Tigers and the St. Louis Cardinals. Greenberg was a star of the Tigers.

I don't know why I took a fancy to the Tigers, but I did. I could name all the players on that team. It was the team of Charlie Gehringer, Schoolboy Rowe, Tommy Bridges, and, mostly, Hank Greenberg. Not that he was my favorite player. Babe Ruth was still Number One, but Hank was right up there.

Certainly, the man enjoyed a remarkable career. He drove in an astonishing 183 runs in 1937, and the following year he hit 58 home runs. And after he was discharged from the service in the summer of 1945, all he did was hit a grand slam on the final day of the season to clinch another American League pennant for the Tigers. He even led the league with 44 homers in 1946, at the age of 35.

Understandably, I was thrilled when the Pirates acquired him in 1947 with the promise of a huge salary and a thoroughbred racehorse donated by Darby Dan Farm, whose owner, John Galbreath, was a minority stockholder in the baseball team. Since I had led the National League with 23 homers in 1946, we were asked to pose together for pictures on the first day of spring training. He said, "Let's go out to dinner." Hank had recently married Carol Gimbel, heiress to the department-store chain, and the three of us dined that night at one of the posher restaurants in west Florida.

He lived first class, and he taught me to do the same. But once at the ballpark, no one worked harder. On that very first day of spring training—a day usually devoted to trying on the uniform, running a couple of laps around the field, and smiling for the cameras—he took extra batting practice. Naturally, so did I.

That was my first lesson. He did a lot of work with me that spring. I had spent the previous winter—and it seems ludicrous to me now—hitting hundreds of balls to right field in an attempt to cut down on my strikeouts. I thought that was the answer. Greenberg straightened me out in a hurry. He moved me from way back in the batter's box to a spot on top of home plate, where I would be able to pull even pitches on the outside corner and utilize my home-run power.

The theory was excellent. My execution was something less. After two months of the season, I had hit the grand total of three home runs. The low point occurred in a game against the Chicago Cubs when I struck out four times against Hank Borowy. My confidence was shaken, and manager Billy Herman wanted to demote me to the minors.

That's when Hank intervened. He went to Frank McKinney, then the majority stockholder in the Pirates, and told him not to send me out, that I still was capable of having a terrific season. In fact, he bet McKinney a suit of clothes that I would finish with 30 home runs.

At the time, it seemed like a terrible gamble. But he knew hitting and he knew what was inside me. Well, I hit a pair of home runs on June 1, and from that day until the end of the season, I hit 48, a four-month stretch that topped anything in the major leagues before or since. I finished the year with a .313 average and 51 homers. For my achievement, he bought me a money clip with the number 51. I'll never forget that.

I flew home with Hank from Pittsburgh to New York after his last major-league game. It remains a sweet memory.

He had invited me to be his guest at the 1947 World Series between the New York Yankees and the Brooklyn Dodgers, a treat for me. Hank had an apartment on Park Avenue, and I would visit him whenever the Pirates came to town after he retired from baseball. He went into the brokerage business and I went on with my baseball career, but we continued our friendship.

When I married Nancy Chaffee, I asked him to be the best man at our wedding. In fact, he served as best man at my first two weddings. When I mentioned my plans to marry my present wife, DiAnn, he said he wasn't going to be held responsible a third time. I told him it wasn't necessary, that I wasn't going to ask him this time. Actually, it was a very small wedding and I didn't have a best man. But Hank and his wife, Mary Jo, did attend. It just wouldn't have been the same without him.

Shortly after my first marriage, Hank and I found ourselves on opposite sides of a table at baseball's winter meetings. By then, he was affiliated with the management of the Cleveland Indians. I was the player representative for the National League, and Allie Reynolds of the Yankees held the same position in the American League.

The year was 1952. For the first time, the players were attempting to bring an attorney, J. Norman Lewis, into negotiations for the pension plan that had originally been enacted five years earlier. The owners refused to allow his presence. We walked out. They then softened their position, but it wasn't until they appointed Greenberg and Galbreath, who by then had become the majority owner of the Pirates, to sit down with the three of us that a compromise was effected.

Hank was also responsible for my first full-time broadcasting job. In 1961, I received similar offers from the Cincinnati Reds and the Chicago White Sox. Largely because of Hank, who had joined Bill Veeck in operating the White Sox, I chose Chicago. I knew he wouldn't steer me wrong, and he didn't. The following year, I was contacted by the Mets. The rest is history.

Once I took the Mets' job, Hank convinced me I should live in New York year-round. Ironically, the year I finally chose to move to the metropolitan area, he packed up his apartment on Park Avenue and moved to Southern California. Still, we remained the best of friends. His standards were very high, and his were the standards by which I chose to conduct myself.

Our only year as teammates, 1947, happened to be a momentous year for baseball. It marked the debut of Jackie Robinson with the Dodgers. As the first black man in the major leagues, he suffered some cruel taunts and insults. It was only later that I learned that Hank had fortified Jackie.

Jackie was playing first base when we met the Dodgers for the first time that season. Robinson singled through the jeers and stood next to Greenberg. "Don't let them get you down," Hank told Robinson. "You're doing fine. Keep it up." Afterward, Robinson said Hank was the first opposing player to offer encouragement.

That was Hank Greenberg. He had a better idea than most what Jackie was going through. He, too, had been singled out for slurs, hate mail, and death threats as a prominent Jew in the 1930s. It was even said by some that Hank was a victim of anti-Semitism when he reached 58 home runs with five games to play in 1938, after which no one gave him a decent pitch to hit. I do know, if it was true, Hank never said he was cheated. That would have been a cop-out. Hank taught me to live with dignity and class.

Despite his bearing, he was a tough, hard-nosed guy. He never started a fight, but he finished quite a few, occasionally against one of his own teammates. He faced prejudice head-on and never backed down.

At a memorial service for Hank held in November 1986 at the Wadsworth Theater in West Los Angeles, actor Walter Matthau recalled the time Hank and some fellow soldiers were seated in a nightclub during the war. A loud patron inspired by one too many drinks stood up and shouted: "Anybody here named Ginsberg, Rosenberg, or Goldberg?" No one moved.

Finally, after a dramatic pause, Henry Louis Greenberg, all 6 feet 4 inches and 220 pounds, arose from his chair. "I'm Greenberg," he said. "Will I do?"

The sneer disappeared from the patron's lips. "No," he said, nervously. "I'm looking for a Ginsberg, a Rosenberg, or a Goldberg."

Steve Greenberg said he once asked his father for an autographed picture to hang in his office. The picture was delivered a few days later. It bore the inscription: "To Steve: Rudyard Kipling said it all." The inscription referred to Kipling's famous poem, "If," which ends with the phrase, ". . . then you will be a man, my son."

To me, one person was the embodiment of that poem. It was my best man, Hank Greenberg.

The Birth of a Franchise

From today's perspective, it is difficult to conceive of New York without the Mets. Imagine what it must have been like for New Yorkers to face the summer without a single National League team. That was the state of affairs in the nation's largest city in 1958.

National League baseball had thrived in New York since the turn of the century, and suddenly, where there had been two teams, there were none. The flight of the Dodgers and Giants following the 1957 season left a large void in the Big Apple. The Yankees were still in the Bronx, of course, but they might as well have been in Tibet as far as patrons of Ebbets Field and the Polo Grounds were concerned. Embrace an American League team? Never.

Mayor Robert F. Wagner knew a political liability when he saw one. Soon after the Dodgers and Giants made their breaks with the city, he contacted William A. Shea, a prominent attorney, a personal friend, and a political ally. Wagner appointed Shea chairman of a select four-man committee charged with bringing National League baseball back to New York.

Bill Shea was a former athlete, skilled enough at basketball to have earned a scholarship to New York University. Upon graduation from Georgetown University Law School, he joined the firm that handled the legal affairs of the Brooklyn Trust Company. It so happened that the bank, headed by George McLaughlin, served as administrator of the debt-ridden Dodgers for the Ebbets and McKeever estates. Among Shea's colleagues in the firm was Walter O'Malley.

The job of overseeing the operations of the Dodgers might have fallen to Shea. Instead, it went to O'Malley, who was older and more interested in business than the practice of law. In time, O'Malley acquired a controlling interest in the team. And then one day, he and his team were gone.

At first, Shea thought it would be simple to lure another National League team to New York. There was the promise of a new municipal stadium to be constructed in Flushing Meadow, Queens, adjacent to the site of the 1938–39 World's Fair. And there was a ready-made fandom of considerable size. He sat back and waited for volunteers from among baseball's marginal franchises. None came forward.

So Shea began a hard sell. He contacted the Cincinnati Reds, Pittsburgh Pirates, and Philadelphia Phillies, teams with old ballparks and declining attendances. The Reds and Pirates expressed some interest but decided to stay where they were for a variety of reasons. The task was going to be more challenging than Shea had envisioned.

His next plan of action was to persuade baseball to expand, including in its plans an NL club for New York. The catch was that an expansion partner would have to be found so the league would be evenly balanced at 10 teams.

It was then that McLaughlin, who had vainly attempted to buy the Dodgers from O'Malley for the purpose of keeping them in Brooklyn, suggested to Shea that he contact Branch Rickey. Although 77, Rickey was still vigorous, and he had some interesting ideas, McLaughlin said, about forming a third major league.

Rickey, a former major-league catcher, had later managed the St. Louis Browns and St. Louis Cardinals with no appreciable success. As an executive, however, he was a brilliant innovator. It was Rickey who launched baseball's first farm system for the Cardinals in the 1920s. As general manager and part-owner of the Dodgers, he not only laid the foundation for a National League dynasty but he broke baseball's color line by signing Jackie Robinson, whose skills and unquenchable spirit earned him a place in the Hall of Fame. More recently, Rickey had served as chief executive officer of the Pirates.

From the meetings between Shea and Rickey was born the Continental League, a confederation that never played a game but which nevertheless had a profound influence on baseball. Shea's first responsibility to the new league was the formation of a New York franchise. His initial contact was with Dwight F. (Pete) Davis, Jr., whose father had been the donor of tennis's famed Davis Cup. Davis was a dedicated baseball fan who journeyed from coast to coast for important games. A second recruit was Mrs. Charles Shipman (Joan) Payson, a lifelong Giant fan who had been genuinely saddened by Horace Stoneham's decision to seek a new home for his club in San Francisco.

Joan Payson was one of the wealthiest women in the world. Her interest in sports was legendary. With her brother, John Hay (Jock) Whitney, she owned the famed Greentree Stable. She backed her support of the Giants with money, gradually amassing 10 percent of the team's stock. When the Giants' board of directors met to consider the transfer of the franchise, there was only one negative vote. It was cast by M. Donald Grant, representing Mrs. Payson's 10 percent.

She was, first and foremost, a fan. So when a last-minute attempt to purchase controlling interest in the club was rebuffed, she flew to San Francisco to attend the Giants' first game in their new surroundings. Still, New York was her home, and she was only too happy to join in a project that would return the National League to the city. Grant, her financial adviser and also an abandoned Giant fan, seconded the notion.

With the consent of Davis and Mrs. Payson, Shea added a third major backer. She was Mrs. Dorothy Killiam, a wealthy Montreal widow who had failed in an attempt to purchase the Dodgers. She had been recommended to Shea by one of his clients, Canadian millionaire Jack Kent Cooke.

Others to be included in the syndicate were Grant, G. Herbert Walker, whose father had been the donor of golf's Walker Cup, and William Simpson, president of a travel agency. Eventually, Mrs. Payson was to buy out Davis and Mrs. Killiam, leaving her in control of approximately 80 percent of the stock.

In midsummer 1959, Shea announced the creation of four more Continental League franchises—Houston, Denver, Minneapolis–St. Paul, and Toronto, which would be headed by

Cooke. Later in the year, franchises were added in Atlanta, Dallas–Fort Worth, and Buffalo, and Branch Rickey was appointed president of the paper league. An application was submitted for acceptance by organized baseball.

Club owners in both the National and American Leagues had little desire to share their good fortune with a third group. But there was the implied threat of a congressional investigation into their favored antitrust status if they rejected the new league. Furthermore, several of its prospective candidates, New York among them, appeared ripe for picking by an existing major league.

On Aug. 1, 1960, organizers of the Continental League were summoned to Chicago, where a compromise plan was offered. If the new league agreed to disband, four franchises would be admitted to the major leagues as expansion teams. An agreement was struck.

Shortly after the World Series, the expansion committees of both leagues convened. On Oct. 17, it was announced that the National League had granted franchises to New York and Houston, effective with the start of the 1962 season. Nine days later, the American League voted to allow Calvin Griffith to transfer his Washington Senators to Minneapolis–St. Paul, then authorized franchises for Washington and Los Angeles. In its eagerness to divide the expansion booty, the American League announced it would begin to play as a 10-team league the very next season.

Three years after Bill Shea had begun his quest to return the National League to New York, his mission was accomplished. It had taken all of his considerable powers of persuasion, but at last the deed was done. A bond issue for the new stadium in Flushing Meadow had passed the legislature. Now it would be up to Mrs. Payson, Grant, and the people of New York to fill it.

For the privilege of outfitting a team, Mrs. Payson was called upon to invest some $3 million. And she regarded it as just that, a privilege. "What ever would not make me buy them?" she said. "Wouldn't anybody, if they had the chance?"

The franchise now had a league. As yet, it had no organization. Enter George Weiss.

Weiss had spent a lifetime in baseball in an executive capacity, starting in the low minor leagues and working his way through the Yankees' farm system until, in 1947, he assumed the role of general manager. An aloof man whose efficiency and knowledge were remarkable, Weiss presided over the most successful chapter in the Yankees' history. Together with Casey Stengel, a longtime friend whom he had hired as manager following the 1948 season, he gained credit for the club's 10 pennants and seven World Championships from 1949 through 1960.

However, that World Series defeat at the hands of the Pirates in 1960 convinced Dan Topping and Del Webb, the Yankees' owners, that it was time for a change. Stengel and Weiss, they announced, were entering voluntary retirement. "I was discharged," Stengel grumbled before heading home to Glendale, Calif. Weiss said nothing as he closed out a career and prepared to settle into another phase of life in Greenwich, Conn.

Retirement, voluntary or otherwise, befitted neither man. At least Stengel had a bank to run. Weiss was at a loss. His inactivity soon began to trouble his wife. "I married him for better or for worse," Hazel Weiss said, "but not for lunch."

Thus, Grant and Mrs. Payson did not have to look far when they sought an experienced man to run their franchise. Weiss was ready, willing, and very able.

Grant and Weiss met in Florida to discuss details. The announcement was made in Miami on May 14, 1961, the day after Floyd Patterson knocked out Ingemar Johansson of Sweden to regain the world heavyweight boxing championship. Weiss would become president of the new team, and Grant, the financial man, would serve as chairman of the board.

Weiss wasted no time in building an organization. There were scouts to be hired, a farm system to be constructed, free agents to be signed. Johnny Murphy, the old Yankee relief ace who was later to become the Mets' general manager, served as Weiss's chief lieutenant. Jim Thomson, another former Yankee executive, was given the task of supervising stadium operations. Bill (Judge) Gibson, who had stayed behind when the Dodgers fled Brooklyn, took over the ticket department.

In May, the Mets officially became the Mets, at the discretion of Mrs. Payson, who pored over the hundreds of nicknames entered in a public contest the previous year. The identification immediately led to some confusion.

The first ticket office of the Metropolitan Baseball Club was established in the Martinique Hotel, near the old Metropolitan Opera House. The sign over the door said simply, "Met Ticket Office." So, quite naturally, a man approached the counter one day and requested two tickets for a performance of *La Traviata.* And the Judge, in the best Brooklyn tradition, replied, "Where would you like them, on the first-base or the third-base side?"

There was no secret whom Weiss wanted as the Mets' first manager. Stengel, who at one time or another had worn the uniform of all three of New York's major-league baseball teams, was immensely popular with the city's baseball fans and press. Weiss had known Stengel since 1925, when Casey was running the Worcester team in the Eastern League and Weiss was operating New Haven. It was to Stengel that Weiss had turned in 1948 with the Yankees, and it was to Stengel that he turned again in 1961.

Stengel had to be persuaded to close his comfortable home in sunny Southern California and return to baseball. But he was too much the showman to turn down the chance for another whirl in the spotlight. Finally, after Joan Payson called personally in an effort to convince him, Stengel agreed. On Oct. 2, the Mets announced that Casey Stengel, 71 years young, would give the Mets the benefit of his experience.

Four days later, the club signed a 30-year lease for the use of the municipal stadium rising in Queens. They would play in the Polo Grounds, the abandoned home of the Giants, until the new stadium was ready for occupancy. The matter of a spring-training site was simplified by the Yankees' decision to leave their longtime base in St. Petersburg and move to new quarters in Fort Lauderdale, where Topping maintained a residence.

The course of events for the Mets could not have been more fortuitous. The Yankees, the most successful organization in baseball, had played right into the competition's hands. The Mets needed a general manager, a manager, and a place for spring training. The Yankees provided all three, free of charge.

Now all the Mets needed was a team.

Branch Rickey

I had more than a passing interest in the evolution and, eventually, the expiration of the Continental League. For it was Branch Rickey, the man behind the proposed venture, who some years earlier had taught me the value of money. My own.

This was back in the days when I was leading the league in home runs and the Pittsburgh Pirates were leading the league in games lost. We didn't have a whole lot going for us then. I was the cleanup hitter, and my family always arrived in the second inning because I never batted in the first.

I was making a comfortable living at the time, even driving a Cadillac, although the line attributed to me ("Home-run hitters drive Cadillacs") was actually uttered by Fritz Ostermueller, a teammate. The Pirates were spending a lot of money in a frantic search for talent, even to the point of offering a California schoolboy the then-unprecedented sum of $100,000. In addition to the bonus, Paul Pettit also received an all-expenses-paid honeymoon in Hawaii for signing a Pittsburgh contract. The Pirates saw to it that the fine print specified Pettit had to provide his own bride.

A left-handed pitcher, Pettit was rushed to the major leagues the following year. He lasted for parts of two seasons, appeared in 12 games, and, in repayment for monies rendered, won the grand total of one game. Clearly, a new policy was needed.

John Galbreath, a construction magnate who assumed the presidency of the club in 1951, had just the man for the job. The man was Rickey, a former fraternity brother at Ohio Wesleyan University.

Rickey had sold his 25-percent share in the Brooklyn Dodgers to partners Walter O'Malley and John Smith for $1 million. That represented a clear profit of some $650,000. Rickey was a shrewd businessman as well as an outstanding judge of baseball talent.

During his years with the Dodgers, Rickey had established a reputation as a tough man in negotiations. Many a Dodger, it was said, had marched into his office determined to extract a large raise and emerged some time later thankful his salary had not been slashed. In Brooklyn, Rickey had all the money and all the players. He just didn't believe in letting the two mix.

His first season in Pittsburgh was notable mainly for a trade he initiated with the St. Louis Cardinals. The Pirates sent pitcher Cliff Chambers and outfielder Wally Westlake to St. Louis for catcher Joe Garagiola, pitchers Howie Pollet and Ted Wilks, infielder Dick Cole, and outfielder Bill Howerton. The deal was consummated on June 15, and what made it so memorable for me was the luncheon Westlake and I had attended earlier in the day.

It was held at the Duquesne Club in honor of Pittsburgh businessmen who had supported the club. During the course of the luncheon, Rickey announced that two players on the 1951 Pirates would never be traded. Those two, he said, were Ralph Kiner and Wally Westlake. That evening Wally packed his bags for the trip to St. Louis.

Nineteen-fifty-one marked the first year of Rickey's famous five-year plan designed to transform the Pirates into National League champions. In truth, it wasn't a particularly bad year for the team. We won 64 games and lost 90, climbed above the Chicago Cubs to finish seventh, and drew more than one million fans. I hit 42 home runs to lead the league for the sixth consecutive season, batted .309, and enjoyed amiable salary negotiations. It would never be so good again.

The '52 Pirates suffered through the worst season that any major-league team had the misfortune to endure. The club won

42 games and lost 112 for a .273 percentage. That left us 22½ games behind the seventh-place Boston Braves, who were so embarrassed by their year they moved to Milwaukee. "We were rained out three consecutive days," Garagiola said in recalling that season, "and we had a victory celebration."

We also dropped below one million in home attendance for the first time in six years. Despite the fact I had once again led the league in homers with 37, I was expecting the worst when it came to contract time. My expectations were fulfilled.

Rickey offered me $70,000 for 1953, a cut of 22½ percent from my top salary of $90,000. I protested, holding out through the first two weeks of spring training. But Rickey was unwavering. "Son," he said in that stentorian voice which gave him instant command of every conversation, "we could have finished last without you."

That's precisely what they did do that season after Rickey traded me, along with Garagiola, Pollet, and George (Catfish) Metkovich, to the Chicago Cubs on June 4, 1953, for six utilitarian players and $150,000 in cash. I have to believe the cash was the major selling point for Rickey. Of the 35 home runs and 116 runs batted in I amassed in 1953, 28 home runs and 87 RBIs were on behalf of the Cubs. And we finished 15 games ahead of the Pirates.

The dissolution of the Continental League temporarily severed Rickey's connection with baseball, but the expansion it forced within the major leagues played a pivotal role in my life. Even before New York, there was Los Angeles. Almost.

At the time the American League conferred franchises on Washington and Los Angeles, it granted Hank Greenberg permission to go to the West Coast and negotiate nonconflicting playing dates for the new team in the Memorial Coliseum, where the Dodgers had just completed their second season while awaiting the construction of their own stadium in Chavez Ravine. Greenberg was a partner of Bill Veeck in the Chicago White Sox operation, and the plan, provided the negotiations went smoothly, called for Greenberg and Veeck to sell the Sox and join C. Arnholt Smith of San Diego in a syndicate that would operate the new Los Angeles team.

Smith was then my boss. The owner of the Padres, he had given me the chance to become a general manager and work near where I had been raised. As a result of my relationship with both Greenberg and Smith, I was to become a limited partner in the new venture.

I met Greenberg in Los Angeles, and we began negotiations with O'Malley and the Coliseum Commission, which operated the facility, to effect the peaceful coexistence of the two teams. The Coliseum, with its preposterously short left-field fence, was once described as a "stadium with room for 90,000 fans and two outfielders." It had been built for the 1932 Olympic Games and, in the intervening years, had earned fame as the home of the Los Angeles Rams and the football teams of UCLA and the University of Southern California.

In the course of negotiations, however, Commissioner Ford Frick suddenly appeared on the scene. He flew to Los Angeles, conferred with O'Malley, one of baseball's power brokers, and then announced that Los Angeles was no longer open territory. Any team moving into the area, he said, had to pay damages to the Dodgers and could not operate within 25 miles of the National League franchise.

That ruled out the Coliseum as a playing site and necessitated the construction of a new stadium. An alternative was to sign on as a tenant in Dodger Stadium, due to open in 1962, a move that would assure the team of second-class dates and citizenship in town. With the change in conditions, Greenberg decided it would no longer be feasible to operate an AL club in Los Angeles and pulled out of the negotiations.

Greenberg had already contacted radio station KMPC concerning the team's broadcast rights. KMPC, which had broadcast the Dodgers' games upon the team's arrival from Brooklyn and later lost the account, was owned by Gene Autry, the cowboy movie star. Once Greenberg withdrew his offer, Autry moved in, purchased the franchise, which he named the Angels (after the city's onetime Pacific Coast League team), and hired Fred Haney, who had been my last manager in Pittsburgh before the trade, as his general manager.

Our plans, which we never got the chance to implement, included the hiring of Casey Stengel as manager. So our failure in Los Angeles left Casey available to manage the New York Mets the following season. And it left me available to sit behind the microphone and watch Casey and his team achieve a special place in baseball lore.

Casey

The firm of George Weiss and Casey Stengel was not back in business long when it became evident that business was not so good. On Oct. 10, 1961, eight days after Stengel's appointment and one day after the Yankees completed a five-game World Series triumph over the Cincinnati Reds, an expansion draft was conducted in Cincinnati's Netherland Hilton Hotel.

The management of the Mets and the new Houston club, the Colt .45s, certainly had not expected to be gifted with gems at this National League auction. But they were hardly prepared for the quality of the merchandise. The NL's eight incumbent franchises had taken the intervening year's time to hide their best prospects under the fine print. What the new members were getting were the expendables.

A coin flip to determine the order of selection preceded the start of the draft. The Mets lost the toss, beginning a slump that would take years to reverse. Houston, picking first, chose Eddie Bressoud, a San Francisco infielder. The Mets countered with Hobie Landrith, a San Francisco receiver, on the theory, as stated by Stengel, that "if you don't have a catcher, you're gonna have a lot of passed balls."

In all, the Mets chose 22 players in four hours at an initial outlay of $1.8 million. The premium choices, at $125,000 apiece, were pitchers Jay Hook (Cincinnati) and Bob Miller (St. Louis), infielder Don Zimmer (Chicago), and outfielder Lee Walls (Philadelphia). Pitcher Sherman Jones (Cincinnati) and outfielder Jim Hickman (St. Louis) were so-called "bargain" picks at $50,000.

Landrith was the first of the players claimed in the $75,000 regular phase. He soon was joined by pitchers Craig Anderson (St. Louis), Roger Craig (Los Angeles), Ray Daviault (San Francisco), and Alvin Jackson (Philadelphia); first basemen Ed Bouchee (Chicago) and Gil Hodges (Los Angeles); infielders Elio Chacon (Cincinnati), Felix Mantilla (Milwaukee), and Sammy Drake (Chicago); outfielders Gus Bell (Cincinnati), Joe Christopher (Pittsburgh), John DeMerit (Milwaukee), and Bobby Gene Smith (Philadelphia).

It was not the start Weiss had imagined. Quickly, he appropriated Mrs. Payson's checkbook and purchased first baseman Jim Marshall from the Giants, slugger Frank Thomas from the Braves, and center fielder Richie Ashburn from the Cubs. Shortly thereafter, he sent Walls—a premium pick—and $100,000 to the Dodgers for Charlie Neal, an infielder. Before Christmas, Weiss had achieved his objective, filling the Mets' uniforms with recognizable players. At least, the team would give the appearance of professionalism.

This was, of course, a calculated hedge. Hodges, one of the most popular men ever to play in Brooklyn, had a bad knee. The skills of Ashburn and Bell, all-stars once upon a time, had eroded with age. But, for the moment, the Mets were tied for first place with nine other teams. Reality was still months away.

Stengel was not to be deterred by the quality of his new team. He baptized them "the Amazin' Mets" and set out to spread the word of the National League's stepchild. There was no man in America better equipped to perform the task Stengel was undertaking, to sell an expansion team to the public and have them love it.

From the outset of his baseball career, Stengel had been among the most resourceful of men. Frozen out of batting practice by the veterans when he reported to the Brooklyn Dodgers as a 22-year-old outfielder in 1912, he thought to have calling cards printed. These he passed out to the older players by way of introduction and soon got to take his swings without interference.

Appointed as player-manager-president of the Worcester team in the Eastern League in 1925 by Judge Emil Fuchs, owner of the Boston Braves, Stengel soon received a more lucrative offer from Toledo. When permission to leave was denied, Casey executed a slick triple play. First, as manager, he released Stengel, the right fielder. Then, as president, he dismissed Stengel, the manager. Finally, he resigned his position as club president.

Casey was born in Kansas City, Mo., July 30, 1890, and christened Charles Dillon Stengel. His nickname at Central High School and later at the Western Dental School, where he spent time attempting to master the intricacies of left-handed drilling, was Dutch. It was only during his playing days in New York that people turned the initials of his hometown (K.C.) into a whole new identity.

The Stengel home was located across the street from the house of Charles Augustus (Kid) Nichols, an ironman major-league pitcher who later would be elected to the Hall of Fame. Stengel participated in all sports as a youth, but it was baseball that captivated him. In 1910, he set out for Kankakee, Ill., which fielded a team in the Northern Association. When the league folded in midseason, young Casey headed for Maysville, Ky., and its Blue Grass League team, the second stop in what was to be a nomadic existence.

In his first major-league appearance, Stengel rapped four successive hits for the Dodgers off Pittsburgh's Claude Hendrix, a right-handed pitcher. Sherry Smith, a left-hander, was pitching when Stengel stepped to the plate for the fifth time. "Okay, you bush phenom," yelled Pittsburgh manager Fred Clarke from the dugout, "let's see you cross over to the other side."

Stengel, who loved challenges, did just that, batting right-handed even though he had never practiced the art. "I was just cocky enough to do it," he said in later years. He also was lucky enough to draw a base on balls.

He spent five full seasons with the Dodgers, earning a reputation as a passably good outfielder, solid hitter, and clown, not necessarily in that order. Among his most celebrated antics was the time he doffed his cap to a group of Ebbets Field hecklers, releasing a sparrow which flew away. The incident quickly turned the jeers to cheers. Even then, Casey knew how to play to an audience.

Wilbert Robinson, the Dodgers' manager whom almost everyone called Uncle Robbie, enjoyed a good joke himself. But Stengel went a bit far one day in spring training at Daytona Beach, Fla. Gabby Street, the catcher for the Senators, had recently caught a ball dropped from the top of the Washington Monument, more than 500 feet high. Stengel and Robinson argued whether a man could catch a ball dropped from an airplane. Stengel said it couldn't be done. Robinson, an outstanding catcher in his playing days with the Baltimore Orioles, said he could do it.

The Dodgers obtained the services of aviatrix Ruth Law, who was to circle the ballpark and drop the baseball, supplied by Stengel. Except that Casey substituted a grapefruit for the ball. Robinson did indeed get his glove on the falling object, but the impact knocked him flat on his back. As he wiped the seeds and juice (which he perceived to be his teeth and blood) off his face, his players doubled over with laughter. The only man who found no humor in the ploy, it was reported, was the victim. Stengel later surmised it may have led to his appearance in a Pittsburgh uniform in 1918.

Stengel played two years for the Pirates and two forgettable seasons for the Philadelphia Phillies before being traded back to New York. This time the team was the Giants, the manager was the harsh John J. McGraw, and there was no call for a comedian. As a platoon outfielder, Stengel helped the Giants win two consecutive pennants and a World Championship in 1922.

His moment of personal glory occurred in the 1923 World Series, which the Giants lost in six games to the Yankees. Stengel's inside-the-park home run, on which he lost a shoe rounding third base, was the winning run in the first game. His homer was the only run in the third game. Indeed, Casey might have become a national hero if it hadn't been for a large Yankee outfielder named George Herman Ruth, who hit three homers as his team won the first Series played in Yankee Stadium.

Stengel found more than a measure of fame with the Giants. He also found a bride. Edna Lawson was a Californian who attended several Giant games at the Polo Grounds in the summer of '23 in the company of a friend, the wife of outfielder Bob Meusel. At 33, Stengel's legs were going, and he frequently was replaced by McGraw for defensive purposes in the late innings. On those occasions, he showered quickly, dressed, and watched the end of the game from the grandstand, where he made the acquaintance of the woman who would be his wife.

The following year, Stengel was dealt to Boston, where he and Edna took time off for a wedding. Casey finished his playing career with the Braves early in the 1925 season, bowing out of the majors with a .284 batting average in 1,277 games. The Braves sent him to Worcester to run their Eastern League club, the start of a managerial career that would carry him from the depths of despair to the height of success and back down again, and would span some four decades.

After a six-year stint in Toledo, where he also was part-owner of the franchise, Stengel returned to the Dodgers in 1934. Brooklyn still had no shortage of clowns, but, as manager, he took a less charitable view of the proceedings.

There was the day at Philadelphia's cramped Baker Bowl when pitcher Walter (Boom Boom) Beck was justifying his nickname (one boom for the crack of the bat, the second for the sound of the ball striking a hard object). Stengel finally had heard enough for one day and walked to the mound to remove his pitcher.

Instead of handing the ball to the manager, the enraged Beck wheeled and heaved the ball on a fly to the sheet-metal fence in right field. The resounding noise startled Hack Wilson, the right fielder, whose head was down and whose body was recovering from a hard night. Acting instinctively, Wilson fielded the carom deftly off the wall and fired a strike to second base while the fans howled and Stengel fumed. "I'd have left you in there," he told Boom Boom, "if I knew you could throw that hard."

The Dodgers finished sixth, fifth, and seventh among eight teams in Stengel's three years as manager. They finished sixth in 1937, when Casey was paid not to manage. It was then that the Braves beckoned. They were no better than the Dodgers and even less funny.

In Stengel's six seasons in Boston, the Braves never landed in the first division. For four successive seasons, they were seventh. Such was Stengel's popularity in the final year of his term that while he was recovering from a badly broken leg suffered in a collision with a taxicab, a caustic Boston columnist nominated the cab driver for a special award as "the man who did the most for baseball in Boston in 1943."

After his recovery, Stengel went back to the minors, managing a year in Milwaukee, a year in Kansas City, and three seasons in Oakland before the call came from George Weiss. Casey returned to New York, stayed 12 seasons, and departed with the reputation of a genius. He had to have been at least that to have made the Mets respectable. And he was perfectly willing to try. To heck with his reputation, he said. Casey needed the action, and the Mets needed him. As he explained the day he accepted the job, "Most people my age are dead."

From the moment he set foot in St. Petersburg for the start of spring training, he was hailed as a hero returned from the wars. It didn't hurt that, at 71, Stengel was approximately the age of the average resident. "Well," he said, "those people are elderly, and I've got a few wrinkles in my face myself."

The coaching staff had almost as much experience as the manager. Rogers Hornsby, 66, one of the great hitters in the history of the game, had been inducted into the Hall of Fame 20 years earlier. Red Ruffing, the 58-year-old pitching coach, had been an outstanding pitcher for the Yankees and was himself a candidate for the Hall of Fame. Cookie Lavagetto and Solly Hemus had managed at the major-league level the previous year.

Stengel went right to work on the fundamentals the first full day of camp. He marched his new team onto the field and led a guided tour of the bases, pausing to explain the function of each. When he reached home plate, Casey said, "You can make a living here." He must have had another team in mind.

The Mets were surprisingly mediocre that first spring, to judge by the record. They won 12 and lost 15 in Florida, beating the Yankees once. But that was not indicative of things to come. More prophetic was a game attended by Mrs. Payson, who arrived after one half-inning had been played. The Mets trailed, 7-0. "We're getting beaten rather badly, aren't we?" she asked Stengel from her box seat alongside the dugout. "How should I know?" Casey replied. "We haven't been to bat yet."

The Mets' turn at bat was coming. Not even Stengel, it developed, was prepared for the consequences.

Growing Up

My first exposure to Stengel predated my association with the Mets and even my career as a professional baseball player. It occurred about 1938, in the winter. I was a high school kid playing ball at Griffith Park in Los Angeles. The Pirate scouts were following me, and they asked Casey, who was managing the Boston Braves in the summer months, to teach me some of the rudiments of playing center field. Well, Casey was forever offering advice to anyone and everyone, and he said he'd try.

I'll never forget his comment about me: "That fellow must not drink whiskey because he's always over at the water fountain." It was only much later that I understood that he meant I was taking a lot of breaks to get out of work.

The fact that I had made a favorable impression in the fast semi-pro leagues of southern California was remarkable in itself, given my background. I was born on Oct. 27, 1922, in the copper-mining town of Santa Rita, N.M. My father, it was said, was such a poor athlete he never played on the mining-camp teams. Yet he was a major figure at the local games. That's because he held the bets wagered by the opposing teams. They trusted him.

Ralph Macklin Kiner had owned a bakery in Farmington,

N.M., and later was a steam-shovel operator at the largest open-pit mine in New Mexico. He died when I was four. My mother, Beatrice, had served as a nurse in France during World War I, and she returned to the nursing profession after my father's death. She landed a job with the Southern Pacific Railroad at a salary of about $100 a month, and we moved into a small house in Alhambra, Calif., a town of some 30,000, directly east of Los Angeles.

Although she taught me a great deal about hard work and dedication, my mother knew nothing of sports. She couldn't understand why I wasted my time playing games, time which might be better spent in directing myself toward the goal of becoming a doctor or lawyer. Fortunately, we lived across the street from the Bodkins, whose appreciation of baseball was no less acute than my own.

The family consisted of Bob Bodkin, his wife, Rose, and one son, Robert. I was several years younger than the son, who played for the Alhambra High School team. His father had been a semi-pro pitcher and frequently threw batting practice to Robert in one of the many vacant lots in our neighborhood. I stood around and watched until one day Bob Bodkin tossed me a glove and asked me to shag flies.

I did this for some time until it occurred to me that it might be more fun to hit a ball than to chase it down. Because of my age and my stature, this proposal was vetoed. But my persistence wore them down, and finally, at 11, I got to swing a regulation bat against a regulation baseball. After some experience with softball, it took a while to overcome the shock of timing a pitch thrown overhand by a man standing 60 feet away. Soon, however, I got the knack and started to hit with some regularity. My tutors were astonished.

Now it was Kiner at the bat and Bodkin in the field, a circumstance that I enjoyed more than he. Thus began my love affair with hardball. You could hit the ball so much farther than you could a softball.

The Bodkins became my surrogate family. I was always hanging around, always nearby in case an impromptu batting-practice session was called. In retrospect, it was amazing that Robert Bodkin put up with me. But he had a great love for baseball, too, and when we weren't hitting, we were playing pepper on the front lawn. This was discouraged, but not strenuously, by Rose Bodkin. Since my mother worked during the day and I was at home alone after school, I was practically adopted by the Bodkins.

Mr. Bodkin taught me how to sew up a baseball when it had been ripped. He also taught me how to nail bats back together after they had been broken. And it was he who introduced me to Sunday morning baseball with an otherwise all-men's team. Rose Bodkin was later to teach me how to drive a car. As for Robert, not only did we play ball together but he allowed me to tag along when he and his friends went to the Pasadena Civic Auditorium. That's where I learned to dance.

But before I was totally seduced by baseball, before I became absolutely certain that my destination in life was the far-off major leagues, I had to weather two crises. The first involved money. Remember, this was the depths of the Depression. My mother, understandably, decided I should contribute to the support of the household.

What she had in mind was a magazine route. I was given the task of selling the *Saturday Evening Post,* the most famous weekly of its era, door-to-door. Each week I took possession of 20 magazines, to be sold at five cents apiece. My profit was a penny per magazine, or 20 cents per week.

The problem with the job was that it cut severely into my playing time. It didn't take me long to figure out that I had to change the course of my suddenly boring existence. Since I lived in California, there was a sensible solution. It came in the form of a lawnmower.

My neighborhood consisted of single-family homes built on lots of 100 feet by 50 feet. Each house had a small lawn, and these lawns needed mowing at least twice a month. Since I had to pay four cents for every magazine, all I had to do was mow four lawns a week at 25 cents per lawn and I would have the 80 cents for the distributor plus the 20 cents for my mother. The lawns required only 30 minutes of work apiece, which left plenty of time for the playground.

The game plan was formed and executed. Everything would have gone smoothly except for one small oversight. Since I didn't sell any magazines, I had to dispose of the evidence. It so happened we had a big pine tree in the backyard. It served the purpose of blocking our view of the incinerator which was used to burn off rubbish accumulated during the week. The obvious choice was to burn the magazines. But the day of delivery was not a burn day. The next best means of disposal, I decided, was to bury them, and that I did, under the pine tree with the low-hanging branches.

For a time, the system worked well. The magazine distributor was getting his 80 cents. Because I was turning over 20 cents to her each week, my mother thought I was becoming a super salesperson. And I was hitting .400 on the local playground.

Then came the fall. It may not have equaled the stock market crash of 1929, but it was no less devastating to me. My burying ground filled up. While burning trash one day, my mother saw something unusual about the roots of the backyard pine tree. Magazines appeared to be sprouting from the earth. I was tried, convicted, and sentenced in one afternoon. On New Year's Day, 1933, I was involuntarily enrolled in the Long Beach Military School, where the supervision was continual.

Out on good behavior after six months as a cadet, my love for baseball landed me in trouble again. The field at Fremont Grammar School was bordered in left field by the sixth-grade building. Prior to my appearance, no one had managed to break any of the second-floor windows which fronted the diamond. In the course of the summer of '33, I had a wonderful time, hitting eight home runs and breaking school windows. Legally, of course, since the league was supervised. The school provided the bats and balls; I furnished the power.

My display went unappreciated by Miss Bloomingdale, the sixth-grade teacher. I don't know whether it was the sight or sound of shattered glass that irritated her. Or perhaps it was the fact that she conducted the glee club and I couldn't sing a lick. All I know is that the day after the summer league had ended, I was at home working on my swing in front of the bedroom mirror when the doorbell rang. I peeked through the venetian blinds and got the scare of my life. The police were at the door.

If the police came to your house in 1933, it meant someone in your family had died—and I was an only child—or someone was going to jail. In this case, it was the latter. During the 10-minute drive to the city jail, I determined my future was behind me. Even military school seemed a joyride by comparison to what lay ahead. The thought of my mother's reaction frightened me even more than the men in uniform.

So there I sat, in a cell at the Alhambra jail, envisioning the worst. My deliverance didn't take long. I was told to appear before the truant officer for my misdeeds. I stood before his desk and saw him reach for a book. He opened it to a preselected spot and proceeded to read aloud, "Casey at the Bat." While there was no joy in Mudville, my heart soared at the police station in Alhambra. Officers had checked out the complaint and decided the only problem was that the baseball diamond had been placed in the wrong area of the school grounds. The diamond was subsequently moved and the infraction removed from my record.

But "Casey at the Bat" remained a part of my life. My first daughter was named Kathryn Chaffee, and we called her K.C. My job as a broadcaster with the Mets placed me in close and wondrous company with Casey Stengel. And, oh yes, the truant officer who read me the poem was Lieutenant John Casey.

I've often wondered whether Lieutenant Casey ever connected that scared little kid who stood before him with the guy who hit all those home runs for the Pittsburgh Pirates years later without breaking a single window.

My dad, Ralph Macklin Kiner, looked like Will Rogers. He was a steam-shovel operator and this was in the mining town of Santa Rita, New Mexico. He died when I was four. *(Kiner Collection.)*

I was six when this was taken in Alhambra, California. My mother told me the photographer charged 25 cents. A day's work.

(Kiner Collection)

In the winter of 1949, after my 51-homer season, I was swamped with mail. That's my mother helping me sort it. I had a secretary to answer the letters. She was the daughter of Al Mamaux, who twice won 21 games for the Pirates—unfortunately not when I played for them.

(Wide World)

My big date with Liz Taylor in 1949. *(Wide World)*

Janet Leigh starred with Paul Douglas in *Angels in the Outfield* in 1951. This was in Pittsburgh, where they shot a number of scenes with Pirates in the background. I dated her for a while. It was serious. *(above)*

(Kiner Collection)

Hank Greenberg was the best man when I married Nancy Chaffee on October 13, 1951, in Santa Barbara, California. *(top right)*

(Wide World)

Nancy was a world-class tennis player. She's playing here at Wimbledon in 1951. Nancy was a three-time winner of the National Indoor Championships. She ranked fourth in the U.S. in 1951. Nancy's the mother of my three children. *(bottom right)*   (Wide World)

Esther Williams came for a swim one day at our home in Palm Springs, California. This wasn't the time she went skinny-dipping. Esther's husband was Ben Gage, the radio announcer. *(top left)* *(Kiner Collection)*

I'm never far from a golf course. The foursome here at the Thunderbird Country Club: (from left) Bing Crosby, Phil Harris, me, and Bill Higgins. *(bottom left)* *(Kiner Collection)*

I hit four home runs in a doubleheader against the Boston Braves in 1947 and my teammates—(from left) Bill Sullivan, Pete Castiglione and Jim Bagby—gave me the star treatment. *(below)* *(Wide World)*

The 1950 All-Star Game in Chicago was one of the most dramatic ever. My home run tied the score in the ninth and Red Schoendienst (next to National League manager Burt Shotton) won it, 4-3, with his homer in the 14th. This is the game in which Ted Williams broke his elbow making a catch on my drive against the left-field wall. He claimed he could never hit after that. *(top left)*   *(Kiner Collection)*

Spring training with Branch Rickey in Havana, Cuba, in 1953. I held out for two weeks. Pleading poverty, Rickey wanted me to take a 22½ percent cut from my $90,000 salary. He said "we could finish last without you." I ended up accepting the cut. *(bottom left)*

(Kiner Collection)

Manager Fred Haney hands me the ball I hit for my 300th home run in 1953. I'm pointing to Babe Ruth and I'm supposed to have said, "That's the man I've got to beat." *(below)*   *(Kiner Collection)*

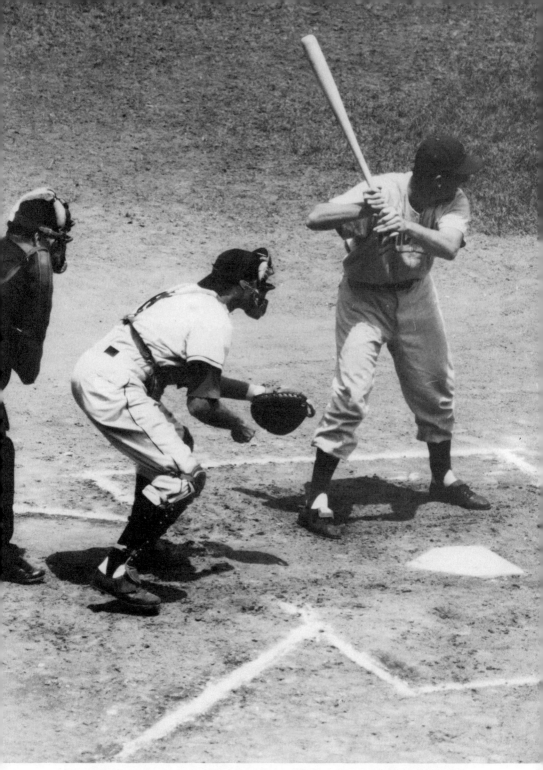

I'm popping out in my first at-bat as a Cub after being traded in the summer of 1953. *(Wide World)*

Starting at the Bottom

The 1962 National League schedule, the first one drawn to include the Mets, determined that New York's newest team should open on the road. It was an eminently wise decision. The Mets were to play their inaugural game against the Cardinals in St. Louis on April 10, but the game was rained out.

Their luck, however, was not to last. The rain abated before they could get out of town, and on Wednesday night, April 11, the Mets' ordeal began in earnest. They sent Roger Craig, a lanky, pleasant man who had enjoyed some fine seasons with the Dodgers, to the mound. Craig promptly yielded two runs in the first inning, one on a balk. Gil Hodges and Charlie Neal homered, but the Mets were beaten soundly, 11-4.

That didn't diminish their triumphal entry into New York the following day. The Mets were honored with a ticker-tape parade up lower Broadway and officially welcomed to the city by Mayor Robert Wagner. The reception was made all the more enjoyable by the fact the Mets were not scheduled to play.

On Friday the 13th, of all days, the Mets played their first game in New York. The Polo Grounds had undergone extensive renovation since the Giants had departed the oddly shaped park in 1957, but still it seemed a dark green ghost of summers past. The fans went right to work brightening up the place with bedsheet banners.

The first banner extolled Hot Rod Kanehl, an itinerant minor-leaguer who had caught Stengel's eye with his hustle and aggressiveness in a Yankee camp some years back and who had won a special place on the Mets with his brash attitude. Kanehl, who had never played a game in New York, studied the sign and decided, "My fame preceded me."

Despite terrible weather, a crowd of 12,447 reported in hopes of seeing some old heroes, foremost among them Gil Hodges. But he was unable to play because of a knee injury. So Stengel sent Jim Marshall to first base. The fans greeted the unfamiliar figure with jeers. He is believed to be the first player ever booed while playing for a team that was yet to engage in its first home game.

"I was booed heavier than anybody I knew before the start of a game," Marshall recalled later. "Usually, it's the way you play or what happens. I was glad Mayor Wagner was there. We were in a class by ourselves." New Yorkers, it should be noted, traditionally boo politicians in such public settings.

The timing of the boos was only slightly premature. The first batter for the Pittsburgh Pirates hit a bouncer to third baseman Don Zimmer, who promptly heaved the ball over Marshall's head and into the seats. The Mets were off and fumbling. They lost that game, 4-3, despite the late intervention of snow.

The Mets continued to lose. They lost two more to the Pirates, one to Houston, two to the Cards, and began their second road trip, to Pittsburgh, with a record of no wins, seven losses. *Sports Illustrated* had assigned a reporter to the Mets for the purpose of recording their first victory for posterity. He had recently been married, and, when the team reached Pittsburgh, Stengel advised him, "There's a chance you may not see your bride until October."

Sure enough, the Mets lost the next two games to the Pirates. That put them in the unique position of trailing the first-place team by 9½ games after playing only nine themselves. The Pirates had played 10 and won them all.

On the night of April 23, the fight crowd at the St. Nicholas Arena in New York listened intently as Johnny Addie, the veteran boxing announcer, prepared to present the winner of the feature bout. "Ladies and gentlemen," Addie said after returning from a brief conference with Western Union operator Howie Smith, "before I give you the winner of tonight's main event, I would like to give you the latest baseball news provided by Western Union telegraph direct from Pittsburgh, Pennsylvania. At the end of six innings, the score is New York Mets 6, Pittsburgh Pirates 0."

A cheer echoed throughout the arena. The Met mystique was already taking hold. The Mets won their first game that night, 9-1, behind Jay Hook. "I may pitch Hook every day," Stengel said. He did not, and the Mets lost their next three games.

The manager's mind was working overtime in an effort to win games. One day, looking down the bench for a pinch-hitter, Stengel yelled, "Blanchard, go up and hit." Johnny Blanchard was Casey's best pinch-hitter on the Yankees, but the man he was addressing happened to be Marshall.

"Casey," Marshall said, "my name's not Blanchard, but I'll be glad to hit."

"Hey, Blanchard," Stengel said, paying no heed to Marshall's comment, "there's something you ought to know. Son, you see them foul lines, the ones on first base and third base that run all the way out to the building [stands]? You know what they're there for? Those are for the hitters to shoot at. When you get in the batter's box, I want you to try to hit that ball as close to those lines as you can because, you see, all those opposing players are standing in the middle."

Blessed with that knowledge, Marshall walked up to the plate and struck out.

George Weiss, faced with such a disastrous start, went to work buying and selling players at a feverish pace. He purchased catcher Harry Chiti from Cleveland for a player to be named later. Then he turned around and acquired Sammy Taylor, another catcher, from the Cubs for Bobby Gene Smith. The reason for the stockpiling was the discovery that Hobie Landrith, who could catch, could not throw; that Chris Cannizzaro, who could throw, could not catch; and that Choo Choo Coleman could catch low pitches but little else.

When asked why he kept Coleman when the only pitches he could catch were those in the dirt, Stengel replied, "Them are the only ones the other teams ain't hitting."

In other transactions, the Mets acquired Cliff Cook, a third baseman, from Cincinnati in exchange for Zimmer, who had typified the team's futility by failing to hit safely in 34 at-bats. They also added a left-handed pitcher by the name of Robert G. Miller to go with right-handed pitcher Robert L. Miller, drafted the previous fall.

Bob Miller, the left-hander, had retired from baseball, but scout Wid Matthews talked him into joining the Mets, promising enough time on the roster to qualify for the major-league pension fund. Miller was only a few days short of the required five years.

Lou Niss, the Mets' traveling secretary, deftly handled the dilemma posed by two Bob Millers on the same team by pairing them on road trips. The theory was that anyone wanting to contact Bob Miller would at least get the right room. The second Miller, for his part, worked hard to get into shape. His first appearance came against the Milwaukee Braves. Del Crandall was the batter. Crandall hit Miller's first pitch for a game-winning home run. His second pitch for the Mets, in a later game, also resulted in a home run. Miller had grasped the true spirit of the team sooner than anyone had a right to expect.

Marshall, who never fully recovered from the crowd reaction to his first appearance, was traded to Pittsburgh for Wilmer (Vinegar Bend) Mizell, a veteran left-handed pitcher who would lose his only two decisions with the team but later became the first Met elected to Congress. Hodges required surgery on his knee, and, with Marshall gone, the Mets needed another first baseman. The new man was Marvin Eugene Throneberry.

Throneberry, acquired on May 9 from the Baltimore Orioles, had modeled every gesture of his appearance after his idol, Mickey Mantle. He had been in the Yankee organization for a number of years and, after hitting more than 40 home runs one season at Denver, was considered a fine prospect. But he had not fulfilled his promise.

With Weiss's revolving door operating at high speed, the Mets started to win, two games at a time. On May 16, upon the completion of a 13-inning game which had begun the previous night, the Mets moved past the Cubs into ninth place. Then they proceeded to win four of their next five, including a doubleheader against the Braves, raising their record to 12-19. It was to be the high point of the season.

Following the 7-6 and 9-6 triumphs over the Braves on May 20, the Mets were scheduled to fly to Houston, where they were to play a two-game series. Departure time for the flight was 9 P.M., but their chartered aircraft failed to reach Milwaukee to pick them up until after midnight.

Estimated time of arrival in Houston was pushed back to 4 A.M. but the Mets, glowing with success, seemed not to mind the delay as they boarded in the wee hours of the morning. The plane did touch down at 4 A.M. Unfortunately, the point of landing was Dallas. The airport in Houston, the Mets were informed, was closed because of fog.

At 6 A.M., with Stengel still holding court on subjects great and small, the flight resumed. The team arrived in Houston in time to encounter morning rush-hour traffic and didn't reach its hotel until 8:30. Casey stopped to pick up the morning paper and, turning to Niss in front of the elevators, said, "If anyone wants me, tell 'em I'm being embalmed."

That was to be the Mets' last celebration for some time. It was followed by a 17-game losing streak.

The Mets lost games in every conceivable manner. One of the more bizarre involved Elio Chacon, the shortstop, and Richie Ashburn, the center fielder. Chacon, a Venezuelan, had first attracted attention the previous fall, when he stole home against the Yankees in the World Series. With the Mets, he was gaining quite a different reputation.

Chacon had two problems at shortstop. He attempted to catch every ball, no matter where it was hit, and he understood little English. On occasion he ran into the third baseman. Other times it was the second baseman. He also had several close calls with Ashburn while pursuing pop flies. Finally, the center fielder went to Joe Christopher, a bilingual teammate, and asked the Spanish expression for "I got it."

"Yo lo tengo," Christopher told Ashburn.

The chance to use it came in a game against Cincinnati. The Mets led by two runs but the Reds loaded the bases. The batter was the dreaded Frank Robinson. He hit a high fly to short left-center field. Chacon scurried back and Ashburn raced in. *"Yo lo tengo,"* Ashburn yelled, and, sure enough, Chacon pulled up. Ashburn settled under the ball and was just about to make the catch when he was bowled over by Frank Thomas, the burly left fielder. Thomas spoke only English. Naturally, the Mets lost.

Strange things were also happening in the front office. When the Mets acquired Harry Chiti the previous month, the terms of the contract specified that they send a player to Cleveland's Jacksonville farm club at the end of 30 days. The player shipped to Jacksonville was Harry Chiti. He was, it appeared, the first player in major-league history to be traded for himself.

The Throneberry deal also took an unusual twist about that time. When the acquisition had been announced, it was said to be a cash arrangement. But a month later, Landrith left for Baltimore to complete the transaction.

The Mets lost their last eight games on that wearying road trip and returned home to drop seven more to the Dodgers and Giants, making their first official appearances in New York since fleeing the city in 1957. In the second game of the Dodger series, the Mets completed a triple play as Chacon speared Willie Davis's line drive and threw to second baseman Neal to double one runner. Neal's throw to first was in time to beat the second runner. Undaunted, Davis homered in the ninth inning for the winning margin.

Two more losses in Philadelphia extended the streak before the Mets righted themselves with a 4-3 victory over the Cubs in Chicago. The 17 consecutive losses fell short of the record 24 straight defeats suffered by the Phillies the previous year. The Phillies later explained that particular slump by saying they were playing marginal major-leaguers while protecting their best prospects from the forthcoming expansion draft which would stock the Mets and Colt .45s.

On June 17, the Mets carried a four-game losing streak into a doubleheader against the Cubs at the Polo Grounds. The first baseman was Throneberry, rapidly developing into a cult figure known as Marvelous Marv. Throneberry had the knack of making the wrong play at the right time, and his place in Met history would be assured that afternoon.

Early in the first game he was charged with obstruction of the basepath. The Mets had been working with Throneberry on rundown plays. The pickoff at first base was not one of Marv's strengths. Whenever it led to a rundown, he could be counted upon to foul it up. On one such occasion earlier in the season, he had done everything right, hanging up the runner and timing his throw to second just in time for the out. There was, however, one small oversight. He had failed to prevent the winning run scoring from third base.

This time the obstruction call helped the Mets to a 3-0 deficit. However, he had a chance to negate the damage when he came to bat with two runners on in the bottom half of the inning. He promptly blasted a high drive off the distant right-center field wall and pulled into third base with what appeared to be a triple.

In Marv's case, appearances frequently were deceiving. The Cubs put the ball in play, the pitcher threw to Ernie Banks, and the first baseman stepped on the bag. Throneberry was called out for failing to touch the base.

Quickly, Stengel hobbled out of the dugout to rail at the first-base umpire. He was kicking up some dirt when Dusty Boggess, the second-base umpire, gently tapped the manager on the shoulder and said, "Casey, it's no use. He didn't step on second base, either." To which Stengel replied, "Well, I know damn well he didn't miss third. He's standing on it."

Throneberry had a lucid explanation for his failures. "It was so long since I was down there," he said, "that I forgot where it was."

A legend was born then and there. His excesses of incompetence were to symbolize the early Mets, and, at the urging of the sharp-witted Ashburn, who occupied the adjoining locker, Throneberry learned to live with the image and even add to it with his comments. The fans treated him as a hero, five of them arriving at the Polo Grounds one day in lettered T-shirts which, when placed in the proper order, spelled M-A-R-V-! Naturally, the newspapers were obliged to note that Marv's initials were M.E.T.

The Mets made another solid contribution to their reputation in the second game of that doubleheader when a slender Chicago outfielder named Lou Brock drove a ball into the bleachers to the right of the center-field clubhouse, more than 450 feet from home plate. That had never been done before in all the years the Polo Grounds had served the National League.

In the very next game, Henry Aaron of the Braves deposited a pitch into the bleachers to the left of the clubhouse, a feat accomplished only once previously. Some time later, Stengel was seated at a dinner alongside Bill Terry, a Hall-of-Fame player and later manager of the Giants. "Bill," Stengel asked Terry, "what was your pitching strategy at the Polo Grounds?"

"You got to pitch everybody outside," Terry replied. "With those short foul lines and that deep center field, you can't let anyone pull the ball. Make them hit it to center."

"We've been trying that," Casey said, "and they're hitting them into the bleachers."

On June 30, in the 73rd game of their existence, the Mets attained a new low in achievement. They managed no hits and no runs against the Dodgers, and their historic efforts in Dodger Stadium were appreciated back in New York through the wonder of television. For Sandy Koufax, it represented the first of four no-hit performances. For the Mets, it represented a 53rd defeat. The final score was 5-0.

The steady stream of losses was interrupted briefly by the All-Star Game. Since each team had to be represented by at least one player, Ashburn was added to the National League team. Fred Hutchinson, manager of the defending champion Reds, also nominated Stengel as first-base coach.

Stengel took the occasion to engage in conversation with John F. Kennedy, the president of the United States. Casey went on at length before terminating the discussion. "Mr. President," he said, "I'd love to stay, but I got to go because I'm not working for myself but the other fellow." And, with that, he limped off to his position in the first-base coaching box.

It was Stengel who made that first season worthwhile. Upon replacing a starting pitcher with Yale graduate Ken McKenzie, Casey turned to his left-handed reliever and said, "Pretend they're the Harvards."

His memory for everything but names was remarkable. In a trip to Chicago, he was stopped by a man who appeared to be well over 80.

"Casey," the man said, "you won't remember me, but I knew you years ago."

"Just keep on talking," Stengel said, "and I'll tell you if I remember you."

The man said, "I'm from Kankakee. I used to be in the restaurant business."

Stengel, who began his professional career in the Illinois

town 52 years earlier, shook his head. "Don't tell me that," he said. "It wasn't a restaurant. You had a diner. Right?"

"Right again," the old man said.

"I'll tell you one thing more," Stengel said. "That league folded in the middle of the week and you still owe me $2.50 on my meal ticket."

The Mets, of course, were eager to capitalize on the nostalgia evoked by Stengel, the team's lineup of former Dodgers and Giants, and the Polo Grounds itself. So, on July 14, they staged an Old-Timers Day, which had been a well-established promotion of the Yankees. The theme chosen was the most famous game in the history of the park, the epic third playoff game between the Dodgers and Giants in 1951.

Ralph Branca pitched for the Dodger oldtimers and Bobby Thomson batted for the Giant oldtimers. And, fittingly, Thomson hit a home run, duplicating the drive that tormented Brooklyn, won the National League pennant for the Giants, and earned distinction as "The Shot Heard 'Round the World." The 37,253 fans were delighted by this flight of fancy. Reality returned in the regularly scheduled game as the present-day Dodgers drubbed the Mets, 17-3.

In a season of countless failures, the Mets could and did rise to dramatic heights on occasion. One of the more memorable occurred on Aug. 21 against the Pirates. Solly Hemus, the first-base coach, had been ejected from the game and replaced by Gene Woodling, one of Stengel's former Yankee stars who was finishing his playing career as a part-time outfielder.

In the ninth inning, with the Mets trailing by three runs, Woodling was sent to the plate as a pinch-hitter and Throneberry was instructed to replace him on the coaching lines. This he did to the accompaniment of a tremendous roar from the crowd. Woodling reached base safely and the Pittsburgh lead was cut to two runs.

When the Pirates brought in Elroy Face, their right-handed relief ace, Stengel waved once again to the coaching box and Marvelous Marv became the pinch-hitter. With the bearing of a man who has known many such moments, Throneberry proceeded to drive a three-run homer into the right-field stands, providing the Mets with a 5-4 victory. It marked the start of a two-game winning streak, the seventh such streak compiled by the Mets in 1962. Also, the last.

After Sept. 1, when the roster limit was raised to 40, the Mets added such stalwarts as Rich Herrscher, Dave Hillman, Willard Hunter, Galen Cisco, Larry Foss, and Joe Pignatano. Pignatano, a Brooklyn boy who had made one appearance in Ebbets Field before the Dodgers invited him to accompany them west in 1958, arrived early at the Polo Grounds on the day he was to report and was sitting on the bench when Stengel walked into the dugout.

Stengel and Pignatano talked for nearly an hour before the rest of the team arrived for pre-game workouts. Then, Pignatano joined the other Mets on the field. Shortly thereafter, a reporter asked Casey the identity of his catcher that evening. "Joe Pignatano," the manager replied, "if that fellow ever gets here."

Later in the month, Pignatano was down in the bullpen when the phone rang. "Get Nelson ready," the raspy voice ordered. The catcher hung up the receiver and looked around at the assembled cast of relief pitchers, but recognized no one by that name. With ingenuity typical of the Mets, Pignatano marched to the pitching slab, placed a baseball thereon and yelled, "Nelson!"

Bob Miller, the right-handed Bob Miller, walked to the spot and began his warm-up throws. It seems Casey always called Bob Miller "Nelson" and called Lindsey Nelson, my colleague on the broadcast team, "Miller."

On the next-to-last day of the season, "Nelson" drew the starting assignment. With a little bit of bad luck, he would qualify for a place in the record book. No pitcher in major-league history has lost as many as 13 games in a season without winning at least one. Miller's record was 0-12.

He appeared doomed in the seventh inning when, with the score tied at 1-1, Frank Thomas fell down rounding third on a single to left field by Jim Hickman and was tagged out in the ensuing rundown. But Throneberry sliced a two-out double and Hickman managed to stay on his feet around the bases. Miller safeguarded the lead and finished with a 2-1 victory.

There was an entirely appropriate conclusion to the 1962 season. Pignatano hit into a triple play in what was to be his last at-bat in the major leagues, and the Mets were defeated by the Cubs, 5-1. It marked their 120th loss in 160 games, enabling them to surpass comfortably the record of 112 losses set by my Pirates 10 years earlier.

The postscript wasn't bad either. Throneberry and Ashburn both received power boats, the former for his expertise in hitting a certain advertiser's sign on the outfield wall and the latter for being selected the team's Most Valuable Player. Alas, the ill-starred Throneberry had to pay taxes on his prize because, it was ruled, he had won it in a game of skill. Ashburn's craft was tax-free because it was an honorary award.

Even then, however, Ashburn did not totally escape the curse of the Mets. He placed the boat in the water off Ocean City, N.J., and watched it sink to the bottom. No one had thought to install the drainage plug.

Choo Choo and The Beagle

Forbes Field, when I first joined the Pittsburgh Pirates in 1946, was among the most massive baseball parks. The distance down the line to the brick wall in left field was 365 feet. It measured 457 feet from home plate to deepest center field. The park certainly was not built with a right-handed slugger in mind.

When the Pirates purchased Hank Greenberg from the Detroit Tigers at the conclusion of the 1946 season, however, management moved to rectify the situation. In order to encourage home runs, the bullpens were transplanted from foul territory into a space in front of the left-field wall. The enclosure was fronted with a 14-foot-high screen. This altered the dimensions to 335 feet down the line and 355 to the power alley in left-center. The area soon was labeled Greenberg Gardens.

Hank hit 25 homers that year, his last as an active player. Upon his retirement, Greenberg Gardens remained in everything but name. The writers began to call it Kiner's Korner.

I resented the name while I was playing because many people who never saw a game in Forbes Field incorrectly assumed that Kiner's Korner was a target for cheap home runs. I would gladly have traded my seasons in that park for a few more shots at the seats in Ebbets Field. But the identification stuck with me. So when it was determined I would host a post-game television show for the Mets, only one name seemed suitable: Kiner's Korner.

This was a whole new ball game for me. Even my interview with Phil Harris at Pebble Beach did not fully prepare me for what was to follow. There was, for instance, our first show from a dank area beneath the stands at the Polo Grounds. My first guest was Casey Stengel. After entertaining viewers for some 15 minutes with his nonstop comments, Casey got up to leave. Unfortunately, he had neglected to remove the small microphone clipped to his uniform. As he walked off the temporary set, he commenced taking the fixtures with him.

Perhaps the most memorable show that first season involved Choo Choo Coleman, the catcher whose conversations usually ran to one word. Coleman, whose first name was Clarence, simply was not responsive to questioning. Once, when Stengel had asked him the nature of a pitch an opponent had just hit over a building (one of Casey's favorite expressions), Coleman replied, "I don't know, Bub."

"Well," the manager advised him, "the next time you give a sign out there, take a peek yourself so you'll know what pitch you were calling."

Coleman had hit the first unofficial home run in club history. It occurred in the team's second exhibition game, and since then I had been needled about having him as a post-game guest. Finally, after running through virtually the entire roster, I surrendered to the inevitable. As a precautionary measure, I also invited Roger Craig, among the more articulate of the Mets' players.

I introduced Coleman as one of the most popular Mets and then turned to ask him, "Choo Choo, how did you get your nickname?" I had anticipated the answer that as a child he liked to play with trains or that his father worked for the railroad. Instead, Coleman said, "I don't know, Bub."

The reply stunned me. I was inexperienced handling interviews and I could feel the panic rising inside. I managed to blurt out the first question that came into my mind.

"What's your wife's name and what's she like?" I asked.

"Mrs. Coleman," he said, "and she likes me, Bub."

Roger Craig received more air time that day than both he and I had anticipated.

Charlie Neal roomed with Coleman during that first season. On the day he reported to spring training the following year, Neal joined a group of us behind the batting cage. There he pointed to Coleman, standing nearby, and said, "I'm going over to say hello to Choo Choo. I'll bet he doesn't even remember my name."

We thought he was kidding, so we followed him over.

"Choo Choo," Neal said, "it's good to see you."

"Hi, Bub," Coleman replied.

"You know my name?" Neal asked.

"Yep," the catcher answered.

"I'll bet you don't," Neal said.

"I know you all right," Coleman said. "You number four."

One of the highlights of Choo Choo's career with the Mets occurred in spring training when Clarence Coleman fielded a telephone call in the Mets' clubhouse intended for Clarence Thoman, an advertising executive assigned to the account of the Mets' major sponsor.

"Hello, Bub," Coleman said.

"Clarence, we want to check these contracts with you," the caller said. "We got to get them clarified, okayed, and into the mail. Now take the second paragraph, the last sentence. Is that exactly the way you want it?"

"Yep," Choo Choo said.

"You've had a chance to read it thoroughly?"

"Yep."

"And you want it to stay this way?"

"Yep."

"If we get them in the mail today, do you think you can have them signed and back here in time?"

"Yep."

By this time, the man on the other end was getting suspicious. "Are you sure this is Clarence Thoman?"

"Yep," Coleman replied. Then, hanging up the phone, Choo Choo said to Herb Norman, the team's equipment manager, "That man's crazy."

There was one other unforgettable character associated with the original Mets. His name was Homer, he had four legs and he wore a mournful expression. Homer was a beagle and the Mets' first mascot.

The idea originated with Phillip Liebmann, whose Rheingold Beer was the major sponsor of our telecasts in 1962. No expense was too great for Homer. He lived in the Waldorf Towers, had a tutor recruited from Hollywood, and occupied a stage set atop four box seats behind home plate at the Polo Grounds. His room and board, including the price of those box seats, was estimated to run $20,000 per year.

Homer played an important part in our telecasts. During the course of a game, the television cameras would focus on Homer at every opportunity. Rudd Weatherwax, the man who had trained Lassie, taught Homer to hold a banner in his mouth which said, "Let's Go, Mets." Then Homer learned to bow his head so a Met cap would show, to do backflips, to bark on cue, and to wave the banner back and forth.

His popularity grew with each routine. His fan mail equaled that of any of the Mets' players. He was about to become a full-fledged star.

The day chosen for Homer's ascendency was Miss Rheingold Day at the Polo Grounds. For weeks, Weatherwax had secretly been training Homer to run around the bases, thereby acting out his own name. Early that morning, he had performed the routine again and again until Weatherwax had been satisfied the dog was ready.

At the appointed hour, Lindsey Nelson made the announcement from home plate and Homer was led out of the stands to resounding cheers. The trainer gave the sign and Homer was off.

The beagle dashed to first base, scooted over the bag and turned for second. So far, so good. The cheering grew louder with each step. He touched second base, something Marv Throneberry had not always remembered to do, and the crowd roared. But suddenly, without slowing down, Homer veered toward home plate and, while thousands laughed, cut across the pitcher's mound. He had skipped third base entirely. He was a true Met, after all.

Homer retired after the season to the home of Al Moore, a Rheingold vice president who lived on Long Island. There it was discovered that, despite his high standard of living and his extensive formal education, Homer was not housebroken.

Farewell to the Polo Grounds

Marv Throneberry had expected a financial reward for his contributions to the 1962 Mets. He had hit 16 homers and driven in 49 runs in 116 games. And all those banners extolling his occasional malfunctions represented paid customers.

"I brought some people in," he argued.

"You also drove some away," countered Johnny Murphy, assistant to George Weiss.

Finally, Marv settled on the club's terms. But a number of other familiar faces were missing as the Mets assembled for spring training in 1963.

The roster which once boasted two Bob Millers now had none. Robert G. Miller, the left-hander, had been "fired" (Stengel's term), and Robert L. Miller, the one called "Nelson," had been traded to the Dodgers for first baseman Tim Harkness and second baseman Larry Burright. Ashburn had retired to a broadcasting booth in Philadelphia, and Mantilla had gone to the Red Sox for infielders Pumpsie Green and Al Moran and pitcher Tracy Stallard, the man who had yielded Roger Maris's 61st home run in 1961. Chacon had gone, period.

There were changes on the coaching staff as well, following the deaths of Rogers Hornsby and Red Kress. Clyde McCullough was hired to work with the catchers, and Ernie White was named pitching coach, replacing Red Ruffing, who was assigned to tutor the youngsters in the organization.

Norm Sherry, a catcher, and Dick Smith, an outfielder, had become the sixth and seventh Dodgers of recent vintage wearing Met uniforms. As a result of a spring-training transaction, there soon was an eighth. This was an authentic Brooklyn hero, none other than the Duke of Flatbush himself. Edwin Donald Snider was 36, paunchy, and ill-disposed to the Mets' image of lovable clowns. Near the end of training camp, the Mets also purchased Carlton Willey, a useful right-handed pitcher, from the Milwaukee Braves.

Stengel spent much of the spring talking about his "Youth of America" program, and two of those youths were to win places on the team. The foremost was Ed Kranepool, who had been signed out of James Monroe High School in the Bronx the previous year for an $85,000 bonus after breaking Hank Greenberg's school home-run record. The second was a personable relief pitcher from St. John's University named Larry Bearnarth. Kranepool, who had one hit in six at-bats in a brief visit to the majors in 1962, was 18. Bearnarth was 21.

The most important addition to the team that year, however, was a scrawny infielder purchased from the Braves' organization on a conditional basis. At the suggestion of coach Solly Hemus, the Mets had paid $5,000 to take a look at Ron Hunt, an aggressive but injury-prone second baseman. Stengel, who admired the brashness of Billy Martin in his Yankee days, saw similar qualities in Hunt, and Weiss had to surrender $35,000 more of Mrs. Payson's fortune. It would be money well spent.

On Opening Day, Stengel presented a lineup that had only one player in the same position in which he had started the 1962 season. That was Frank Thomas, the left fielder, who had found the peculiar dimensions of the Polo Grounds so much to his liking that he succeeded Roger Maris as the home-run champion of New York with 34. Thomas was still with the Mets because the Polo Grounds was still with the Mets, construction on the new stadium having been stalled by a series of labor problems.

Roger Craig, who had won 10 and lost 24 the previous season, had the dubious honor of throwing the first pitch. Curt Flood of the St. Louis Cardinals had the pleasure of hitting it. Charlie Neal, the second baseman turned third baseman, had the misfortune of fielding it. His throw sailed down the right-field line, Flood scurried to second base, and the Mets came to bat for the first time in 1963 trailing, 2-0.

Burright led off the Mets' first with a single. He also led off the Mets' ninth with a double. Those were the only hits the Mets collected off Ernie Broglio. The Cards won the game, 7-0. "We're still a fraud," Stengel rasped. "The attendance got trimmed again."

The Mets were also shut out in the second game as Ray Washburn limited them to four hits. They managed their first run of the season in the third game on a Duke Snider home run. It was their only run in a 6-1 loss to Warren Spahn and the Braves. In the fourth game, Snider homered again, Jim Hickman added another circuit, and the Mets managed a 5-2 defeat. Another shutout, a 1-0 loss that required 10 innings to complete, followed.

The Mets set a season high in the sixth game, scoring three runs to take a 3-2 lead into the ninth inning. Stallard had replaced Al Jackson on the mound in the seventh inning and retired the first six Brave batters. He displayed no hint of weakness in the ninth, striking out both Eddie Mathews and Joe Torre for the first two outs. But Mack Jones singled, Lee Maye homered, and the Mets were still seeking their first victory.

Cincinnati was the next stop. Only the scores changed. The Reds defeated the Mets, 7-4, in the first game of the series, and Jim O'Toole recorded a 5-0 shutout in the second game, the fourth time the Mets had been blanked in eight contests. One more defeat and it could be said of the Mets that they had not improved even a little from one year to the next.

The ninth game of the season was scheduled for the Polo Grounds. The Braves took a 4-3 lead into the ninth inning, apparently dooming the Mets to another 0-9 start. But in the bottom of the inning, Hunt slapped a two-run double against the team that could find no use for his services and the Mets triumphed over the ghost of season past.

So overwhelmed at her team's dramatic victory was Mrs. Payson that she ordered a bouquet of roses sent to Hunt's apartment. Unknown to the thoughtful owner, Hunt was troubled by a bewildering variety of allergies. After hours of noisy suffering, the tough second baseman had to throw out the flowers in order to get some sleep.

The Mets won again the following day, 3-1, and actually swept a doubleheader from the Braves on Sunday by scores of 8-5 and 9-2. It represented the first four-game winning steak in club history. The team continued to win with some regularity until, after stretching another streak to five games on May 10, they had jumped into seventh place with a 13-15 record.

In the second game of a doubleheader on Mother's Day, the Mets overcame the Reds, 13-12, at the Polo Grounds. It prompted Stengel to say, "Just when my guys are commencing to hit in this ballpark, they're going to tear it down." However, the Mets were to stop hitting long before the demolition began.

The losses mounted as the team reverted to 1962 form. In one game, Stallard twice was belted for home runs into the right-field stands. Upon the occasion of the second homer, Stengel trudged to the mound. "Doctor," he addressed Stallard, "at the end of the season they're going to tear this joint down. The way you're pitching, the right-field section will be gone before they get to it."

Throneberry, the marvelous one from '62, was already gone. On May 9, the Mets announced that the quiet folk hero from Tennessee was being farmed out to Buffalo. One of his last acts as a Met was turning a single into a two-run error from his new position in right field.

"I ain't gave up yet," Marv said when he learned of his demotion. "I'm going to leave my name up there above my locker." After everyone had said goodbye and the clubhouse had emptied, he pulled off his New York uniform for the last time, showered, dressed, packed his gear, and began his journey.

He didn't get far. The clubhouse door was locked from the outside. It was only after a half hour of commotion that his cries for help were heard and he was allowed to leave. No Met ever went out in more fitting style.

On May 22, while the team was playing the Dodgers in Los Angeles, it was announced that the Washington Senators had sought permission to talk to Gil Hodges about their managerial vacancy. At the time, Hodges was on the disabled list, where he spent the greater part of his term with the Mets.

Hodges welcomed the opportunity and a deal was struck. The Mets received Jimmy Piersall, a controversial but talented outfielder who had suffered a nervous breakdown early in his career and had won fame as much for his zany stunts as for his acrobatic catches. Piersall also had one problem characteristic of all Mets who had made reputations elsewhere. It was age. Piersall was 33 and no longer the gazelle he had been.

He did have one moment of inspired lunacy with the Mets. He hit his 100th career homer in the Polo Grounds and, as he had vowed some time before, jogged around the bases in reverse gear although not in reverse order.

Stengel was not amused. Nor did Piersall's .194 average help his cause. The Mets released Piersall after two months. "There's only room for one clown on this team," the manager said.

Piersall did last long enough to star in the game that represented the highlight of the season. Maybe the Mayor's Trophy Game didn't count in the standings, but then the Mets never had much use for the standings. A crowd of nearly 50,000 fans descended on Yankee Stadium on the night of June 20 for the first meeting of the Mets and Yankees in New York, and if any of them were Yankee fans, it was a well-kept secret.

Many of the banners with which Met fans customarily traveled were confiscated by security guards. But there was no regulation about making noise. The fans blew horns, set off firecrackers, and generally conducted themselves as if the great ball atop the Times Tower were about to drop, signaling the start of a New Year. The Old Man had a pretty good time himself.

The game marked Stengel's first trip to the historic stadium since he had been requested to leave three years earlier. He was prepared, exhibition or no exhibition. The Yankees, en route to their fourth consecutive American League pennant, fielded reserves. Casey not only led with his regulars but had Jay Hook and Carlton Willey, two of his best pitchers, primed for the charity contest.

Piersall led off with a two-base hit and later scored the first run on a wild pitch. The Yankees tied the score, 1-1, in the third with another hit. Hook pitched the first five innings and Willey the last four. The Mets won, 6-2. They were champions of New York, sort of.

Ralph Houk, the Yankee manager who was known as the Major for his exploits in World War II, said, "It wasn't as bad

as the Battle of the Bulge." And then he laughed aloud, something he rarely did after losing games.

The Mets made several personnel changes as they sank
deeper and deeper into last place. It was decided that Kranepool, who was batting .209, simply wasn't ready for major-
league pitching, and he was optioned to Buffalo in July. Always
in the market for another catcher, the Mets traded Neal and
Sammy Taylor to Cincinnati for Jesse Gonder, a heavy-legged
left-handed hitter who handled a bat a lot better than he did a
glove.

Banners, which the management once had regarded with
suspicion, became an integral part of a game at the Polo
Grounds. The craze received official recognition in 1963 when
Jules Adler, the franchise's first promotions director, staged the
inaugural Banner Day.

Among the winning banners in that first bedsheet parade
was one that stated, "Up a Tree in '63, Off the Floor in '64." The
Mets unfurled a banner of their own. It read, "To the Met Fans:
We Love You, Too." And, at the very last moment, Stengel
popped out of the dugout, carrying an exclamation point to its
inevitable conclusion.

The real drama of 1963, of course, was inspired by defeat.
The man on trial was Roger Craig, the pleasant gentleman
whose ill fortune it was to be the Mets' ace pitcher. Being the
ace gave him the chance to lose more often than anyone else.

On May 4, Craig had been blasted in a 17-4 loss to the Giants.
It was the start of a routine that was to last three months. Craig
would start every fifth game; Craig would lose every fifth game.
He wasn't pitching badly, but the Mets were averaging only one
and a half runs in each game he pitched.

As the streak grew, so did the number of suggestions as to
how he might break the evil spell. After he had lost his 13th
consecutive decision, he readily acceded to a request that he
change his uniform number from 38 to 13. He promptly lost his
14th and went back to his old number.

The cards and letters sent by Met fans offered encouragement, but what Craig really needed was runs. In one game, he
was locked in a scoreless tie when he marched up and down the
dugout between innings begging for just one run. By the eighth
inning, it was apparent that he was asking too much, so Roger

altered his plea. "All right, you guys," he said, "get me half a run." The Mets got no runs and lost.

Craig suffered his 18th successive defeat on Aug. 4. That left him one shy of the major-league record for one season last achieved by Jack Nabors of the Philadelphia Athletics in the summer of 1916. Not just New York but the entire country was now interested in Roger's plight.

The Mets were scheduled to open a series against the Chicago Cubs on the night of Aug. 9. The pitcher was Craig, and this time the team responded with an all-out assault on his behalf. Which is how the Mets and Cubs came to be tied, 3-3, in the ninth inning.

With two men out and a runner on first base, Al Moran doubled. Now there were runners at third and second. Craig was due to bat, but Stengel sent up Harkness as a pinch-hitter. He was walked intentionally. The next batter was Jim Hickman, the mild-mannered outfielder who took so many called third strikes that he had inspired this ditty by Stengel: "Oh, you can't improve your average with your bat upon your shoulder, tra-la, tra-la."

Hickman didn't hit the ball very far, but he did hit it high and parallel to the left-field line, where the seating began at the 280-foot mark. Billy William settled under the ball near the wall, but, as it drifted lazily down, it brushed the facade of the overhanging upper deck, one of the park's architectural oddities, and the umpire waved his right arm in a circle. Hickman, to the surprise of everyone, had hit a grand-slam home run. Roger Craig was a winner, at last.

"I've won World Series games and other big games," the pitcher said. "But this one ranks with my greatest thrills."

Stengel accepted some credit for the victory, acknowledging that he had given Chicago relief pitcher Lindy McDaniel his famous "Whommy" in the ninth. The Old Man explained that he had crossed his fingers and shouted, "Whommy, whommy," at the suitable time.

To keep the losing tradition alive, the Mets recalled pitcher Craig Anderson from Buffalo late in the season. Anderson had lost his last 16 decisions of 1962 and promptly dropped two more in 1963. That left him on an equal footing with Craig in the category of club records, but, since the streak was set over two seasons, he was no threat to Jack Nabors.

The final baseball game in the historic Polo Grounds was played on Sept. 18. The Mets, of course, lost. The opponent was Philadelphia and the final score was 5-1. The Mets lost seven of their last nine games, played on the road, and finished the season with a record of 51-111. That left them 15 games behind the ninth-place team, the Colt .45s.

In relation to 1962, the season had been encouraging. In relation to the rest of the National League, the season had been embarrassing.

Breaking In

I might have been a Yankee. I guess I was, in a sense. For three seasons, corresponding to my varsity years with the Alhambra High School Moors, I was an infielder and pitcher for the Yankee Juniors.

This was a team of young prospects in the Los Angeles area sponsored by baseball's most successful franchise. The Yankees supplied the bats, the balls, and even the uniforms, which were hand-me-downs from the big-league club. I wore a uniform that once belonged to George Selkirk, the outfielder who had the unenviable task of replacing Babe Ruth in right field. Fortunately, I didn't have to run the bases in his shoes. Although a well-proportioned man, Selkirk was famed for his tiny feet. They were size five. Hence his nickname, "Twinkletoes."

Dan Crowley, who had been a minor-league player, was the manager of the team, and the operation was overseen by Bill Essick, the Yankees' influential West Coast scout and the man who recommended that the club purchase Joe DiMaggio from the Pacific Coast League. There was an unwritten rule in those days that the sponsoring major-league club had first crack at the players. And the Yankees were interested in signing me to a contract.

It was tempting to join an organization that in 1939 had won the World Series for the fourth consecutive year, and without the loss of a game. The other side of the coin was that the Yankees were deep in talent all the way through their minor-league system. It might be years before I struggled up to the big leagues. And, like most organizations at the time, they were planning to start me in Class D ball.

I also had an opportunity to sign with the Pirates. The Pittsburgh scout, Hollis Thurston, knew something about home-run hitters, having contributed to Ruth's record home-run total as a pitcher for the Chicago White Sox and Washington Senators. Thurston, known as Sloppy for his sartorial splendor, was a persuasive man. He argued that I could advance much faster in the Pirates' chain, and he offered a contract that guaranteed I would start in nothing lower than a Class A league. He also offered a $3,000 bonus, a huge selling point in 1940, and $5,000 more when I made the big-league roster.

There was a third option. The Pacific Coast League was a prosperous operation at the time, and the Hollywood Stars were on the lookout for local talent. Babe Herman, who had been a great hitter with the Brooklyn Dodgers, was scouting for the Stars, and he proposed an unusual deal whereby I would play for them and then collect 50 percent of whatever they made in selling my contract to a major-league club.

It was Herman who was responsible for my one meeting with Ruth. The Brooklyn Babe was performing as Gary Cooper's double in *The Pride of the Yankees,* the story about Lou Gehrig's life and death. The baseball scenes were being shot at Wrigley Field in Los Angeles. He got me onto the set one day and brought me over to Ruth, who, of course, was playing himself in the movie. "Babe," Herman said, "this kid might break your home-run record. He can hit it a long way."

Ruth looked at me and shook my hand. "Good luck, kid," he said. "Nice to meet ya."

My mother preferred none of the three alternatives. She wanted me to go to college, an angle covered by the Yankees, who said they were willing to underwrite a scholarship to the University of Southern California during the winter months. The decision was made by a committee of three—my mother, me, and Harry Johnston, the father of my high school teammate Lefty Johnston and the man who was my unofficial baseball guidance counselor in those days. Of the three, I had the least to say about my future course. What did I know at that age?

Harry Johnston had been a minor-league pitcher, and he ran a semi-pro team in the Los Angeles area. He understood the workings of the sport, and it was he who convinced my mother that the Pirates' offer was best for me. The day I signed the Pittsburgh contract, my mother and I, Harry and his wife, Vera, and Lefty all drove to La Cienega Boulevard, known as the place "where the elite meet to eat." For the first time in my life, dinner was on me.

I had to wait until the following spring training to begin my pro career, as was the custom then. The Pirates invited me to the big-league camp at San Bernardino, about 60 miles east of Alhambra. It didn't take long to see that I could hit the ball farther than anyone Pittsburgh had on its roster.

But first, I had to find a sponsor. It was common practice at the time for veteran major leaguers to monopolize the batting cage, to prohibit rookies from taking their cuts. Bob Elliott, beginning his second full season as a regular, finally gave me my opening, handing me his bat and telling me to go hit. I'm sorry to say that, years later, I would repay his kindness by firing him from the post of manager of the San Diego Padres in the Pacific Coast League.

Once I got my chance in the cage, I opened a few eyes. Even Frankie Frisch, the hard-bitten manager who had been captain of the rowdy Gas House Gang in St. Louis, liked me, and he sure could be tough. After sizing up my potential, he made sure I got my swings every day. And he put me in the starting lineup—at first base—for the first exhibition game of the spring.

What made it memorable for me was that the game, against the White Sox, was played at Brookside Park in Pasadena. As a youngster, I had bicycled seven miles from my house just to watch similar exhibition games. Adding to the sense of occasion that day was the location of our locker room. It was in the famed Rose Bowl nearby.

I couldn't have imagined a better debut. I had four hits in five at-bats, including two home runs. I hit one off Bill Dietrich, a right-hander who had pitched a no-hitter against the Browns four years earlier, and the other off Thornton Lee, a left-hander who would win 22 games that season. Naturally, I was thrilled with myself.

It wasn't until late in the exhibition season that I concluded pro ball was not going to be a joyride. We had just taken a pounding from the Cubs at Wrigley Field in Los Angeles, and Frisch was angry enough to order laps after the game. I hadn't played, so I decided not to participate in the extracurricular activity. Frisch found me seated in the bullpen.

"Why aren't you running?" he shouted.

"Mr. Frisch," I said (I was barely 19), "I only have one pair of baseball shoes, and if I wear them out running, I won't have any for the games."

Apparently, the answer didn't satisfy him. "Well, that's fine," he said. "You can take those shoes to Barnwell, South Carolina, because that's where you're playing your next game."

That's how I discovered I was being sent to the camp of the Albany (N.Y.) Senators of the Class A Eastern League. It so happened a next-door neighbor of mine, Bobby Jones, was reporting to a Class D team in Lake Charles, La., and he had a car. So we set off cross-country in pursuit of the American Dream.

We were so square and eager then that we'd drive for three hours, stop the car, and play catch along the side of the road to keep our arms loose. We must have been quite a sight, something along the lines of the Norman Rockwell covers for the *Saturday Evening Post* that I had buried in my backyard nine years earlier.

En route to Louisiana, we picked up a hitchhiker. I would have cause to remember him, but not fondly. Once we arrived in Lake Charles, I took a train to Barnwell, where I arrived with the measles, courtesy of the extra passenger in the back seat of Bobby Jones's car.

I missed a week of training because of the illness but proceeded to hit a baseball over the 440-foot left-field fence in my first game back. I hit 11 home runs for Albany that season. That might not seem like a lot, but the Eastern League was a pitcher's league. The parks were big, the lights were bad, and the ball was dead. I played a second year at Albany, increasing my home-run output to 14, sufficient to provide me with my first title as a professional.

The war was at its height in 1943, and I was eligible for

duty. I decided to enlist in the Navy before I was to be drafted. By then, I had been promoted to Toronto of the International League, one step from the majors. I could really run at the time, which may surprise those who saw me near the end of my career, when my back was giving me fits. But I played center field in the minors.

In my last game before reporting for duty, I even managed to hit an inside-the-park home run. The Ralph Kiner who went off to flight school at 165 pounds in mid-1943 was a far cry from the man discharged after the war.

Although a number of athletes continued to play baseball after entering the service, I barely touched a bat during my hitch. I spent most of my time in the Pacific flying antisubmarine missions. I really filled out in that time. I added about 30 pounds. Unfortunately, what I gained in strength, I lost in speed.

Bob Lemon, who would become a Hall-of-Fame pitcher with the Cleveland Indians, had played against me in the minors, and he was amazed at my appearance when we met during spring training in 1946. "I remember you," he said. "I used to have to guard against the bunt when you batted. Now you can't run a lick."

Well, I wasn't *that* slow. But it was obvious that I would go only as far as my bat would carry me. Fortunately, that was pretty far.

Shea Hey

In just two years, the Mets had gained a solid foothold in New York without any success on the field. What they did in 1964 enabled them to sink roots even deeper into the city's consciousness. They moved.

The new stadium was a reality. The five-tiered, symmetrical structure would be ready for Opening Day. It was more than a year behind schedule, but, like the Long Island Rail Road which ran nearby, it was better late than never. Throughout the winter and early spring, workmen on the site raced workmen across the street who were busy preparing exhibits for the World's Fair.

Flushing Meadow was, in many respects, an ideal place for a ballpark. It was served by an elevated subway line that fed directly into Manhattan, and it was surrounded by parkways serving heavily populated Long Island. The Bronx and the northern suburbs beyond were a short ride away via the Bronx-Whitestone Bridge. There was parking for thousands of cars.

In recognition for his tireless (and unsalaried) efforts in bringing National League baseball back to New York, Bill Shea was granted a singular honor. The edifice was proclaimed William A. Shea Stadium at the dedication ceremony. "I feel highly honored that Mayor Wagner and members of the City

Council have seen fit to put my name on this wonderful structure," the attorney said. "Now I hope I live long enough to see a World Series played here."

That possibility appeared remote as the Mets prepared to play the first game in their palatial home on April 17. This third Met team already had bowed to tradition by losing its first two games of the season in Philadelphia.

George Weiss had revised the cast extensively during the previous winter. The coaching staff now included Wes Westrum, a top defensive catcher with the New York Giants during their championship seasons of 1951 and 1954, Don Heffner, Mel Harder, and Sheriff Robinson. Roger Craig had been rewarded for his two years of silent suffering by being traded to the Cardinals, a pennant contender, for powerful outfielder George Altman. Craig's place in the starting rotation was filled by Jack Fisher, whom the Mets had purchased for $30,000 from San Francisco in a special draft designed to aid the league's floundering expansion teams.

Fisher, a right-hander of ample girth who was called Fat Jack by his friends and those larger than he, had reached the majors at 20 with a Baltimore Orioles team so rich in young talent it was known as the Baby Birds. He had gained considerable fame for two pitches he had thrown on behalf of the Orioles. The first of those, in 1960, resulted in Ted Williams's 521st home run, on the occasion of Williams's final at-bat. The second enabled Roger Maris to hit a record-equalling 60th home run in 1961.

With the addition of Fisher to a staff that already included Tracy Stallard, the benefactor of Maris's 61st homer, the Mets now had the two pitchers who had made the greatest contributions to the fall of Babe Ruth's historic record. They were to form the nucleus of a staff whose other starters were Al Jackson and Jay Hook. Carlton Willey, who had enjoyed a fine season in 1963, suffered a broken jaw when hit by a line drive in an exhibition game and would not win a game for the Mets in 1964.

The Mets also had purchased Bob (Hawk) Taylor, a catcher, and Amado Samuel, an infielder, from the Braves during the off-season, and they were to figure in the club's immediate plans. The team's 10-17 spring training record wasn't very promising, but, at least, they had the satisfaction of winning two of three games played against Mexican League opponents in Mexico City.

After the Mets had lost the first of those three games south of the border, a journalist asked Casey Stengel whether the altitude had bothered his team. Ever aware of the Mets' deficiencies, Stengel snapped, "The altitude bothers my players at the Polo Grounds, and that's below sea level."

Shea Stadium also appeared to be below sea level, judging by the soggy turf. It had been constructed on landfill near the waters of Flushing Bay, and its heavy outfield would be a source of complaints by visiting players. But, for the Mets, it was home, sweet home.

En route north, the Mets bade farewell to Duke Snider, sending him to the San Francisco Giants. Snider a Giant? It seemed unthinkable. The last attachment to another era of New York baseball had been severed. The Mets would have to develop their own heroes in the future. They already had one in Ron Hunt, the tough second baseman Stengel had shifted to third in spring training in an effort to plug a gaping hole.

Fisher drew the starting assignment for the first game at Shea. Characteristically, the first hit in the new park was by a member of the opposition. Willie Stargell homered for the Pirates in the second inning. Tim Harkness supplied the Mets' first hit, a single in the third. Fisher was knocked out in the seventh, and Pittsburgh scored a run off reliever Ed Bauta in the ninth, dealing the Mets a 4-3 defeat.

However, the real news of the day was not made on the field. The citizens of New York once again had proven themselves more amazing than their team. A total of 50,312 braved crowded subway cars and massive traffic jams to attend the Friday housewarming.

More than 31,000 returned the following day, and the Mets lost, 9-5. The change of scenery was welcome but not inspirational. Then, just when it appeared the Mets were primed to make a run at their 1962 mark of nine consecutive losses, a strange thing happened. Jackson shut out the Pirates on six hits in a 6-0 victory on April 19.

Success was short-lived. The Mets lost 12 of their next 14 games for a 3-16 record, enabling them to pull even with their 1962 pace. The stadium was new, the Mets' record was not. But, at least, they were losing in better style.

The inauspicious start mandated changes. Hunt was moved back to second base, the position he favored, and the Mets acquired third baseman Charley Smith from the Chicago White Sox. Then, on May 8, the club completed its most important trade to date. The Mets sent battle-scarred Jay Hook to the Braves for Roy McMillan, a veteran shortstop with all-star credentials and a thorough streak of professionalism.

Only four days earlier, the Mets had engaged in a brawl against the Braves in Milwaukee. It was instigated by Hunt, who smashed into catcher Ed Bailey in a futile attempt to score the tying run in the ninth inning. But it was elevated to legend by that little old battler, Casey Stengel.

Stengel had rushed onto the field as fast as his bowed legs would carry him and quickly wrapped his arms around the first available Brave, Denis Menke. Feeling himself shackled, the Milwaukee shortstop whirled around, knocking his adversary to the ground. His first thought, as he gazed upon the prone figure of the Mets' manager, was, "Omigod, I killed the Old Man." Stengel soon dusted himself off, however, and the battle abated with no reported injuries.

At 73, Stengel was the oldest combatant ever to participate in a major-league fight. "I laughed so hard when I saw Casey fall on his back," Stallard said, "that I couldn't hit anybody." Stallard did not say it to Casey's face.

The Mets battled on, losing two for every game they won. Although they were failures, they were anything but dull. The first in a series of bizarre games occurred on May 26, a Tuesday afternoon, at Wrigley Field.

On that day, the Mets amassed 23 base-hits, five by Dick Smith. They breezed into the ninth inning with a stunning 13-1 lead and promptly scored six more runs. "That's when we knew we had them," said Stallard after the 19-1 victory.

In the evening, a man involved in a weekly run pool called a radio station in New York. "How many runs did the Mets score today?" he inquired.

"Nineteen," the operator answered.

"Man, that's great," the caller said. "Did they win?"

His pessimism was justified. The Mets scored a total of one run in the next two games and lost the series.

The question of just how far the Mets would go in losing a game was answered emphatically on May 31 in the second game of a holiday doubleheader against the Giants. Victories on Friday night and Saturday had helped to lure a record crowd of 57,037 to Shea Stadium. Not unexpectedly, the Mets lost to Juan Marichal, 5-3, in the first game. There was more to come, much more than anyone anticipated.

The Giants took a 6-1 lead in the second game, but the Mets rallied and eventually tied the score, 6-6, on Joe Christopher's homer in the seventh inning. The game remained tied after nine innings. Also after 10, 11, 12, and 13 innings.

In the 14th inning, the Giants threatened. But with runners on first and second and none out, McMillan speared a line drive hit by Orlando Cepeda and converted it into the second triple play in Mets' history. The game continued.

Thousands remained in their seats as 10 o'clock came and went. The two teams were taking aim at the record for the longest game in major-league history, a 26-inning affair staged in 1920 between the Brooklyn Robins and Boston Braves which ended in a 1-1 tie. Thousands more at home tuned in after being advised of the remarkable encounter by a panelist on "What's My Line?" the popular television quiz show. Introduced by moderator John Daley at the top of the show, publisher Bennett Cerf said, "I've been backstage watching the most amazing game I've ever seen." Click went the dials in living rooms throughout the New York area.

Gaylord Perry, who had entered the game in the 13th inning, was still pitching for the Giants as the 23rd inning began. Later, much later, he would confess that this was the game when he first experimented with the illegal spitball. Galen Cisco had been pitching for the Mets since the 15th.

Jim Davenport led off the Giants' 23rd with a triple into the right-field corner. After an intentional walk, Del Crandall pinch-hit for Perry and doubled, driving in the first run by either team in 16 innings. A single by Jesus Alou produced a second run, and Bob Hendley set down the Mets in order in their half of the inning. The game had lasted 7 hours, 23 minutes, the longest in major-league history from a standpoint of time.

The doubleheader, which had consumed 10 hours and 17 minutes, ended at precisely 11:25 P.M. Ed Kranepool, for one, was disappointed. He had been recalled from the Mets' Buffalo farm team after playing in a doubleheader on Saturday, and had played all 32 innings of Sunday's marathon. Apparently, it affected his mind. "I wish it had gone longer," he said. "I always wanted to play in a game which started in May and ended in June."

The umpire behind home plate for that second game was Ed Sudol. It would not be his last encounter with the Mets' madness.

If that defeat marked a shining hour for the Mets, there was another three weeks later which many felt was more representative. On Father's Day, in the first game of yet another doubleheader at Shea, the Mets conspired to send 27 men to the plate against Jim Bunning of the Phillies without managing a single baserunner. Only Jesse Gonder threatened even remotely, but his ground smash in the fifth inning was knocked down by second baseman Tony Taylor. Gonder's lack of speed made possible the fine recovery and throw by Taylor.

Bunning completed a 6-0 victory by striking out pinch-hitter John Stephenson, a rookie catcher. By then, the 32,026 fans were on their feet, cheering an opponent with every pitch. His perfect game was the first since Don Larsen's in the 1956 World Series, the first in regular-season National League play since 1880 and only the eighth in the history of the major leagues.

A tough competitor who had pitched a previous no-hitter for the Detroit Tigers, Bunning was not the sort to be overcome by emotion. Although his wife and one of his seven children—who had been seated in the stands—joined him on the field, Bunning retained his poise when our producer, Joe Gallagher, sought to make arrangements for an interview between games. "How much is in it for me?" Bunning inquired.

Once it was explained that it was for the good of the game, Bunning agreed to the interview, which was televised in New York and also transmitted to Philadelphia. And he didn't have to wait long for a financial reward. That evening he made a paid appearance on "The Ed Sullivan Show."

It was not the first time Met fans had cheered an opponent. On June 9, they had displayed their appreciation for the game's finer points in the course of a memorable performance by Billy Cowan, an outfielder for the Cubs.

Cowan struck out four times in the first game of a doubleheader, won by the Mets, 6-5, in 12 innings. He struck out a fifth time in the second game and received a round of applause.

Then, facing Cisco, Cowan struck out again, tying a league record for ineptness. The crowd accorded him a standing ovation. If anyone needed proof negative of the Met fans' knowledge of the game, this was it. Without aid of any scoreboard information, they knew a record when they saw one.

With his sixth strikeout, Cowan had become an instant hero. On his next trip to the plate, he topped his performance by smashing a home run. Again, he received a standing ovation. It was essential, of course, that the Mets acquire a player capable of such entertaining extremes. This they did the following season.

On a positive note, the fans were rewarded for their dedication when the All-Star Game was staged at Shea Stadium in July. What made the day so enjoyable to the faithful was the inclusion of their favorite, Ron Hunt, in the National League's starting lineup. Hunt, batting above .300 and battling everyone in another uniform, had become the first Met ever voted to the squad by his peers.

The fans lavished their affection on Hunt when he was introduced before the game. Hunt appreciated it. "I just hope I can hang around here until we get into the World Series," he said. "Look at the way these fans are now. Can you imagine what it would be like if we won the pennant? They wouldn't let us go home. It would be wild."

Hunt had a single in the game, which made the fans happy, and the NL rallied for a 7-4 victory when John Callison of the Phillies slammed a three-run homer in the ninth inning off Dick Radatz, the 230-pound relief ace of the Boston Red Sox.

The Mets closed out their home season on Sept. 27 with a 3-1 loss to the Reds. The paid attendance for the year was an unbelievable 1,732,597, certainly a record for a last-place team. The club's record was 51-104 as it left on its final road trip. The Mets needed only one victory to make this their most successful season.

After a three-game series in Milwaukee, they still needed one victory. And it wasn't going to be easy. The last opponent on the schedule was the Cardinals. Suddenly, the Mets found themselves in a pennant race. It wasn't *their* pennant race, but it was a pennant race nonetheless.

On Sept. 21, the Phillies held a 6½-game lead with 12 games remaining. They appeared assured of their first pennant since

1950, the season of the Whiz Kids (or Quiz Kids, in Stengel's lexicon). They promptly collapsed, losing their next 10 games and slipping behind the Cardinals and the Reds. As the three-game series opened Friday night, Oct. 2, the Cards led the Reds by a half game, the Phils by 2½, and the Giants by three. A four-way tie was a distinct possibility.

It remained a possibility as the Mets defeated the Cards, 1-0, behind Jackson's five-hitter. Kranepool's third-inning single had produced the only run against Bob Gibson, the St. Louis ace. The Mets had their 52nd win, their highest total ever, and three other teams still had a chance for the title, the Phils having defeated the Reds and the Giants also having won.

Again on Saturday, the Mets rose up, knocking out 20-game winner Ray Sadecki in the first inning and breezing to a 15-5 victory. The Giants lost, eliminating them from competition. The Phils and Reds were not scheduled. As a result, the Cards and Reds shared first place, with the Phils only one game back.

Never before had the Mets so thoroughly enjoyed playing baseball. For a change, they were being celebrated for their triumphs instead of their failures. This was a new scene, the first time they had been taken seriously. Respect was in the offing.

In the fifth inning of the third game, the Mets took a 3-2 lead and knocked out starter Curt Simmons. Johnny Keane, the Cards' manager, had no choice but to call upon his ace, Bob Gibson, who had started and lost the first game of the series. It would take the Cards' best to beat the Mets, and that was a tribute of sorts.

Cisco, the captain of Ohio State's Rose Bowl team six years earlier, faltered in the fifth and was removed as the Cards scored three runs to regain the lead. St. Louis won the game, 11-5, and clinched the pennant as the Phillies clobbered the Reds, 10-0.

The most successful of Met seasons was history. Oh, yes, in the course of the year, Craig Anderson was recalled from Buffalo. He made one start and lost his 19th consecutive decision. At one point in his career, he was the team's most successful pitcher, with a 3-1 record. Now the record for futility was his alone.

There was a strange fallout from the 1964 season, and it had an immediate impact on the Mets. Although the Cardinals won not only the pennant but also the World Series, in seven games from the Yankees, both field manager Johnny Keane and general manager Bing Devine declined to continue their associations because of what they considered interference from my old friend Branch Rickey, who had been hired as a special consultant by owner Gussie Busch. Meanwhile, the Yankees fired the popular Yogi Berra, who, in his first year as manager, had guided the team to within one game of the World Championship. The final bizarre note was sounded a week after the Series when the Yankees announced their new manager for 1965. It was none other than Johnny Keane.

Devine, an able baseball man who had worked his way from the bottom to the top of the St. Louis organization, was quickly snapped up by the Mets. He would serve as George Weiss's assistant and be groomed to take over the general manager's job when Weiss decided to retire.

One month later, the Mets called a press conference to announce another public relations coup. They had signed Berra as a player-coach. As they had four years earlier in the case of Stengel, the Yankees played directly into the Mets' hands.

Stengel had referred to Berra as "my assistant manager" while with the Yankees. Now the odd couple of baseball was reunited.

"Mr. Berra always knew the pitchers," Casey said, "and he liked to talk to the hitters. And besides which, he got them into the World Series, so you'd have to say he ain't failed yet. And maybe he can still swing the bat for me."

There were other changes, both in the front office and on the field. Eddie Stanky, the former Giants' infielder who had worked under Devine in St. Louis, became director of player development. He was assisted by Joe McDonald, who had joined the Mets as statistician for our broadcast team and then moved into the minor-league department.

The project of recycling older stars continued with the acquisition of Warren Spahn from the Braves. He was to pitch and also to coach the other pitchers. Spahn was the winningest left-handed pitcher in the history of the game, but he was also 43 and the Braves wanted to rebuild.

Billy Cowan, who had already made his mark at Shea, was added over the winter in a trade that sent George Altman to the Cubs. At Devine's recommendation, the Mets also dealt for another outfielder, Johnny Lewis, assigning Tracy Stallard to the Cardinals. But the major excitement in spring training was generated by a third outfielder, a husky youngster named Ron Swoboda.

Swoboda was the first of Stengel's so-called "Youth of America" to play his way onto the team. He was homegrown, signed by the Mets out of the University of Maryland, and he had led the Eastern League in home runs in his first professional season. Although his talent was raw and his defensive play was heartstopping, Swoboda drew Stengel's attention. He had prodigious power, of a kind rarely seen, and he was willing to work at his deficiencies.

In outfield practice one day, Swoboda continually heaved the ball high to home plate instead of making the acceptable one-bounce throw. Finally, Stengel shuffled all the way to the outfield to make the point. "You have to get the ball down," the manager said. "You have to throw to home plate on one bounce."

Swoboda got the message. On his very next throw, he kept the ball down. And he almost hit himself in the left foot.

Yet, Swoboda was among the final 25 who went north with the Mets for Opening Day. Naturally, the Mets lost their first game, 6-1, to the Los Angeles Dodgers. They also lost their second game, 7-6, to Houston despite a pinch-hit home run by Swoboda in his second major-league at-bat.

Victory came sooner, if no easier, to the Mets in their fourth season. Against Houston, in the third game, Lewis started an unusual triple play—from right field to the catcher to the shortstop—and Bobby Klaus, a weak-hitting utility infielder acquired from Cincinnati in mid-1964, belted a 10th-inning home run. The Mets won, 5-4.

The masterful Juan Marichal shut out the Mets, 4-0, in the fourth game, and the Giants also won the opener of an Easter Sunday doubleheader, 4-1. The Mets earned a split with a 7-1 victory in the second game, during which Swoboda, making his first start, hit his second homer.

Interest centered on Spahn as the Mets flew west on their first road trip of the season. He was scheduled to pitch the first game against the Dodgers on April 20, three days prior to his 44th birthday. A tough competitor, Spahn had remained in excellent physical condition and was determined to prove he could still be an effective starting pitcher.

He got no argument that night. Spahn matched Claude Os-teen of the Dodgers zero for zero through seven innings and was granted a 1-0 lead in the eighth. The Mets scored two insurance runs in the ninth, and now Spahnie was three outs away from vindication.

Then Wes Parker singled and an error by Ed Kranepool placed runners at first and third. A single by Tommy Davis drove in one run and a single by John Roseboro cut Spahn's lead to 3-2. The tying run was on third base, the winning run on first base, and soon Stengel was at the mound for a talk with his pitching coach.

A right-hander and a left-hander were warming up in the bullpen. Stengel asked Spahn which man he wanted. Spahn, the coach, stared blankly at the manager. "How do you feel about yourself?" Stengel asked. Spahn, the pitcher, saw the opening. "I'll pitch," he said.

The batter was Jim Lefebvre. Spahn struck him out. Then he got Ron Fairly to tap to the mount, hanging up Davis between third and home, where he was tagged out. Finally, Spahn fanned John Kennedy. He had held off the Dodgers and won his first game for his new employers.

His teammates, suitably inspired, lost the next two games to Sandy Koufax and Don Drysdale. But in San Francisco, they seemed to be a different club. They rallied from an 8-2 deficit to defeat the Giants, 9-8, in 11 innings on Friday night, then staged another amazing comeback the following day.

The Giants led, 6-4, entering the ninth inning, but Charley Smith started a rally with a bunt single. One out later, Chris Cannizzaro hit a checked-swing grounder on which no fielder could make a play. Stengel was down to his last left-handed pinch-hitter, who also happened to be his pitching coach. Spahn grounded out, both runners moving into scoring position.

Lewis, a left-handed batter, was next in the order. Herman Franks, the Giants' manager, elected to grant Lewis an intentional walk, putting the potential winning run on base. Stengel then sent Danny Napoleon to bat for Roy McMillan against the right-handed Bob Shaw. Napoleon was a right-handed batter. He was also a veteran of two at-bats in the major leagues, and he appeared overmatched against Shaw, who got two quick strikes.

But to the surprise of Shaw and Franks and Napoleon himself, the rookie drove the next pitch to the fence in right-center field for a three-run triple. The Mets won, 7-6. "Viva la France," shouted Stengel, walking around the clubhouse with his right hand tucked inside his uniform shirt in the manner of Napoleon Bonaparte. It didn't seem to matter that Napoleon was a black from Pennsylvania.

The Mets split a doubleheader the next day, Spahn winning his second complete game and Swoboda slamming his fourth homer. Optimism was rising to the surface. The team's record, as it began a two-game series in Houston, was 6-7. It was a chance at .500, the chance of a lifetime.

There was an added dimension to the game. The Colt .45s had been renamed the Astros in honor of their new home, the spectacular Astrodome. This would be the Mets' first indoor game, and they would have cause to remember it for a long time.

In the first few games played in the Dome, outfielders frequently had lost fly balls against the backdrop of a plexiglass ceiling which was designed to admit enough light to encourage the growth of grass. The mistake soon was acknowledged and the glass panels were painted opaque to help fielders. (It also aided the manufacturers of a new artificial field surface which became known as Astroturf after its installation in the Dome.) The Mets resisted such help. Asked how he thought the Mets would react to fly balls in the Dome, Stengel replied, "We're still working on grounders."

Jack Fisher started for the Mets and was pitching one of his better games. After seven innings, he held a 2-0 lead, but two hits and a Mets' error in the eighth cut the margin in half. Fisher retired the first batter in the ninth, but Cowan, who had entered the game for defensive purposes, failed to grab Bob Aspromonte's drive to center field. It was ruled a double.

Rusty Staub, a dangerous left-handed hitter, stepped to the plate, and Stengel replaced Fisher with his best lefty pitcher, Al Jackson. Mike White, a right-handed hitter, batted for Staub and flied out. One out away from .500, Stengel called for Dennis Ribant, his best right-handed reliever, to face Ron Brand. On a 3-2 count, Ribant walked Brand. It was an ominous sign.

The Houston pinch-hitter was Eddie Kasko, a veteran with a minimum of power. Ribant threw one pitch and Kasko lofted a fly ball to left field. It was deep but catchable, and, from the broadcast booth, it looked like the final out. Apparently, it looked quite different from Joe Christopher's vantage point underneath the ball, because he started in, hesitated, and then raced back. The ball fell behind him, both runners scored, and the Mets waved goodbye to .500. They lost their next five games.

Berra was "activated" about this time, started a couple of games behind the plate, but soon proved to everyone's satisfaction that he had not retired prematurely. He was deactivated permanently.

There were other problems. Kranepool, who had hit over .400 in the giddy first two weeks of the season, began his descent. Swoboda, a terror for a month, was seeing more action and hitting fewer home runs. Spahn was showing his age.

Then, in what may have been the fatal blow, Hunt suffered a shoulder dislocation in a basepath collision with Phil Gagliano of the Cardinals. The Mets acquired Chuck Hiller from the Giants as a replacement. Hiller, a skillful batter, was no Hunt around second base.

In true contradictory fashion, a 10-game losing streak in early June served as a prelude to the high point of the season. It occurred in the course of a no-hit performance by an opposing pitcher, another marvelous twist.

The date was June 14. The place was Crosley Field in Cincinnati. Jim Maloney, a hard-throwing right-hander, was the Reds' pitcher, and he never was faster than he was that night. Maloney overpowered the Mets for nine innings. He allowed only two baserunners—Kranepool, who walked in the second inning, and Smith, who reached first on a missed third strike in the third. But the Reds failed to score against veteran Frank Lary over the first eight innings, and Larry Bearnarth held them off in the ninth.

So Maloney went back out for the 10th inning and again held the Mets hitless, raising his strikeout total to 17. His teammates failed to score against Bearnarth in the bottom of the inning. How long could Maloney maintain his mastery? The answer was not long enough.

Johnny Lewis, the leadoff batter in the 11th, took two balls and a strike and then lined a home run over the center-field fence. Maloney made Swoboda his 18th strikeout victim, and, after McMillan slapped a single, Jesse Gonder bounced into a double play. Bearnarth preserved the lead in the last of the 11th, and all Maloney had to show for his magnificent effort was a two-hit, 1-0 defeat.

The season soured after that. Spahn was released in mid-July with a record of 4-12. The future course of the Mets was permanently altered in the early morning hours of July 25. At a party thrown for the honored guests of the Mets' annual Old-Timers Day at Toots Shor's restaurant, Stengel slipped and fell on his hip. The Old Man, whose tolerance was amazing, picked himself up and continued the celebration.

Stengel was living nearby at the Essex House, but since Edna was back in California at the time, he accepted an invitation to spend what was left of the night at the home of Joe DeGregorio, the club controller, who lived near Shea Stadium. The wake-up call was a piercing pain at the spot where he had fallen.

A birthday ceremony for Stengel, who would be 75 on July 30, was to precede the doubleheader against the Phillies. By then, however, Casey was lying in Roosevelt Hospital with a broken hip. The following day, at Stengel's suggestion, Wes Westrum was designated interim manager for the remainder of the season. Casey underwent surgery and was hospitalized for three weeks.

On Aug. 30, at a press conference in the Essex House, he announced his retirement. "If I can't walk out there to take out the pitcher," he said, "I can't manage. I can't pull him out with this here crooked cane." He was given the title of vice president and West Coast representative of the Mets.

"I'm disappointed in the ball club," he said in review. "I'm not disappointed in the staff or the fans. They were wonderful. I'm proud to be connected with this club. When I started, I would have liked to finish higher. I wanted to leave behind eight or nine men who could last 10 or 12 years. Well, there's Hunt, and I know he's first-division. There's Swoboda, and nobody will laugh at him in another year. The shortstop, Roy McMillan, was wonderful. Then there are some young ones."

Edna Stengel, who had flown in from California to take care of her husband after the injury, said, "I know it's going to be rough for Casey to take off the uniform, but I never wore a uniform."

Casey paid a visit to Shea before accompanying his wife back home to the big house in Glendale. He took the occasion to give the Mets, his Mets, a final pep talk. George Weiss announced that number 37, the uniform to which Casey Stengel had given life, was being retired.

"This uniform," Weiss said, "will be put under glass to be reviewed by fans who come to Shea Stadium." Stengel, as ever, had the last line. "I hope," he said, "they don't put me under glass, too."

There were a few bright moments under Westrum late in the season. Very few. Tug McGraw, an exuberant 20-year-old left-hander, provided one when he outdueled the great Koufax for one of his two victories. It marked the first time the Mets had beaten the Dodgers' ace in four seasons.

But the Mets suffered through an 11-game losing streak in August and won only 19 of 67 under the new manager. Jack Fisher was saddled with 24 defeats, tying Roger Craig's club mark. As was the case with Craig, his fault was that he was so dependable. The overall record of 50-112 was the second poorest in the team's brief history, and now there was no Stengel to entertain the media and to distract the public from the truth.

The Celebrity Game

Not unlike hundreds of thousands of incredulous fans, I watched the finish of that remarkable 23-inning game against the Giants on television. In fact, I watched the last four hours on television although never stepping outside the ballpark. It wasn't by design.

As I did at every televised home game, I left the broadcasting booth in the eighth inning and went down to our studio near the Met clubhouse to prepare for my post-game show, "Kiner's Korner." If the game ended quickly, I had to be ready. By the time this one ended, I was never so ready in my life.

At the start of the 14th inning, I considered returning upstairs and relieving either Lindsey Nelson or Bob Murphy, who were handling the television and radio broadcasts by themselves. But just as I was about to leave the studio, the Giants got two runners on base and I sat down again in expectation of a decision. That's when Roy McMillan started the triple play. I resigned myself to a long wait.

The Mets and Giants finished 19 innings, and producer Joe Gallagher thought we should inject some humor into the proceedings. First, we discussed setting up a stack of our sponsor's empty beer cans and taking a shot of me passed out alongside. The plan was vetoed as an example of bad taste. What the viewers at home ultimately did see was a picture of me stretched out on the studio couch, apparently asleep.

Not that I wasn't tempted. But I still had work to do. As it was, the post-game show ended at 11:45, only 15 minutes to June.

There were any number of amazing stories connected with the telecast of that doubleheader. Among my favorites was the one involving Richard Burton and Elizabeth Taylor.

Burton, the celebrated Welsh actor, had spent considerable time in New York earlier in the decade while appearing in the musical *Camelot.* In the course of his stay, he had taken an interest in baseball. When he left the play, he was given a book on the sport by the producer, and he took it home with him to Switzerland.

"I'm a voracious reader," he later explained. "I'm even an expert on the backs of sauce bottles . . . The more I read, the more interested I got in the sport of baseball."

As fate would have it, Burton was back in New York on that memorable Sunday. He was appearing in *Hamlet* and living in a hotel suite with his actress-wife, Liz Taylor. Baseball had never been one of her consuming passions.

While Elizabeth paced about the room in an agitated condition on May 31, Burton was seated in front of the television set, watching the Mets and Giants. "A wife should be interested in her husband's hobby," Burton said. "Sit down and I'll explain the game to you."

The explanation was wasted. She began dressing for dinner. Finally, she was ready but Burton was not. "It's the eighth inning," he assured her. "The game will be over in a few minutes."

He would regret those famous words. Dinner that evening was almost as cold as his wife.

I'll never forget the occasion of my one date with Liz Taylor. I was playing for the Pirates and she was a rising young star in the movies. I had visited Bing Crosby, one of the Pirates' owners, at Paramount Studios following the end of the season. Crosby asked me if I'd like to accompany Miss Taylor to a Hollywood premiere. It sounded like a terrific idea.

I picked her up at her home and we had a police escort to Graumann's Chinese Theater. The picture was *Twelve O'Clock High,* and the list of invitees had drawn several thousand curious fans. Temporary bleachers had been set up outside the theater, which was lit by powerful searchlights. We pulled up behind several long limousines and received an ovation when we stepped out and an attendant took the car. It was quite an experience.

After the show, we walked outside. A man stood at a public-address system, paging the cars of celebrities. "Paging Mr. Grant's car," he said. And, swiftly, there appeared the limousine which had delivered Cary Grant and his date.

I asked the man to call for my car and then rejoined Elizabeth. In the meantime, cars belonging to Jimmy Stewart, Gregory Peck, and several other stars pulled up, received their occupants and sped off to a reception. My car was nowhere to be seen.

Once again, I asked the man to page my car. He did. Still no sign of it. The crowd was dwindling to a precious few and I was squirming. I approached the man a third time.

"Mr. Kiner," he said. "I've paged it twice already. Your chauffeur must be asleep."

"Chauffeur?" I said. "I don't have a chauffeur."

"In that case," he replied testily, "it's that way." And he pointed us in the right direction. The car was sitting in an otherwise vacant parking lot two blocks from the theater.

Even though my first date with a movie star ended in embarrassment, I was not so discouraged as to swear off the species entirely. Perhaps if I had encountered Liz Taylor on my turf instead of hers, I would have been more comfortable with the situation. Certainly, that was true in the case of Janet Leigh.

We met in 1951 in Pittsburgh, not Hollywood. In fact, we became acquainted at Forbes Field. She had a featured role in the motion picture *Angels in the Outfield,* which was using the ballpark for background shots. The producers were also filming game action of the Pirates, including me. for authenticity. The players received not a cent. I expect Branch Rickey, who arranged the deal, did somewhat better financially.

But it was an enjoyable experience for all of us, and for me in particular. I was still single. Janet and Tony Curtis were an item, but he was off on location in Europe or somewhere. The movie company stayed in town for the better part of six weeks, during which time I started going out with Janet.

She was a tremendous person, and we established a relationship that wasn't just another studio publicity stunt. We developed a genuine interest in each other. Of course, given our notoriety, we made all the Hollywood gossip columns. I don't know if the rumors influenced Curtis or not, but shortly after Janet left town, he flew to meet her and they were married.

I became engaged that summer to Nancy Chaffee, who was among the top women tennis players in the world. We married in October and moved into a house I had built at Thunderbird Country Club in Palm Springs, Calif. Our neighbors included many celebrities with whom we became close friends. Of course, there were a number of others who would come to the desert community for brief periods of rest and relaxation during the winter months.

Among the latter was Esther Williams. She arrived one day in Palm Springs with her husband, Ben Gage, who was a famous radio announcer in Chicago. I had known Ben before his marriage, and when he came to town, he gave me a call. I invited him and his wife to dinner.

When I was growing up, Esther Williams was one of the great stars in show business. She was a terrific swimmer and a beautiful woman, not necessarily in that order. The four of us got along famously, and one night we decided to go out to a local night club that had Las Vegas-style acts.

Well, we might have exceeded our capacity, a condition we compounded when we got back to the house about two o'clock in the morning. After another round or two, Esther and Ben decided to take a swim in our pool. Now, despite her attraction to water, Esther neglected to carry a bathing suit along with her everywhere she went. In this instance, she didn't even bother to ask if there was one she could borrow.

The next thing I knew, Esther Williams was swimming naked in my pool. Nancy and I were at the bar, and I remember trying not to look because I knew that would get me in deep trouble. Did I peek? Well, from that moment on, when anybody has asked what I remember about her, I say, "She had the greatest backstroke I've ever seen." And she did.

Not long thereafter, she became involved in a restaurant in Los Angeles and invited us to the grand opening. She was really a nice lady. Later, she divorced Ben Gage and married Fernando Lamas, and I never saw her after that.

I never saw Janet Leigh again, either, after our time in Pittsburgh. But there's a wonderful postscript to that story.

In the summer of 1985, 34 years after the making of *Angels in the Outfield,* I was at Veterans Stadium in Philadelphia with the Mets, when someone told me that Jamie Lee Curtis, Janet's daughter, who has become a big star in her own right, was in the press room. I decided I should say hello. She was sitting with her husband, and my wife, DiAnn, was with me. So I went up to her and said, "Jamie Lee, my name is Ralph Kiner. I broadcast the New York Mets' games. I dated your mother just before she married Tony."

With that, she jumped up, threw her arms around me, and said, "Daddy! At last I've found you. I've been searching for you all my life." It was the most spontaneous reaction I've ever seen, and it certainly caught me by surprise.

The best part of it all was that DiAnn was there counting. "Let's see: You got married . . . She could be . . . How many years did you say it was . . . ?"

A Terrific Future

While Wes Westrum, who had been rehired as manager, plotted to make the Mets more competitive in the field in 1966, the front office made two decisions that were to have a lasting impact on the future of the club. They involved a right-handed pitcher named Tom Seaver and a left-handed pitcher named Jerry Koosman.

Seaver, a standout at the University of Southern California, had been selected by the Atlanta Braves in the January free-agent draft and signed to a $51,500 contract that included a $40,000 bonus. As he prepared to celebrate his good fortune, however, Seaver received a telephone call from the office of the commissioner of baseball. The contract, he was informed, had been voided because it was in violation of a rule that prohibited the signing of a college player during the course of his season. USC already had played two games in 1966. It didn't matter that Seaver had appeared in neither.

Furthermore, since he had signed a professional contract, Seaver now was ineligible under the National Collegiate Athletic Association rules. That led to the revocation of his scholarship. Suddenly, he was a pitcher without a team.

The commissioner's office proposed that Seaver could be signed by any organization other than the Braves willing to meet the terms of the original contract. Only three clubs applied. They were the Cleveland Indians, the Philadelphia Phillies, and the Mets.

Nelson Burbrink, the Mets' area scout, had been favorably impressed in his last look at Seaver. He strongly recommended the pitcher to Bing Devine, who persuaded the conservative Weiss to join in the bidding. The names of the three teams subsequently were placed in a hat, and Baseball Commissioner William D. Eckert pulled out the piece of paper that awarded Seaver to the Mets.

Koosman, a husky farm boy from Minnesota, had been signed to a Mets' contract late in 1964, after John Luchese, his catcher on an Army team at Fort Bliss, sent home a glowing report. The catcher's father, a Shea Stadium usher, passed on the notice to Joe McDonald in the minor-league department.

Despite his apparent physical ability, Koosman had been a disappointment in his first pro season, 1965. After a lackluster spring in 1966, it was the opinion of several minor-league managers and officials that he should be released. A dissenting vote was cast by McDonald, who reasoned that Koosman still owed the organization money advanced after an automobile accident and that he should be kept at least until he paid off the loan.

The wisdom of those two decisions would become apparent in the next two years. But there were immediate problems to be solved in George Weiss's final year on the job. The Mets were in 40th place, Stengel's terminology for finishing 10th for four years. The fans were looking for evidence of progress.

Westrum's staff included Yogi Berra and Sheriff Robinson as well as two new coaches, Whitey Herzog and Harvey Haddix. The pitching coach, Haddix qualified as a Met by hurling 12 perfect innings for the Pirates against the Braves in 1959 and losing the game, 1-0, in the 13th. There also was one significant change in the front office caused by Eddie Stanky's departure to become manager of the Chicago White Sox. He was replaced as director of player development by Bob Scheffing, the former manager of the Detroit Tigers.

During the winter, the Mets acquired several new faces, the most prominent of which belonged to Ken Boyer, a third baseman who had been the league's Most Valuable Player in 1964. The reason they were able to entice him from the Cardinals, at the cost of Al Jackson and Charlie Smith, was his age. Boyer would be 35 in May.

The Mets also added a young catcher, Jerry Grote, from the Houston organization, and picked up an experienced infielder in Eddie Bressoud and an experienced flake in Dick Stuart. The latter listed his occupation as first baseman although his performance in the field had earned him the nickname Dr. Strangeglove. But he was a powerful batter who once hit 66 home runs in a minor-league season and never let the world forget it. Jack Hamilton, a hard-throwing veteran, was the one prominent pitching acquisition.

Westrum was from the school of positive thinking. Inspirational messages were sprinkled everywhere. His maxim was: "You can if you think you can."

The new manager counted on a fast start, meaning he thoroughly expected the Mets to win on Opening Day. There was an added bonus in 1966. The Mets were scheduled to play their first game in Cincinnati, where the season traditionally began a day early. A victory on Monday would give the team undisputed possession of first place, at least for 24 hours.

Well, it rained Monday. It also rained Tuesday. And Wednesday. The series was postponed. On the record, it was the best start in Mets' history, but that was a negative assessment. The manager thought it ruined the team after a fine spring training record of 14-10. "We lost our momentum," he decided.

So the Mets' opener was shifted to Shea Stadium on Friday. The opponent was the Braves, who had just set up house in Atlanta after their second franchise shift in 13 years. The Met team that took the field had Stuart at first base and Boyer at third, with Ron Hunt at second and Roy McMillan at shortstop. The outfield was comprised of Ron Swoboda in left field, Jim Hickman in center, and a promising young hitter from Mobile, Ala., named Cleon Jones in right. Jerry Grote was the catcher and Jack Fisher, the durable one, was on the mound.

The Mets led, 2-1, after eight innings. Was this another tease or were they ready for a major breakthrough? The Braves answered the question in the ninth when Joe Torre doubled off the center-field fence and scored on Lee Thomas's single. Thomas reached third when Jones's throw disappeared from play. Denis Menke then dropped a squeeze bunt, and Thomas scored as Fisher threw the ball past Grote. The Mets lost, 3-2.

Yet, on the following day, the Mets triumphed, 3-1, on a five-hitter by Hamilton, marking their first time at the .500 mark. Surprisingly, they also defeated the Braves, 5-4, on Sunday with two runs in the eighth inning and one in the ninth. Westrum had done something Stengel had been unable to accomplish in four years. His team actually had won more games than it had lost.

The rarified air proved too thin for the Mets. They lost their next five games and never approached .500 again all season. But they were receiving competition for last place from the Cubs, who finally had scrapped an unorthodox system of rotating head coaches and appointed Leo Durocher manager. Durocher set out to rebuild the team from top to bottom after a succession of eighth-place finishes.

"This is not an eighth-place team," he said. The Cubs promptly proved it, losing 16 of their first 20 games and settling into 10th place.

Weiss attempted to repair the Mets' erratic pitching staff in the following six weeks. First, he added veteran left-hander Gerry Arrigo from Cincinnati and promoted Dick Rusteck, another left-hander, from the top farm club in Jacksonville. Both men soon landed on the disabled list, so Weiss went back to work. On June 10, he signed 35-year-old Bob Friend, who had just been released by the Yankees but who had been among the most lethal of Met-killers in his years with the Pirates. Five days later they bought Bob Shaw from the Giants. Shaw was a successful right-handed pitcher who, at 31, appeared to be in his prime.

The Mets now had an all-veteran starting rotation, and the team stabilized behind them. They set a club record in July with an 18-14 mark, their first winning month ever. And, on Aug. 21, they recorded victory number 54, an all-time high.

Jones and Kranepool were making major contributions at bat, and, late in the season, a scrawny youngster named Bud Harrelson arrived from Jacksonville to replace the injured McMillan. He had benefited from the veteran's tutelage during spring training and now was prepared to take over at shortstop.

It seemed there just might be a future for this team. Although they lost their last two games, the Mets finished with 66 victories and had a new place—ninth—to call their own. The World's Fair had closed and Casey was back in California, but, miraculously, the Mets had drawn a home attendance of 1,932,693.

Not only had it been a good year on the major-league level but help was on the way. Seaver, that fellow the Mets won in a bizarre lottery back in April, had posted a 12-12 record at the Triple-A level and was poised for the jump to Shea. Koosman, saved for the Mets by a car accident, had straightened himself out and enjoyed a banner year at Auburn in the Class A New York–Penn League, compiling a 12-7 record and striking out 174 batters in 170 innings. He would bear watching.

At the conclusion of the season, Westrum was rehired for 1967. Shortly thereafter, Weiss confirmed he was retiring. At 75, he would be home for lunch again. Bing Devine ascended to the post of president and set about to make some sweeping changes.

Devine had studied under Frank Lane, whose love of trading was such that he once initiated an even exchange of managers at the major-league level. When Devine succeeded Lane as general manager of the Cards in 1957, he proved the lessons were not wasted. At St. Louis, he obtained Curt Flood, Julian Javier, Dick Groat, Bill White, and Lou Brock, the nucleus of a World Championship club, through trades. Now he was starting all over with the Mets.

Within two weeks of his appointment, Devine lopped three players off the roster, acquired outfielder Larry Stahl from the Kansas City A's, and picked up outfielder Tommie Reynolds in the minor-league draft. That whetted his appetite.

He got down to serious business on Nov. 29 when he dealt Jim Hickman, the last original Met, and Ron Hunt, the fans' favorite, to the Los Angeles Dodgers. In return, the Mets received infielder Derrell Griffith and outfielder Tommy Davis, a Brooklyn native who had twice won the National League batting championship. A broken leg had robbed Davis of his speed but not his ability to hit.

While the fans digested that deal, Devine dispatched Dennis Ribant, a young pitcher who had won 11 games in 1966, to Pittsburgh. By return mail, the Mets received the contracts of Don Cardwell, a veteran right-handed pitcher, and Don Bosch. The latter was a small, prematurely graying center fielder who was said to be the defensive equal of Willie Mays by his minor-league manager, Larry Shepard.

The shuffling continued. Eddie Bressoud was sent to the Cards for Jerry Buchek, another utility infielder. Ralph Terry, a World Series hero for the Yankees in 1962, was added to the pitching staff. So, too, was Ron Taylor, a relief pitcher who had a save for the Cards in the '64 World Series. Chuck Estrada and Jack Lamabe were later acquisitions.

Westrum settled on a lineup that had Davis, Bosch, and Jones in the outfield. Swoboda was moved to first base, where he would platoon with Kranepool. Chuck Hiller was the second baseman, Harrelson the shortstop, Boyer the third baseman, and Grote the catcher.

Cardwell, a big man who had a no-hit game to his credit but whose reputation was founded on hard-luck defeats, received the starting assignment on Opening Day of 1967 against his former team, the Pirates. The score was tied at 3-3 in the ninth when Gene Alley doubled. Jesse Gonder, the ex-Met, followed with another double and Pittsburgh won. Clubhouse historians noted it was not the first time Gonder had cost the Mets a game.

Things improved dramatically as soon as Westrum handed the baseball to Seaver. The youngster had stepped into the starting rotation in spring training and created the impression he had been facing major-league hitters all his life. He got the call in the second game of the season, and the Mets won, 3-2, although the victory was credited to Estrada in relief.

In his second start, Seaver won with relief help. In his third start, on April 25, he went 10 innings to beat the Cubs, 2-1, for his first complete-game victory. At 22, he was a man on the mound, and the other players seemed to sense this. They were to play their best games behind him.

Despite Seaver's success, however, the Mets were backsliding. Bosch, a nervous 24-year-old who felt the pressure of a big buildup, was no Mays in the field and no help at the plate. Boyer was showing his age, second base was a problem, and Swoboda was a menacing first baseman, especially to any second baseman who wandered too close in pursuit of pop flies.

Devine redoubled his efforts. From Kansas City, he purchased Ed Charles, a third baseman with the soul of a poet and three seasons left in his legs. Bosch was demoted to the minors, and Hamilton, who had been used almost exclusively in relief, was shipped to the California Angels for Nick Willhite. Two more left-handed pitchers, Bob Hendley and Dennis Bennett, were obtained from the Cubs and Red Sox, respectively.

Another addition was Phil Linz, a utility infielder with a genial personality who had gained a measure of fame in New York by playing a harmonica on the team bus following a bitter Yankee defeat in the 1964 pennant race. The music sent manager Yogi Berra into a well-reported rage. Now the two men were reunited.

About this time, the Mets also recalled Greg Goossen, a burly catcher they had acquired on waivers from the Dodgers and then had left in the minors to develop. In two minor-league seasons, he hit 24 and 25 homers although he had shown little in his previous trials with the big club. It was Casey Stengel who had made the hard evaluation of Goossen's talents. "He's 20 years old," Casey once said in describing the catcher, "and in 10 years, he's got a chance to be 30."

Despite Devine's changes, the Mets continued their descent. At the All-Star break, they had a record of 31-47 and were jockeying for last place with the Astros. The only positive note had been sounded by Seaver. He was 6-5 with a 2.68 earned-run average, and he was Dodger manager Walter Alston's choice as the lone Met selected to the National League squad.

The All-Star Game was a festival of strikeouts through 14 innings. Just when it appeared the contest might go on indefinitely, the NL broke the 1-1 tie, which had existed since the sixth inning, when Tony Perez homered off Jim (Catfish) Hunter of the A's. Perez was batting for Don Drysdale of the Dodgers, the sixth pitcher employed by Alston. Now the manager would have to summon a seventh to protect the lead in the bottom of the 15th. The man who emerged from the bullpen was Tom Seaver.

To many in the national television audience, it must have seemed a preposterous joke. Why would a manager allegedly in his right mind call upon a Met at such an important moment? But this Met had no allegiance to Marvelous Marv and the image-makers of the Polo Grounds. He was the new prototype, a confident young man who had earned the designation Tom Terrific in the New York press. "Hey, Pete," he called to Pete Rose as he passed the second baseman en route to the mound, "why don't you pitch and I'll play second base." Rose declined the invitation with a laugh.

The first batter Seaver faced was Tony Conigliaro, the American League home-run champion in 1965. Conigliaro flied out. Carl Yastrzemski, well on his way to the AL's Triple Crown, drew a walk. But Seaver then retired Bill Freehan on a fly ball and struck out Ken Berry. Before a television audience estimated at 60 million, a Met had saved the National League's 2-1 victory.

In the course of the next three months, he was to grow into a national figure. More and more people probed his background in an effort to discover what set him apart from his teammates, why he won while all about him lost. It was an interesting study.

Seaver had inherited athletic ability and the desire to compete from his father, who had played on the football team as well as excelling in golf at Stanford. Tom had an outstanding Little League career, but, while his teammates grew, he made very slow physical progress. As a high-school sophomore in Fresno, Calif., he was 5-6 and weighed 145 pounds.

Without the size or strength, he was unable to throw hard. While his friend Dick Selma made the varsity team, Seaver had to settle for the jayvees. At 14 and 15, he was throwing slow curves, changeups, and even a knuckleball out of necessity.

Seaver made the varsity staff as a senior, but Selma, who had a live fast ball, was the star. One year later, Selma received a $20,000 bonus to sign with the Mets. There were no teams seeking Seaver's signature on a contract and no colleges offering scholarships, either.

While debating his future course, he took a job lifting crates of raisins for the packing company where his father served as vice president. It was backbreaking labor but added to his strength. Seaver decided to enlist in the Marine Corps reserve and, after three months of boot camp, was sent to Camp Pendleton and from there to the Marine base in the Mojave Desert. He had entered the service a 5-10, 160-pound youngster. He emerged six months later a 6-1, 195-pound man.

At the completion of his active duty, Tom enrolled in Fresno City College. Now he had the size, the strength, and another opportunity to pitch. He won 11 games for the school and was contacted by Rod Dedeaux, the hugely successful coach at

Southern Cal. Dedeaux asked Seaver if he was willing to test himself in a good amateur league that summer. Seaver said he was.

The team Dedeaux had in mind was the Alaska Goldpanners, who played out of Fairbanks. They were composed largely of college All-Americans and included Ken Holtzman of the University of Illinois. The Goldpanners enjoyed a banner season and were one of 32 teams invited to the National Baseball Congress tournament at Wichita, Kans.

In a game against a Wichita team, manager Red Boucher summoned Seaver from the bullpen with Alaska leading, 2-0, and the bases loaded in the fifth inning. Two walks and an infield hit later, the Goldpanners trailed, 3-2. However, Seaver was allowed to bat with the bases loaded in the sixth and blasted a home run. He had made an impression.

Dedeaux was sufficiently convinced to offer Seaver a scholarship to USC. In the spring of 1965, Seaver compiled a 10-2 record for the Trojans and was drafted by the Dodgers. Scout Tom Lasorda mentioned a bonus of $2,000, Seaver countered with a figure in the neighborhood of $50,000, and there was a parting of the ways and means. Tom prepared for another summer in Alaska.

His teammates on the Goldpanners that year included Andy Messersmith of the University of California at Berkeley and Danny Frisella of Washington State. The team again was invited to compete at Wichita, and this time it advanced to the semifinals as each of the three star pitchers won a decision.

Seaver was to start the semifinal game. The opposition was the Wichita Dreamliners, who boasted four former major-leaguers. They were Bobby Boyd, Jim Pendleton, Charlie Neal, and Rod Kanehl. The latter two, of course, had performed for the Mets.

It was an education for the young pitcher. Neal led off the game with a triple. Boyd had three hits. Kanehl stole home. The Dreamliners won, 6-3. But, over a few beers after the game, Kanehl told Seaver he thought he had the makings of a big-league pitcher. Kanehl was a good judge of other people's talent.

In January 1966, while still enrolled at USC, Seaver's name

again was selected in the special draft of baseball players. This time it was the Braves who were willing to make a serious offer. The package finally agreed upon called for a $40,000 bonus, another $4,000 for the completion of his education, and a $7,500 incentive bonus ($1,000 for staying 90 days at the Double-A level, $1,500 for 90 days at the Triple-A level, and $5,000 for 90 days at the major-league level).

The problem was that while negotiations were in progress, USC was preparing to open its season. By the time Seaver signed the contract on Feb. 24, Southern Cal had played two games. Jess Hill, the athletic director at the school and a former major-league outfielder, protested the signing as a violation of organized baseball's rule protecting the colleges. The protest was upheld.

Caught in the middle, Seaver contacted the commissioner's office. Since Seaver technically was a professional, a lottery was proposed. The 19 other major-league teams had until April 1 to signify their interest in matching the Braves' offer.

Administrative assistant Lee MacPhail placed a call to the Seaver household on April 2 from Miami Beach. Charles Seaver answered the phone and Tom, his son, picked up the extension in the kitchen. "The three teams have put their names in the hat," MacPhail said, building the suspense with a running commentary. "The commissioner is putting his hand in the hat. The winning team is . . . the New York Mets."

Nelson Burbrink drove from Los Angeles to Fresno the following day and signed Seaver to a Mets' contract. Tom spent some of the bonus money on a car, some more on an engagement ring for Nancy Lynn McIntyre, and then flew to the Mets' minor-league training complex.

Within 16 months, he became the talk of baseball and the Mets' hope for salvation. The team continued to stumble through the second half of the 1967 season, but Seaver continued to win. His final record of 16-12, the best in club history, was remarkable for a rookie on a last-place team. He had 18 complete games, 170 strikeouts, and a 2.76 earned-run average. Seaver was the first National League pitcher to win Rookie-of-the-Year honors in 10 years and the first player on a last-place club ever to be so honored.

The only other record set by the Mets in '67 was a dubious

one. With Devine surpassing himself, the team went through 54 players (including 27 pitchers) in the course of the season. No team had ever done so little with so many.

Westrum offered his resignation in September. Salty Parker, the interim manager, presided over seven losses in the last 11 games. The Mets concluded the season with a 61-101 record. They were back on the bottom now, and in the market for a manager.

Small World

One of the benefits of broadcasting, I discovered, was the chance it gave me to relive the past. Many familiar faces passed through the doors of the Mets' clubhouse in those early years, and that wasn't even counting the men who assembled for the annual Old-Timers Day production.

The parade started with Red Ruffing, an old friend who served as pitching coach that first season. During the same year, the Mets activated Robert G. Miller, a left-handed pitcher who had spent some time with the Detroit Tigers in the 1950s.

I had finished my career in the American League, playing the 1955 season with the Cleveland Indians. A bad back limited my playing time and my contribution, but it was an exciting season nonetheless. Finally, after nine years with an also-ran, I was on a contending ball club. The feeling was invigorating.

I remember playing a Labor Day doubleheader against the Yankees in New York. We gained a split when Whitey Ford uncharacteristically bounced a wild pitch with me at bat, and that night Bob Feller and I celebrated our first-place status at the Stork Club.

Unfortunately, it wasn't long before the Yankees gained the lead. We fell out of the race in the final week. The last appearance of my career was in Detroit, where Hank Greenberg had earned both respect and fame. I wish I could have ended my playing days with a home run. Surely, in that case, I would have remembered the opposing pitcher. But the experience had seemed so anticlimactic at the time, I forgot all about it.

It took a Met to remind me. The Met was Bob Miller. He was, he told me, the opposing pitcher on my final at-bat in Briggs Stadium. I struck out. No wonder I had forgotten.

Other memories were recalled when Clyde McCullough joined the Mets as a coach in 1963. McCullough had been a catcher on some of those terrible Pirate teams. In 1966, it happened again. The Mets acquired Bob Friend. When the Pirates lost a then-record 112 games in 1952, Friend did his share by losing 17.

We didn't win many games in Pittsburgh, but we did manage to have some fun. I was reminded of the 1947 season and the clubhouse record player, donated by Bing Crosby, which continually blared, "Cigarettes and whiskey and wild, wild women . . . They drive you crazy, they drive you insane." I guess you could call it our fight song. It certainly fit the mood on the occasion of Vinnie Smith's wedding. Smith had been a reserve catcher with the club in 1945 and 1946, and a large percentage of the '47 team attended the ceremony and reception which were held on a Saturday afternoon. We were scheduled to play a game against the Cincinnati Reds that night.

Several Pirates served as ushers at the wedding and reported directly to Forbes Field. Jimmy Russell, Billy Cox, Elbie Fletcher, and I forget who else, all showed up in tuxedos. They also showed up in need of black coffee.

Ewell Blackwell, the great sidearm fastball pitcher who was the toughest man I ever faced and a sobering experience for any batter, was the probable pitcher for the Reds. Fletcher, a first baseman whose best years were behind him, wasn't taking any chances. He went next door—the clubhouses in Forbes Field were adjoining—and presented Blackwell with six cigars.

"Blacky," he said, "you're my favorite pitcher and my son thinks you're the greatest. He also thinks I'm a great dad. Under these circumstances, don't come too close."

Well, Kirby Higbe was our pitcher that night. It was difficult to tell if he was pitching well because we kept making errors behind him. Finally, he had taken as much as he could take, and he motioned Billy Herman, our manager, to the mound.

"I can't pitch," Higbe said, "when they're drunk out there."

Herman, who did not have his hand on the pulse of the club, appeared astonished. "Who's drunk?" he said.

"Everyone," Higbe replied.

When my playing career ended, I turned more and more to golf for physical activity. Although I hadn't been associated with the Pirates for several years, I was still friendly with Bing Crosby, and we continued to play golf whenever our schedules placed us both in Palm Springs.

Crosby was a scratch golfer who couldn't bear to lose. He would virtually insist that you keep playing with him until he won. He also had founded the Bing Crosby National Pro-Amateur tournament which, in 1962, would serve as a springboard to my position as a Mets' broadcaster.

I played in the tournament whenever I was able. In 1956, at a time when the Crosby was still a 54-hole event, I was paired at the outset with a gentleman who had been the number one player on the Stanford team that had included the illustrious Lawson Little. He also had been a Walker Cup contestant and the California state amateur champion.

At the conclusion of our round, he asked for my autograph. He said it was for his son, a Little League pitcher who, he felt, was certain to become a major-leaguer one day. Years later, when I heard about the strong, young right-hander who had enjoyed such a fine season at Jacksonville in 1966, it struck a chord.

The golfer's name was Charley Seaver. His son was called Tom. I would have frequent cause to remember that meeting in the next decade.

The Quiet Man

The Mets had three managerial candidates within their own organization. Both Bob Scheffing and Yogi Berra had job experience at the major-league level. Whitey Herzog, who had moved into the minor-league department after a year on the coaching lines, did not.

There was one man who had the universal admiration of the entire Mets' hierarchy. Unfortunately, he also had a long-term contract to manage the Washington Senators. Gil Hodges was the man the board of directors wanted.

Hodges had done a marvelous job with the Senators, another ragged expansion club created hurriedly in 1961 to replace the team of the same name that had moved to Minnesota and now called itself the Twins. Washington had been a last-place club when Hodges took over in the midst of the 1963 season, and, despite what had been labeled inferior personnel, the Senators demonstrated improvement in each succeeding year. They were a formidable sixth in 1967, barely falling short of the first division.

There were other considerations. Hodges had been, if only briefly and ineffectively, a Met. He also had been one of the most popular players in New York baseball history. His ties with the city were permanent. He had met and married a

Brooklyn girl during his playing career, and, through the Dodgers' shift to the West Coast, through his own shift to Washington, he had maintained the family home in Flatbush.

He was a man who ruled with quiet strength. At times, he could be patient; at other times, he could be forceful. He inspired, even demanded respect with merely a stare. All the Mets had to do was sell the Senators on the idea that Gil Hodges should be allowed to come home.

Johnny Murphy, the number two man in the front office, was assigned the task of broaching the subject with George Selkirk, the general manager of the Senators. Murphy and Selkirk had been teammates on the Yankees and had remained fast friends. Murphy was very persuasive.

Shirley Povich, the *Washington Post* columnist, broke the story of the secret negotiations during the 1967 World Series between the Cardinals and the Red Sox. The conversations between Murphy and Selkirk were, Povich said, akin to "asking a man permission to steal his wife."

Two days later, on Oct. 10, in a Boston hotel suite, Hodges was introduced as the Mets' manager for 1968. For their consideration in releasing Hodges from his contract, the Senators received a large sum of cash and Bill Denehy, a young pitcher who had a 1-7 record in 1967.

Hodges received a three-year contract at an estimated $60,000 per year. Berra would remain as a coach, but the rest of Gil's staff would be recruited from Washington. The new coaches were pitching coach Rube Walker, a reserve catcher on the great Brooklyn Dodger teams; Eddie Yost, a New Yorker who annually led the American League in walks during his days as a third baseman with the Senators, and Joe Pignatano, the Brooklyn boy who punctuated his brief career with the Mets by banging into a triple play.

A call from home initiated another major change in the organization before the year was out. Bing Devine had maintained his residence near St. Louis after the parting with the Cardinals. His family had stayed in Missouri, and he, much like Hodges, had expended time and energy shuttling back and forth between cities.

Stan Musial, who was ill-suited to office work, stepped down as the Cards' general manager after the team won the World Series in seven games, leaving the the position vacant. Busch now acknowledged his mistake of 1964 and offered Devine his old job. Devine also wanted to go home.

Devine's departure was announced on Dec. 5. The Mets made another announcement on Dec. 27, one more in a line of hometown decisions. The new general manager would be a man who had served the team well since its earliest days. The new general manager would be a man who was born and raised in New York. The new general manager would be Johnny Murphy.

Murphy first had come to public attention at Fordham University in the Bronx. As a member of the Yankees, he was acclaimed as one of the great relief pitchers of his era. An older brother, Thomas F. Murphy, was police commissioner of New York and later was appointed a federal judge by President Truman.

A quiet gentleman with a taste for Beaujolais wine, Murphy was a popular choice for the position. Although he had started in the front office with the Red Sox organization, Murphy had been the first employee hired by George Weiss in 1961. He knew club policy and operation as well as anyone.

Devine, of course, had not left without some farewell alterations to the roster. He had traded infielder Bob Johnson to Cincinnati for outfielder Art Shamsky. Then, at the urging of Hodges, he initiated a major transaction with the Chicago White Sox. Murphy and Grant completed the deal soon after Devine rejoined the Cards.

Under the terms of the agreement, the Mets surrendered pitchers Jack Fisher and Bill Wynne and outfielder Tommy Davis, who had batted .302 but whose defense was inadequate. They received Al Weis, a utility infielder who let his glove do his talking, and Tommie Agee, an outfielder whom Hodges coveted.

Agee had won Rookie-of-the-Year honors in 1966 when he batted .273, with 22 homers and 86 runs batted in. But he slumped badly (.234, 14, 52) in 1967 and antagonized manager Eddie Stanky with his mannerisms on the field and his sociability off the field. "He never caught a ball standing still," complained Stanky, who hired a private eye to monitor Agee's postgame behavior.

Hodges, who had seen Agee play for two years in the American League, was only too glad to accept responsibility for a player with the speed to play center field and the power to intimidate pitchers. It seemed a particularly good arrangement for Agee, who would be reunited with Cleon Jones, an old friend and former high school football teammate in Mobile, Ala.

Such was the curse of the Mets, however, that when Agee stepped to the plate as leadoff batter in the first inning of the very first exhibition game, he was beaned by Bob Gibson's first pitch. Although the batting helmet protected him from serious injury, Agee received a mild concussion and a lasting impression.

The team assembled by Hodges was the youngest in Mets' history. Seaver, 23, was the ranking member of a pitching staff that included rookies Jerry Koosman and Nolan Ryan as well as such inexperienced arms as Don Shaw, Dick Selma, and Danny Frisella. Selma, of course, had been Seaver's more successful teammate at Fresno High School, and Frisella had been a fellow member of the Alaska Goldpanners. Now all three were together in the big leagues.

Although the Mets were 9-18 in spring training, their worst Florida record, Hodges did not appear disturbed. A positive man who worked hard to instill confidence in his players, the manager said, "I think we will win 70 games."

The Mets were scheduled to open their seventh season on April 9 in San Francisco. However, funeral services were to be held that day in Atlanta for Dr. Martin Luther King, the slain civil rights leader, and the team voted not to play out of respect for the man's memory. The decision was backed by the manager and management, and the Giants, who wanted to play, grudgingly postponed the opener to Wednesday, April 10.

Surprisingly, the Mets jumped to a 4-0 lead behind Seaver as Ron Swoboda singled across one run in the first inning and homered following singles by Agee and Ken Boswell in the third. They succeeded in knocking out Juan Marichal, and Seaver clung to a 4-2 lead as the Giants prepared for their last chance in the ninth. An Opening Day victory was within reach.

But Seaver faltered. A single by Willie Mays, a passed ball, and a single by Jim Ray Hart cut the lead to 4-3, and Hodges replaced Seaver with Frisella. Nate Oliver promptly singled and Jesus Alou doubled, driving in both runs. The Mets lost, 5-4. Opening Day tradition was preserved. The new manager, still preaching confidence, said, "We'll win tomorrow."

And they did. Koosman, the rookie left-hander whose debt to the Mets had long since been paid, threw a four-hit shutout at the Los Angeles Dodgers in a 4-0 victory. Don Cardwell pitched well the following day but not as well as Don Drysdale, and the Mets were defeated by the Dodgers, 1-0. A combined five-hitter by Ryan and Frisella staked the Mets' to a 4-0 victory over the Astros in the first of a two-game series at Houston.

The Mets had played four games and the last three had resulted in shutouts. The fifth game would follow a similar pattern. What would distinguish it was its duration. The game started at 7:30 P.M. in the Astrodome. By the time it ended, breakfast was being served in the press room.

Seaver was matched against Don Wilson, who had pitched the first of his two no-hitters the previous year. Both starters departed with the game scoreless. The futility continued through the 9th, the 12th, the 15th, the 18th, and the 21st innings. Starting the 24th inning, not a run had been scored, and the contest already had set a record for the longest night game ever played.

The Mets' pitcher in the 24th was Les Rohr, a big left-hander who had been the club's top draft choice in the first free-agent draft in 1965. His experience was limited, and he had the added disadvantage of having pitched 20 minutes of batting practice some seven hours earlier.

Norm Miller, the first Houston batter, singled. Jimmy Wynn was ordered to bunt. As he squared around, however, Rohr separated his hands in the stretch position and was charged with a balk. Wynn was walked intentionally. Both runners advanced a base as Rusty Staub grounded out. Then John Bateman was walked intentionally, loading the bases and setting up a force at any base.

What the Mets needed was a double play. Bob Aspromonte obliged with a ground ball to Weis. However, the ball skipped through the shortstop's legs and the Mets, after six hours and six minutes of frustration, had lost another 1-0 game. Swoboda and Agee both were hitless in 10 at-bats, and Agee, who had started well in the first four games, was not to fully recover until 1969. The man who suffered most in the marathon was the home-plate umpire. It was Ed Sudol. Naturally.

Despite, or perhaps because of, the drawn-out defeat, there was a crowd in excess of 52,000 at Shea Stadium for the Mets' home opener against the Giants. It seemed like another long day when leadoff batter Ron Hunt, the ex-Met, singled and Weis booted Jim Davenport's grounder in his first chance since the 24th inning at Houston. A walk to Willie McCovey loaded the bases.

But Koosman, the Mets' starting pitcher, was a rookie in the mold of Seaver. He faced down the challenge by striking out the wondrous Mays on four pitches, retiring Jim Ray Hart on a foul pop, and striking out Jack Hiatt. He pitched eight more scoreless innings, and the Mets won, 3-0, on Jones's home run.

Koosman's initial exposure to baseball occurred on the family farm in Minnesota. His brother, Orville, would pitch to him. Then they would exchange gloves and he would pitch to Orville. In winter, they did their throwing in the barn. Before reporting to the army, Koosman's only game experience was in the summer beer leagues, where the opponents were grown men.

He was strong in the manner of a farmer, and John Luchese had all he could do to hold his fastball at Fort Bliss. The catcher's recommendation had been passed from his father to Joe McDonald to Red Murff, the Mets' scout whose area encompassed the base.

Murff watched Koosman pitch, then invited the soldier for a meal and a few beers. Koosman asked for a large bonus. Murff offered $1,600. Koosman declined. The next time they met, the offer was $1,500, and $100 was deducted with each subsequent visit. Koosman accepted at $1,200. "I decided to sign," he said, "before I owed them money."

Koosman had three starts with the Mets at the outset of the 1967 season and had enjoyed an 11-10 record with a high strikeout ratio at Jacksonville. The Mets expected fine things from him in 1968, but no one anticipated consecutive shutouts in his first two starts. It was an unprecedented feat for a Met pitcher.

It was no fluke, either. Koosman posted two of the club's next three wins, and his four consecutive victories tied a team record. When Don Cardwell shut out the Phillies, 1-0, on April 30, it was apparent the Mets' pitching was as strong as their hitting was weak.

The most notable failure at the plate was Agee. The hitless streak begun that long, long night at the Astrodome had carried through the month of April. On the night of May 1, in his first at-bat, he equaled the Mets' record slump of 0-for-34 set by Don Zimmer in that very first season. Finally, in his second appearance of the night, he bounced a ground ball up the middle for a base hit and was accorded a standing ovation from the Shea Stadium fans.

The shutouts continued, for and against. When Seaver and Selma blanked the Dodgers on successive nights in early June, it marked the 9th and 10th shutouts by the Mets in 55 games. They had been shut out nine times themselves.

The Mets flirted with a .500 mark throughout June and had a respectable 39-43 record at the All-Star break. They were 13½ games out of first place. Their increased stature was confirmed when Jerry Grote, who had learned to control his temper and his bat under Hodges's tutelage, was selected as the National League's starting catcher. Both Seaver and Koosman gained places on the pitching staff.

Grote caught the first five innings of the game, played in the Astrodome. The NL led, 1-0, when Seaver entered the game in the seventh. In two innings, he allowed two hits and struck out five, including Carl Yastrzemski and Mickey Mantle. Ron Reed of the Braves retired the first two batters in the ninth and, with the left-handed Yastrzemski coming to the plate, Koosman got the call. The rookie struck out Yaz to save the victory. The Mets were no laughing matter any more.

The regular season resumed, and so did the shutouts. Selma, who once startled the Mets by scheduling his own shoulder operation, defeated the Cubs, 1-0, in the first game of a doubleheader. The Mets were blanked, 2-0, in the second game. A day later, Koosman came back with a 4-0 shutout, and so on and so forth.

If any one player typified the effort and frustrations of the 1968 season, it was Jim McAndrew. And he didn't even join the team until July. McAndrew was a 24-year-old right-hander who had a degree in psychology from the University of Iowa. He was called up from Jacksonville specifically to start one game of a Sunday doubleheader on July 21, while Ryan was away on weekend reserve duty. His opponent was Bob Gibson.

McAndrew pitched five scoreless innings against the Cards and left after seven innings, trailing 1-0. The Mets lost the game, 2-0, as Gibson struck out 13. McAndrew returned to Jacksonville but, a week later, came back to stay.

On Aug. 4, in the second game of a doubleheader against the Dodgers, he pitched another strong game but lost, 2-0. His next two starts, against the Giants and Astros, resulted in 1-0 defeats. By mid-August, he was saddled with an 0-4 record, and the Mets had yet to score their first run in his behalf.

Finally, in his sixth start, he got the hang of pitching for the Mets. He threw a shutout at the Cards. The final score, of course, was 1-0.

The Mets' staff amassed 25 shutouts in 1968. The opposition threw 23 at the Mets. The Mets won seven 1-0 games and lost six. Their 2.76 earned-run average was the second-lowest in the league.

Koosman had seven shutouts, tying a rookie record established a half-century earlier by Grover Cleveland Alexander, among his 19 victories. Seaver won 16 for the second year in a row and raised his strikeout total to 205. As for McAndrew, he finished with a 4-7 record and a 2.28 ERA, a most unlikely combination.

The Mets set an all-time record by recording their 67th victory on Sept. 13. They finished with 73 wins, three more than Hodges had predicted, and a game ahead of the Astros, whom they finally had overtaken after seven years. It was justifiable cause for celebration, but the Mets would do no celebrating in 1968. While they completed their season in New York, their manager lay in an Atlanta hospital recovering from a heart attack.

Hodges was an intense man who kept his emotions bottled. He was smoking more frequently late in the season, and the strain was beginning to show on his face. On Tuesday evening, Sept. 24, before a game against the Braves in Atlanta Stadium, Hodges pitched batting practice and hit fungoes to the outfielders, as was his custom. Once the game began, he told Rube Walker that he wasn't feeling well and asked the pitching coach to manage the club while he went to the clubhouse. Inside, he complained of chest pains to Gus Mauch, the trainer.

Mauch, who had suffered a heart attack himself a few years earlier, summoned the Braves' team physician. Within an hour, Hodges was in Crawford W. Long Hospital. A medical report issued the following day classified the attack as mild.

Hodges spent a month in Atlanta, where his wife took a hotel room to be near him. From there he went to St. Petersburg for some rest and relaxation. He came home to Brooklyn in November.

Doctors reported there was no reason why he should not make a full recovery and return to work, even work as nerve-wracking as managing the Mets. But cigarettes were out. He would have to observe a strict diet, and he would have to take long walks to strengthen his heart muscle. He was a man strong enough, Casey Stengel once said, "to squeeze your earbrows off," but he was 44 and suddenly vulnerable.

The optimism of the Mets' finest season had yielded to uncertainty. The Mets waited for next year, unsure what next year would bring.

Gil and Me

Ebbets Field was home to many characters in the days when the Dodgers inhabited Brooklyn. The park was intimate and encouraged dialogue among the fans, players, and managers. And, with such eccentric personalities as Wilbert Robinson, Babe Herman, Leo Durocher, and Chuck Dressen in Dodger uniforms, there always was plenty to talk about.

Baseball in Brooklyn was a swirling, mad, exhilarating experience. Hilda Chester rang her cowbell in the stands, and strikeout victims wearing uniforms other than those of the Dodgers were accompanied, musically, back to the dugout by the Dodger Sym-phony Band. Tex Rickard, the public address announcer, had a special way with words, such as the time he noted the coats spread over the box-seat railings and said aloud, "Tenshun, will the fans in the front seats please remove their clothing?"

It was an unlikely setting for Gil Hodges, a man of quiet dignity. He played on a team of outspoken stars—Jackie Robinson, Duke Snider, Carl Furillo—and never raised his voice. I can still remember encountering one of his teammates for the first time. "Greetings and felicitations, welcome to first base," the man said as I arrived following a base on balls. The man was Chuck Connors, who achieved greater fame and prosperity on television as "The Rifleman."

From a personality standpoint, Hodges was one of the last of the Dodgers you might have expected to become a manager. But, as a player, he was extremely perceptive. There was little he missed on the field.

Even though he began his career as a catcher, he was a great first baseman, a master of timing the throw and coming off the bag just as the ball arrived. Gil was constantly accused of cheating with his foot, but I cannot recall an umpire ever calling a runner safe because of the alleged violation. So adept was Hodges at the maneuver that it came to be identified as the "neighborhood play." Anytime Gil Hodges was in the neighborhood of first base, you were out.

It was his slugging ability that entwined our careers. Everyone remembers the 1951 playoffs between the Dodgers and Giants for the home run Bobby Thomson hit in the ninth inning of the deciding game. I remember it for the home run or home runs Hodges didn't hit.

I had finished the regular season with 42 homers, the top figure in the major leagues. Hodges had hit 40, but, according to National League rules, any subsequent homers he hit in the playoffs would be added to his total. Since Gil had hit four homers in just one game in the previous year, there was the possibility I might lose a sixth consecutive home-run title three days after the end of the season.

As it developed, Gil failed to hit a home run in any of the three playoff games. It was acknowledged publicly moments after the Giants' victory achieved on Thomson's dramatic shot. After Russ Hodges had stopped shouting "The Giants win the pennant" eight or nine times on the national broadcast, he turned the microphone over to Bob Prince for the wrap-up. Now Prince happened to be the Pirates' broadcaster and a good friend of mine. And he concluded his remarks by saying, rather incongruously, "And Ralph Kiner is still the home-run king of the National League."

In 1962, Hodges hit his last home run. It was of special interest to me. The game was played at the Polo Grounds and it was televised. The cameras focused on two men as the ball dropped into the stands. They followed Gil as he toured the bases and they zeroed in on me as I described the event. The home run was the 370th of his career, exceeding my total of 369. At that moment, he had hit more home runs than any other right-handed batter in National League history.

I got a rise out of Gil that day, for the first and only time, when I introduced him on the post-game show. "Records are made to be broken," I said, "and Gil Hodges today hit his 370th home run, surpassing my total of 369. And Gil, I just wanted you to know that I'm not happy about it."

He did a double take, checking to see if I was serious, and then recognized a put-on. "Well, Ralph," he said in deadpan fashion, "if I had to break someone's record, I'm glad it was yours." Few people in baseball had Hodges's ability to talk with tongue in cheek.

In his first season as manager of the Mets, he proved to be a demanding and resourceful boss. He was a man of few words, but what he requested he expected to be done. Early that year, Gil had seen four players slip into the hotel well after curfew, and the following day he called a meeting in the clubhouse. He said he wouldn't name names because he didn't want to embarrass the players, but he announced a $50 fine if the violators paid it voluntarily. If not, he said, the fine would be doubled.

An hour later, while Hodges was out on the field, Joe Pignatano rushed out with the news. "Hey, Gilly, you're doing good," the coach said. "You got seven checks already."

That first season, he was asked what kind of manager he would like to be. Typically, his reply was brief and to the point. "There are only two kinds of managers," he said, "winning managers and ex-managers. I like to work."

The heart attack had not altered the man's philosophy. He still wanted to work, and to do that he had to win the most important battle of his life.

Hodges followed doctor's orders carefully. He stopped smoking. He took daily constitutionals, starting around the block and then extending them until they reached around his Brooklyn neighborhood. He dropped 25 pounds, from 225 to the 200 he carried in his playing days. And, in February, he received a clean bill of health.

He stepped up his conditioning program in Florida. Each

morning, he would rise early, and, accompanied by pitching coach Rube Walker, he would walk down Gulf Boulevard, through the business district of St. Petersburg Beach, and across the causeway. On the far side, they would be joined by the other coaches, and all would drive to the Mets' training camp. At night, the manager fished with his wife, Joan, from a bridge south of the beach.

The catch that year would be remarkable indeed.

The First Championship

Gil Hodges was prepared to start spring training in 1969 on schedule. The players were not.

A conflict had arisen between the owners and the Players Association in negotiations for a new pension plan. The Association asked its members to boycott training camp, and the vast majority of members honored that request. So while Hodges and his staff worked with youngsters and a handful of veterans, some Mets worked out on their own in St. Petersburg and others stayed home.

On Feb. 24, the Association agreed to terms with the owners and spring training began in earnest. Among the foremost priorities for the Mets was the conversion of Amos Otis, a lithe speedster who had enjoyed a fine season at Jacksonville in 1968, from outfielder to third baseman. The position had been a trouble spot for the team since that first home game when Don Zimmer threw the ball over Jim Marshall's head.

The Mets also wanted to take long looks at Gary Gentry, the latest in the line of outstanding pitching prospects, outfielder Rod Gaspar, and Wayne Garrett, a 21-year-old infielder who had been drafted from the Braves' organization and would have to be kept on the major-league roster or returned to Atlanta. And then there was Bud Harrelson, who had undergone knee surgery the previous year and whose recovery was being closely monitored.

The name of Joe Torre popped up frequently that spring. Torre, who was born and had grown to prominence in Brooklyn, was the kind of productive hitter the Mets needed, and he was available. Torre and Paul Richards, the Atlanta general manager, had feuded throughout the 1968 season, and the players' boycott, of which Torre had been an outspoken advocate, drove them farther apart. Torre once said of Richards that he always wanted you to kiss his ring, but he always carried it in his back pocket.

Officials of the Mets and Braves huddled in West Palm Beach, where they were scheduled to play an exhibition game. Richards said he would accept Nolan Ryan, the young flame-thrower who still was unproven, and Jerry Grote because he would need a catcher to replace Torre. The Mets nodded. But Richards wanted more. How about Otis? The deal died. Shortly thereafter, Torre was shipped to St. Louis for Orlando Cepeda.

The Mets won 14 games and lost 10 in Florida. Bud Harrelson's knee was coming along fine. Gentry worked his way into the starting rotation. Gaspar and Garrett proved to be welcome additions. And Tug McGraw, profiting from an additional two years in the minors, earned the position of left-handed short relief man.

There was room on the roster because Dick Selma, Larry Stahl, and Don Shaw, in addition to three minor-league prospects, had been selected in the expansion draft to stock the league's two new franchises. The San Diego club, which adopted the nickname Padres used so long by its minor-league predecessor, acquired Stahl and Selma, whom they later traded to the Cubs. The Montreal Expos claimed Shaw and also purchased Don Bosch in a later transaction.

In the aftermath of its second expansion within a decade, the league was split into two six-team divisions. The new alignment, which grouped the Mets with the Cardinals, Cubs, Phillies, Pirates, and Expos in the Eastern Division, ruled out 10th place forever. Even ninth now was beneath New York. And, with a first-year team in the division, the Mets were expected to finish higher than sixth. First place, of course, still seemed out of the question. In Las Vegas, odds on the Mets were fixed at 100-1.

The early schedule favored the Mets. They were to open the 1969 season at home against the Expos, a team training for its very first regular-season game. How could the Mets lose? Let me count the ways.

Ken Boswell committed three errors at second base, Seaver was knocked out, and reliever Cal Koonce was battered. A rally in the ninth fell short when Gaspar struck out with two runners on base. Final score: Montreal 11, New York 10. It was the Mets' first international defeat in National League play.

The Mets proceeded to lose four of their first six games. After 18 games, they were 7-11 and tied for last place with Montreal. The season looked anything but promising on May 4 as they prepared to play a doubleheader against Chicago in Wrigley Field.

The Cubs had turned themselves around under Leo Durocher. They had jumped off to a quick start and led the Eastern Division. They were eight full games ahead of the Mets when the doubleheader started. A crowd of nearly 40,000 was wedged into the old park, with its ivy-covered brick walls. What the Chicago fans witnessed was the first clear sign that these were not the same old Mets.

Seaver, batting in the third inning, was hit between the shoulder blades by a pitch from Bill Hands. In the bottom of the inning, Seaver returned the favor by plunking Hands in the stomach. The umpires interceded before the game got out of hand, and the Mets won, 3-2. Jerry Koosman was shelved with an arm injury, so Hodges started McGraw in the second game and the relief ace beat the Cubs by an identical score.

On May 21, in Atlanta, Seaver stopped the Braves, 3-0, on three hits, boosting the Mets' record to 18-18. They had reached the .500 mark 36 games into the season, and the achievement received a great deal of attention from the news media. But only a few players, those like Ed Kranepool who had suffered through the worst years, appreciated the moment. The vast majority saw nothing to celebrate.

"What's so good about .500?" Seaver said. "That's only mediocre. We didn't come into this season to play .500. I'm tired of the jokes about the old Mets. Let Rod Kanehl and Marvelous Marv laugh about the Mets. We're out here to win. You know when we'll have champagne? When we win the pennant."

Of course, Seaver took quite a bit of needling when the Mets lost their next five games. They were nine games behind the Cubs, and their record (18-23) was identical to that at the same stage in 1968.

It was time for a stand. Koosman, his arm recovered, was the starting pitcher against the Padres. Through 10 innings he did not allow a run, striking out 15 batters. Through 10 innings the Mets managed not to score. But McGraw held the Padres scoreless in the 11th, and the combination of two errors and a single by Harrelson produced a run. The slide had been stopped.

The Mets swept three games from the Giants, and then Koosman struck out eight in beating the Dodgers, 2-1, on June 2. The Mets were back at .500, and this time they zoomed right past. Seaver, with help from McGraw, beat the Dodgers, 5-2, the next afternoon. There followed, on June 4, a bizarre game the likes of which were to distinguish the season.

Again, it was the Dodgers providing the opposition. The teams were scoreless for 14 innings. Jack DiLauro, a left-hander called up from Jacksonville to replace the injured Ryan, had started and pitched splendidly. Now it was up to Ron Taylor, the veteran relief pitcher.

With runners at first and third and one man out in the Dodger 15th, Willie Davis drove a ball off Taylor's glove. However, Weis, reacting instinctively, fielded the ball in his bare hand and, in the same motion, threw to the plate as he flung himself to the ground. The ball arrived on a short hop, but Grote dug it out and tagged Billy Grabarkewitz, attempting to score from third. It was one of the most incredible plays by an infielder I had ever witnessed. The Dodgers failed to score, and, in the bottom of the inning, a walk to Harrelson, a single by Garrett, and Davis's error gave the Mets a well-deserved 1-0 victory.

The winning streak finally ended at 11 games on the West Coast, but by then the Mets had proven something to themselves. On June 15, the day of the trading deadline, the Mets acquired the power hitter who would give them the ability to score runs in clusters. Johnny Murphy announced that the team had obtained first baseman Donn Clendenon from the Expos for utility infielder Kevin Collins, pitcher Steve Renko, and two minor-leaguers. For the first time, there was justifiable reason for optimism.

The Mets were a second-place team, trailing by only three games, as they prepared for a three-game series against the Cubs in early July. It was billed as the first crucial series in the team's history.

Hodges scoffed at the suggestion. "I don't believe you can have a big series in July," the manager said. "Sure, we want to win today, we want to win tomorrow. But our season will not end regardless of what happens. I'm sorry I couldn't make it more exciting, but that's how I feel."

The fans, who didn't know better, were excited. A total of 56,096 filed into Shea Stadium on a Tuesday afternoon for the first game. Joan Payson was excited, too. But, early in the year, she had scheduled a stay at the Elizabeth Arden Health Spa in Maine. So she did the next best thing. She arranged for the telecast of the game to be carried over a local station in Maine.

What she saw was marvelous entertainment. Kranepool homered off Ferguson Jenkins, the Chicago ace, in the fifth inning and Ernie Banks tied the score, 1-1, with a homer off Koosman in the sixth. The Cubs took the lead in the seventh, and then Jim Hickman, an original Met, homered for a 3-1 Chicago advantage. The Mets were down to their final three outs.

Boswell batted for Koosman in the ninth and lifted a shallow fly. Don Young, the rookie center fielder, had difficulty locating the ball in the sun, and it fell for a double. After Tommie Agee fouled out, pinch-hitter Clendenon drove a pitch to deep left-center. Young caught up with the ball on the warning track but dropped it as he rammed the fence. Cleon Jones then doubled into the left-field corner, tying the score. Art Shamsky was walked intentionally, and, after Garrett grounded out, Kranepool hit a soft liner to left-center for a single. The Mets had won their first "big" game.

A record crowd of 59,083, including 50,709 paid, swelled Shea the following night to watch the duel between Seaver and Ken Holtzman, onetime teammates in Alaska. It was no contest. Seaver was devastating. He struck out five of the first six Chicago batters. He retired the first 24 in order. As he walked to the mound in the ninth inning with a 4-0 lead, he needed three outs for a perfect game. The fans were chanting his name.

Randy Hundley, the leadoff batter, tried a surprise bunt, but Seaver was prepared and threw him out easily. Into the batter's box stepped Jimmy Qualls, a rookie outfielder. He was a left-handed hitter who had flied to right and grounded to first in two previous trips to the plate, his 46th and 47th in the major leagues. Seaver wound up and threw a blazing fastball. It arrived belt high and Qualls stroked it on a line into left-center field for a clean single.

On the mound, Seaver turned his back to home plate and stared into the distance beyond the outfield fence. The fans were standing all around the park. They were applauding him, not politely but feverishly. After a minute of reflection, he regained his poise, retired the next two batters, and completed the Mets' second victory of the series. He seemed elated by the experience, not disappointed in losing a no-hitter and perfect game. His wife, Nancy, broke down and cried on the post-game show as I interviewed Tom. It was one of those magic moments in sports that can never be duplicated.

The Mets were due for a letdown, and it occurred in the series finale. They committed two errors and played sloppy ball in a 6-2 defeat. Durocher was asked, "Were those the real Cubs out there today?" "No," the cocksure Chicago manager replied, "those were the real Mets." He would have cause to regret those words.

A week later, the teams were matched again, this time in a three-game set at Wrigley Field. The Bleacher Bums, a boisterous group of fans who wore construction helmets, were in good voice as Seaver and Hands locked in a torrid duel. Seaver, who had won his previous eight decisions, retired the first 10 batters, including Qualls. But, in the sixth inning, Don Kessinger singled, reached second on an infield out, and scored on Billy Williams's single. It proved to be the only run of the game.

Before another standing-room crowd the next day, Gentry drew the starting assignment against Dick Selma, the former Met. The score was 1-1 in the fourth when little Al Weis drove a three-run homer clear over the bleachers and onto Waveland Avenue. It was his first homer of the season, his second as a Met, and his fifth in the major leagues. The Mets won, 5-4, as Taylor saved the game for Gentry.

"Surprised?" said Weis, a man of few words. "I'm always surprised when I hit a homer. Once, when I hit a homer for the White Sox, I came into the dugout and all the guys were lying on the floor like they were dead or passed out from shock."

The Mets opened a 4-0 lead before Don Cardwell got to throw a pitch in the finale. They led, 6-0, after one and one-half innings. But Cardwell was gone after three, and the lead was cut to 6-5. Once again, Weis flexed his muscles and homered. A homer by Shamsky with a man on base completed the scoring in a 9-5 victory. The Mets left Chicago trailing the leaders by only 3½ games.

Someone prophesized there would be a man on the moon before the Mets won a pennant. And, on the night of July 20, after the Mets had split a doubleheader with the Expos and while they watched on television in the Montreal airport, American astronauts first set foot on that surface.

The Mets stumbled for a full month after the All-Star break. Their particular nemesis, as always, was their expansion partner, the Astros. They won only two of 12 games against Houston in 1969 and none of the six played in the Astrodome. On Aug. 13, they concluded a road trip by losing a three-game series to the Astros and returned home in third place, 9½ games behind the Cubs. First place appeared to be a fantasy.

But Seaver beat the Padres, 2-0, in the first game of a doubleheader, and the Mets won the second game, 2-1, on Grote's pinch single. Another doubleheader sweep the following day boosted the Mets back into second place. Their prospects were changing.

The next opponent was the Giants, who were starting Juan Marichal in the first game of the series. Hodges countered with Gentry, who responded with 10 scoreless innings before yielding to McGraw. The teams went to the 13th still scoreless, and, with slugger Willie McCovey at bat and no runners on base, the manager sent third baseman Bobby Pfeil into the left-field corner and challenged the hitter with a four-man outfield.

Hodges had successfully used the same maneuver earlier in the season to combat Richie Allen of the Phillies. McCovey clobbered the first pitch. The ball sailed toward the 371-foot sign in left-center precisely where Jones had been stationed. The left fielder leaped against the fence and speared the drive. In the 14th inning, Agee hammered Marichal's 151st pitch of the game into the Giants' bullpen, and the Mets escaped with a 1-0 victory.

The Mets won 9 of 10 on the homestand and swept a three-game series in San Diego. They were driving. After a 5-0 loss in San Francisco, they responded with an utterly implausible 3-2 victory on Aug. 30. The Mets threw out a baserunner at the plate in the eighth inning and again in the ninth inning. Another Giants' runner was cut down at third base in the ninth. Clendenon homered in the 10th for the winning margin.

By the time the Cubs paid their last visit of the season on Sept. 8, the Mets had pulled to within 2½ games. The two-game series was a big one by anybody's definition.

Bill Hands, the Cubs' starter, showed just how big it was when he sent Agee, the Mets' leadoff batter, sprawling in the dirt with his first pitch. Koosman, the Mets' starter, reacted to Durocher's attempt at intimidation by drilling cleanup hitter Ron Santo on the forearm as he led off the Chicago second. Upstairs in the broadcasting booth, it sounded like Santo had broken his arm. The message was clear. The Mets would not back down.

Agee delivered his personal communique in the third, homering for a 2-0 lead. The Cubs tied the score in the sixth, but in the bottom of the inning Agee stretched a single into a double and slid home safely under Hundley's tag following Garrett's single to right. Durocher and a half-dozen Cubs argued the decision long and loud, but to no avail. The Mets won, 3-2. Before more than 58,000 the next night, Seaver breezed to a 7-1 victory, his 21st of the season. The Cubs left town gasping for breath, their lead reduced to a half game.

The Mets defeated the Expos, 3-2, in the first game of a doubleheader some 20 hours later. At 10:13 P.M., word was received that the Cubs had lost to Philadelphia. The Mets occupied first place for the first time. After 140 games in 1969, after a total of 1,271 games since the franchise was founded, the Mets were on top by one-thousandth of a percentage point. They promptly widened their lead by winning the second game, 7-1.

The Cubs were sinking as the Mets opened a seven-game road trip with a doubleheader in Pittsburgh. Cleon Jones, the team's best hitter, had been sidelined with a leg injury, and military commitments further depleted the Mets' lineup against the heavy-hitting Pirates. So they did the best they could, which was slightly beyond human comprehension.

Jerry Koosman pitched the first game, held the Pirates scoreless, and drove in the only run with a fifth-inning single. Don Cardwell pitched the second game, held the Pirates scoreless with ninth-inning help from McGraw, and drove in the only run with a second-inning single. While the Pirates still were shaking their heads over those developments, Swoboda slugged his first grand-slam homer the following day for a 5-2 victory.

A loss in the series finale at Pittsburgh preceded another in a line of mystifying triumphs. On Sept. 15, at St. Louis, Steve Carlton struck out 19 Mets, establishing a major-league record. However, Swoboda hit a pair of two-run homers, and the Mets won the game, 4-3.

In the final month of the season even some of their losses were amazing, among them a 4-0 no-hitter by Bob Moose of the Pirates. Finally, on Sept. 24, before a paid crowd of 54,928, the Mets reached the end of the rainbow.

Clendenon hit a three-run homer in the first inning, and Ed Charles, who had to earn his spot on the roster in 1969 after being released the previous fall, followed with a two-run drive against the Cardinals. Gentry carried a 6-0 lead into the ninth inning, and, at 9:07 P.M. Joe Torre, rejected by the Mets in spring training because the price was too high, grounded into a double play. The Mets were division champions. Their fans sacked the field, tearing out chunks of sod in a moment of spontaneous combustion.

The Mets partied into the morning, first in their clubhouse and later in the Diamond Club upstairs. They had clinched the half-pennant in the final home game of the year, and 2,175,373 had paid to watch their astounding charge from ninth to first.

Of the many telegrams received by Hodges, one was of particular significance to the manager. "Happy to see you're number one," it said. "Hope your team does as well as your heart." It was signed by Linton H. Bishop, the specialist who had treated Hodges in Atlanta the previous fall. It was exactly one year to the day that Hodges had suffered his heart attack.

Ironically, Atlanta was the next stop for this team with aspirations. The Braves had staged a late rush to capture the Western Division title, and the two teams were scheduled to meet in a best-of-five series to determine the National League champion and World Series representative.

The first game, matching Tom Seaver (25-7) against Phil Niekro (23-13), got out of hand. Tony Gonzalez and Hank Aaron homered off Seaver, and the Braves led, 5-4, in the seventh. But

Atlanta literally threw away the game in the eighth as the Mets scored five runs to claim a 9-5 victory.

The Mets displayed unaccustomed muscle in the second game, taking leads of 4-0, 6-0, 8-0, and 9-1, with Agee and Boswell hitting homers. A three-run homer by the mighty Aaron and a two-run single by Clete Boyer cut the deficit to 9-6, but Jones hit a two-run homer for the Mets in the seventh. McGraw preserved a wild 11-6 victory.

On the occasion of his 23rd birthday, Gentry started the third game of the series at Shea Stadium. He was greeted by Gonzalez's single and an awesome home run off the center-field flagpole by Aaron. Gentry was knocked out in the third, and Nolan Ryan, bothered much of the season with leg pulls, pitched out of trouble.

Agee homered in the Mets' third and Boswell smacked a two-run homer in the fourth for a 3-2 New York lead. A two-run homer by Orlando Cepeda in the fifth pushed the Braves ahead momentarily, but Ryan singled in the bottom of the inning and Garrett, whom the Braves had surrendered to the Mets for the $25,000 draft price, homered for a 5-4 advantage. The Mets added additional runs in the fifth and sixth, and Ryan wrapped it up. At 3:34 P.M. on Oct. 6, the Mets were National League champions. There followed another celebration on the field and a blizzard of ticker tape and computer cards fluttered down on Wall Street.

Only one challenge remained. Ahead lay the World Series and the Baltimore Orioles, who had dispatched the Minnesota Twins in three games in the American League playoffs. They were, it was generally conceded, the finest club in baseball. They had power, speed, pitching, defense, and experience. They also had the home-park advantage for the first two games.

Seaver again drew the first-game assignment. This time, his disappointment began with the second pitch, when Don Buford, another of Rod Dedeaux's pupils from Southern Cal, popped it over the right-field fence. The Orioles scored three more runs in the fourth, capped by Buford's double, and Mike Cuellar baffled the Mets until the seventh, when they scored their only run on Weis's sacrifice fly. After Baltimore's 4-1 victory, the odds in Las Vegas on the Mets jumped from 8-5 to 16-5. Well, it was better than 100-1.

The Mets' outstanding pitching had yet to assert itself in

four post-season games. There was no time like the present. Koosman, 17-9 during the regular season, was at his best in Game Two. He pitched hitless ball through six innings and held a 1-0 lead achieved on Clendenon's homer off Dave McNally.

But the Orioles pulled even in the seventh when Paul Blair singled, stole second, and scored on Brooks Robinson's single. In the Mets' ninth, however, Charles, Grote, and Weis ripped successive singles for a 2-1 advantage. Ron Taylor bailed Koosman out of a jam in the ninth, and the Series was even.

In the course of the second game, a delegation of Met wives had paraded around Memorial Stadium with a banner fashioned from a hotel bedsheet. That was the spirit the Mets were looking forward to as they prepared for Game Three in Shea Stadium. Now they had a remote chance to win it all at home.

Gary Gentry retired the side in the Baltimore first. Agee was the Mets' first batter, and, as he had done so often in 1969, he provided a jolt in the form of a leadoff homer. He had become the inspirational player the Mets had expected a year earlier. New York scored two more runs off Jim Palmer in the third when Gentry, hitless in 28 previous at-bats, blasted a double over the head of Blair, the finest center fielder in baseball. The runs batted in were the pitcher's second and third of the year.

Frank Robinson singled in the fourth for the Orioles' first hit, and Boog Powell followed with a single. After Brooks Robinson struck out, Elrod Hendricks drove a pitch to deep left-center. Agee, who had been shading the left-handed hitter the other way, appeared to cover half the outfield as he closed on the ball. At the last instant, he made a desperate backhanded lunge, caught the ball in the very tip of his webbing, and managed to hang on as he caromed off the wall.

That catch still was a major topic of discussion in the stands and in the broadcasting booth when, with the Mets holding a 4-0 lead, Gentry walked the bases full in the seventh. Hodges, wanting a strikeout, called for Ryan. The youngster got two quick strikes, but then Blair ripped a sinking liner into right-center field. Agee had to travel in the opposite direction this time. He also had to dive for the ball. He made the catch anyway, skidding on one knee. It was a virtuoso performance. Agee had saved at least five runs with two of the great catches in Series history. Kranepool homered in the eighth, and Ryan punctuated the 5-0 victory by striking out Blair two innings later than the manager had planned.

The only man in Met history to lose a World Series game went to the mound the following day. This time Seaver was in command. He carried a 1-0 lead, provided by Clendenon's home run, into the ninth. But, two outs from the end, Frank Robinson and Powell singled and Brooks Robinson hit a sinking line drive to shallow right. It appeared to be a certain base hit.

Again, a Met outfielder was there. Only this time it was Swoboda, who claimed he was so uncoordinated as a kid that it wasn't until he was 18 that he could walk and chew gum at the same time. Swoboda might have played it safe, conceding a single and the tying run. The Mets, however, were conceding nothing. Ron launched himself through the air and made a spectacular, diving, backhanded catch which exceeded even Agee's pair for degree of difficulty. Although Swoboda jumped to his feet and came up throwing to the plate, Frank Robinson alertly tagged up and scored the tying run from third.

The score was 1-1 when Grote's catchable fly fell for a double in the 10th. After Weis was walked intentionally, Hodges sent J.C. Martin, a reserve catcher and accomplished bunter, to bat for Seaver. On the first pitch by Pete Richert, an experienced reliever, Martin dropped a bunt toward first base. Richert quickly fielded the ball and spun toward first. His throw, however, struck Martin on the wrist and bounded into right field. Rod Gaspar, running for Grote, easily scored the winning run in a 2-1 victory.

Some photos later showed that Martin had run on the inside of the baseline, which is illegal, but plate umpire Shag Crawford ruled Martin had touched the foul line with his right foot, and that was good enough for him.

The Mets were one victory away from the most improbable of success stories. Koosman got the call against Dave McNally but experienced difficulty in the early innings. McNally homered following a single by Mark Belanger, and Frank Robinson hit a solo homer in the third for a 3-0 Baltimore lead.

The last of the season's wondrous turning points occurred in the sixth inning. A low, inside pitch by McNally skipped away from the catcher, and Cleon Jones, the batter, claimed the ball hit him on the foot. Plate umpire Lou DiMuro disagreed. But Hodges retrieved the ball, which had rolled into the Mets' dugout, and calmly walked to home plate with the evidence. The ball had a telltale smudge of shoe polish, and DiMuro, confronted by this quiet giant of a man whose integrity was above question, motioned Jones to first base. Clendenon followed with a home run, cutting the Orioles' advantage to 3-2. An inning later, Mighty Mouse Weis homered, tying the score.

By then, it seemed inevitable. The Mets would find a way. Jones, who had batted .340 during the regular season, led off the eighth with a booming double. Clendenon grounded out, but, with first base open, Swoboda doubled down the left-field line and the Mets surged ahead. One out later, Grote hit a smash off Powell's glove, and relief pitcher Eddie Watt juggled the hurried throw at first base as Swoboda scored the Mets' fifth run.

Frank Robinson drew a walk in the ninth, but Koosman was equal to the moment. He got Powell to bounce into a force play and Brooks Robinson on a fly to right.

Davey Johnson, Baltimore's last hope, raised a fly to deep left, and Jones settled under it. It was 3:17 P.M. Oct. 16, 1969. "Keep dropping to me, baby. Keep dropping down," Jones yelled. And then it was in his glove.

The Mets were World Champions, and the fans charged over the barriers in waves. They grabbed the bases, they tore up the sod for souvenirs, and they danced around in jubilation. In Manhattan, showers of paper fell from office buildings, and soon people were in the streets laughing and weeping and hugging and kissing perfect strangers.

"They came slow but fast," explained baseball analyst Casey Stengel, on hand to see the fruition of his labor. Of course, there was no logical explanation for what happened. Perhaps the feeling was best expressed by Karl Ehrhardt, the professional "sign man" of Shea Stadium. At the conclusion of the game, he raised a special sign he had been saving. "There are no words," the message read. And there weren't.

Spring training for the Mets' first season, 1962, with Bob Murphy and Lindsey Nelson. We established a record as the broadcast trio with the longest time together. *(Kiner Collection)*

Our first owner, Mrs. Charles Payson, joins (from left) third baseman Don Zimmer, manager Casey Stengel, left fielder Frank Thomas and right fielder Gus Bell at St. Petersburg, Florida, in 1962.

(Sports Photo Source)

The scoreboard says it for the Mets' first home game—at the Polo Grounds. *(New York Mets)*

A Mets' version of Murderers' Row in 1962: (from left) Rod Kanehl, Jim Hickman, Gil Hodges, Frank Thomas and Charlie Neal.

(New York Mets)

Marvelous Marv Throneberry not only missed a lot of throws at first, he didn't get the ball to second base either. *(New York Mets)*

At least Casey Stengel knew my name. He would usually refer to us as "my announcers." *(top left)* *(Louis Requena)*

Wes Westrum with his coaches at spring training in 1966: (from left) Yogi Berra, Whitey Herzog, Westrum, Sheriff Robinson and Harvey Haddix. *(bottom left)* *(New York Mets)*

One of the Banner Days at Shea. My favorite banner is "Pray for Reign."

(UPI)

Gil Hodges shows umpire Lou DiMuro a smudge of shoe polish to prove Cleon Jones had been hit on the shoe by a sixth-inning pitch in the fifth game of the 1969 World Series. Cleon got his base and Donn Clendenon (left) hit a homer that capped a comeback rally. *(above)* *(UPI)*

The longest night! The fans—that is, the few who went the distance—get a third 7th-inning stretch in the 21st inning of what was the longest night game in major league history. The Astros, playing at home, beat the Mets, 1-0, in the 24th inning. Ron Swoboda and Tommie Agee were each 0-for-10. *(top left)* *(UPI)*

Jerry Koosman won two games to lead the Mets to the World Championship in 1969. He had a great personality to go with his pitching technique. And a great-looking wife. *(bottom left)* *(New York Mets)*

The champs get their ticker-tape parade on Broadway en route to a City Hall reception. *(above)* *(UPI)*

Tom Seaver is a great wine collector, but nothing was sweeter than this champagne. Lindsey Nelson is on the right, Bob Murphy is partially obscured in the middle and I'm somewhere under the bubbly. *(left)*

(Ken Regan/Camera 5)

The 1969 World Champion Mets: **Front row** (from left)—Gus Mauch, trainer; Joe Pignatano, coach; Rube Walker, coach; Yogi Berra, coach; Ed Yost, coach; Joe Deer, assistant trainer. **Second row:** Frank McGraw; Gary Gentry; Al Weis; Cleon Jones; Manager Gil Hodges; Jerry Grote; Bud Harrelson; Ed Charles; Agee; Cal Koonce; Ken Boswell; Tom Seaver; Jerry Koosman; Ron Swoboda; Wayne Garrett; Bobby Pfeil; Lou Niss, traveling secretary. **Back row:** Nick Torman, equipment manager; J. C. Martin; Ron Taylor; Ed Kranepool; Don Cardwell; Donn Clendenon; Nolan Ryan; Art Shamsky; Jack DiLauro; Roy Neuer, club-

Afterglow

There was much to celebrate in 1969, and the Mets didn't miss an opportunity. The scenes after each successive championship were events in themselves. Then there were parades, exclusive invitations, and parties galore.

It all started on Sept. 24 in the Mets' clubhouse at Shea Stadium. I never played for a championship team, so my experience at such affairs was as limited as that of the players. Perhaps because of my age, however, I was more inclined to drink champagne than to pour it over someone else's head.

I had been assigned by WOR-TV to do clubhouse interviews if and when the Mets clinched the Eastern Division title. So there I was on the night of Sept. 24, standing on an improvised platform, looking into the television camera and talking with Gil Hodges. The first assault was led by Tom Seaver.

The bubbly came down on the heads of Hodges and myself, trickling down our faces and onto our clothes. At least Hodges was wearing a baseball uniform. My first reaction was that champagne really burned. We continued the interview, fighting to keep our eyes open, and Hodges said that the team had shown "confidence, maturity, togetherness, and pitching."

M. Donald Grant, the chairman of the board, was next, and while he (and I) took a ritual dousing, he proclaimed, "Our team finally caught up with our fans. Our fans were winners long ago."

The show, and the champagne baths, continued for nearly an hour, after which I still had to conduct "Kiner's Korner." With the help of towels and a collection of loose-tongued Mets, I muddled through. Then I made a terrible mistake.

Before starting the clubhouse interviews, I had placed a tape recorder near the interview stand to capture the broadcast for posterity. I remembered it after the post-game show, so I decided to retrieve it. Well, the champagne was long gone by then, and the players were amusing themselves by tossing clubhouse visitors into the showers. I, too, became a victim.

Fortunately, I had the foresight to bring a change of clothes with me that night. So, after the reluctant shower, I dressed in a dry pair of slacks and a jacket and went upstairs to the party in the Diamond Club. Although I had not actually contributed to the championship, I found myself, like millions of New Yorkers, swept up in the emotion. In 10 years of playing major-league baseball, I had no pennant to celebrate. So this would be it for me, too. I wouldn't have missed it for the world.

The party pace quickened after the Mets defeated the Braves in the National League playoffs. In the time between the end of the playoffs and the start of the World Series, the Mets' players and broadcasters and their families were invited to the magnificent Fifth Avenue apartment of Governor Nelson Rockefeller.

The governor stood atop a coffee table, raised high a glass, and said, "Ladies and gentlemen, join me in a toast to Joan Payson and the New York Mets. It's as good as landing on the moon."

"Better than the moon," suggested coach Joe Pignatano.

"I want to amend that," Rockefeller said. "It's better than the moon landing."

In the course of the reception, we were given a tour of the apartment and its extensive and celebrated art collection. Several of us were examining a particularly famous painting when Pignatano wandered over.

"What's that?" the coach asked.

"It's a Picasso."

"What's so good about that?" he said, thinking the man had said Pignatano. "I've got three of them at home."

Everywhere the Mets went was news. Their departure for Baltimore and the start of the World Series became an event, one which WOR-TV asked me to cover. The Mets' chartered flight was scheduled to leave the Marine Air Terminal, a good distance from the main passenger terminal at LaGuardia Airport. A huge crowd assembled nonetheless. Mayor John Lindsay, who was running for reelection, showed up with a Dixieland band. He also read aloud a poem, a parody of the baseball classic "Casey at the Bat."

It didn't hurt Lindsay's image any. His identification with the Mets, especially the sight of him being doused by Rod Gaspar in the clubhouse following the World Series, helped the mayor retain his office.

The Series was a big thrill for me. I was chosen to broadcast the games in Baltimore over the radio for the National Broadcasting Company while Lindsey Nelson did the telecasts from New York with Curt Gowdy. I can remember sitting in the booth with NBC's Jim Simpson prior to the start of the first game and being visited by Joe Garagiola. "I just want to remind you," my old teammate said, "that over 80 million people will be listening to this game on radio." Thanks for the reminder, Joe.

I got through the Series somehow, and so did the Mets. The next order of business was a special day in New York, Mets' Day. It featured a ticker-tape parade up lower Broadway. The Mets and their wives were assigned four and five to a car and began a procession through the financial district, the "Canyon of Heroes" previously reserved for Charles Lindbergh and Douglas MacArthur and the astronauts. The city responded with enough paper to have wasted a few forests.

At City Hall, Robert Merrill, the Metropolitan Opera star, sang the national anthem and Mayor Lindsay praised the Mets for their contributions to the life of New York. Grant, on behalf of the Mets, said, "When I came to New York in 1925, looking for a job, I didn't dream such a thing would happen to me. From the top to the bottom, to the man who shined Cleon Jones's shoes, it was a team effort."

Kranepool, the only man to have played for the Mets in each season of their existence, said, "We did it for New York. It's been a long eight years."

The motorcade then proceeded to 42nd Street and Bryant

Park, where I had been assigned by the Mets' television station. I was filling time, awaiting the Mets' arrival, by interviewing Pearl Bailey, the famous entertainer who was a fervent Met fan. At the conclusion of the interview, she and Merrill, who had just arrived on the scene, were asked to sing "Take Me Out to the Ball Game." The problem was that they didn't know the lyrics. I can't carry a tune, but I had to lead these two famous singers because I was supplying the words.

Yes, it was a helluva season.

Downfall

The Mets monopolized post-season honors dispensed in the fall of 1969. Donn Clendenon, who had hit three home runs against the Orioles, was selected as the Most Valuable Player in the World Series. Tom Seaver won the Cy Young Award as the outstanding pitcher in the National League and, later in the year, was presented with the Sportsman of the Year Award from *Sports Illustrated*.

"Tom," general manager Johnny Murphy said at the award presentation, "if you and Nancy ever come up for adoption, Mrs. Murphy and I will be only too glad to take you."

Murphy himself was honored by *The Sporting News* as the Major League Executive of the Year, and Gil Hodges received every managerial honor worth receiving. Hodges also had his old three-year contract, which had another year remaining, torn up and replaced by a new three-year pact for a reported $70,000 per year.

It was the best of times for the Mets, who spent the winter finding things to do with their World Series shares of $18,332. But before the year was out, the times abruptly changed. On Dec. 30, Murphy suffered a heart attack in his Bronxville home. He was placed in intensive care, where he remained for two weeks. Murphy suffered another attack on Jan. 14 and died. He was 61 and he had been with the Mets since before Year One.

Before his death, Murphy had made several changes designed to keep the Mets on top. From San Francisco, he had acquired left-handed pitcher Ray Sadecki and outfielder Dave Marshall for minor-league prospects. The big trade had transpired at the winter meetings in Miami Beach in early December. There, he traded Amos Otis, who had spent much of 1969 in the minors and who no longer was an untouchable in the light of Agee's emergence, and pitching prospect Bob Johnson to the Kansas City Royals for Joe Foy. A power hitter raised in the Bronx, Foy was a third baseman and the Mets never could get enough of them. Foy would be the 42nd man in nine seasons to play the position.

The Mets stayed within the organization, as was their custom, in naming a successor to Murphy. He was Bob Scheffing, a former catcher, manager, broadcaster, and scout. Scheffing was a year-round resident of Scottsdale, Ariz., and a passionate golfer, but he also was a professional baseball man.

Wherever the Mets traveled in the spring of 1970, they were greeted by large, enthusiastic crowds and hordes of young autograph-seekers. "It's a feeling," Kranepool said, "of respect." Tug McGraw wore a gold pin in the shape of the number one just so he would not forget 1969.

There was little experimenting in Hodges's third Mets' camp. Foy was placed at third base and stayed there in the course of a 13-12 exhibition season. Never had the Mets appeared so settled.

"Getting there was the toughest part," said Hodges, once again stressing the positive. "If you've shown you've done it, you can do it again. We'll never capture what happened last year. Winning again won't be like winning the first time, but we can still make a second trip to the moon. And that's a pretty good trip."

There was little reason to doubt the manager, especially after the Mets did something they had not done in eight previous seasons. At Forbes Field in Pittsburgh, on April 7, the Mets won the first game of the season, beating the Pirates, 5-3, in 11 innings. Certainly, the Mets were the first team in history to win a World Series before they won on Opening Day.

They did, however, lose their home opener to the same Pirates a week later, evening their record at 3-3. They stayed at or slightly above the .500 mark throughout April and May. The pitching, however, still was spectacular.

On April 22, a bright Wednesday afternoon, Seaver received his Cy Young Award prior to a game against San Diego. In the nine innings that followed, he displayed the skills that made him the National League's top pitcher. Seaver struck out 19 batters, including the final 10 in order, in a 2-1 victory. The 19 strikeouts in one game exceeded the best of Bob Feller and Sandy Koufax and tied the major-league record for a nine-inning game. The 10 strikeouts in succession were two more than the previous major-league mark of eight shared by Max Surkont, Jim Maloney, Don Wilson, and Johnny Podres.

Coincidentally, Podres was seated near home plate throughout the game. The former Dodger left-hander, who had been the winning pitcher in the game that earned Brooklyn its only World Championship, was serving as the Padres' minor-league pitching instructor. "He was fantastic, outstanding," Podres said afterward. "There was no doubt in my mind he'd break that record. He had perfect rhythm, and I don't think he'll ever throw that hard again. It's amazing, as hard as he was throwing, he was still hitting the spots. If you didn't swing, it was still a strike."

Seaver was unhittable at the end. Only three batters made any contact over the final five innings, and he required only 10 pitches to strike out the side in the ninth inning. "I might as well have played without a glove," said Bud Harrelson, who handled no chances at shortstop.

Gary Gentry flirted with a no-hitter in Chicago on May 13, but Ernie Banks singled in the eighth. It was the Cubs' only hit in a 4-0 defeat. Two days later, Seaver followed with a one-hit, 4-0 victory over the Phillies, whose only safety was a third-inning single by Mike Compton. The next day, Jerry Koosman beat the Phillies, 6-0.

By the end of May, the Mets appeared to be following the pattern they had set in 1968. Their staff had compiled six shut-outs, and they had been blanked six times themselves. On June 12, they began a successful stretch of 20 victories in 27 games to move into first place, but by the All-Star break they had fallen back to second, one and one-half games behind the Pi-rates.

The 1970 All-Star Game was played in Cincinnati's unfinished Riverfront Stadium, and Seaver received the starting assignment from the National League manager, who happened to be Gil Hodges. Seaver did his job, holding the American League scoreless for three innings. The Nationals won, 5-4, in the 12th inning when a base hit by Jim Hickman (yes, *that* Jim Hickman) scored Cincinnati's Pete Rose, who bowled over catcher Ray Fosse as he was taking a throw from center fielder Amos Otis (yes, *that* Amos Otis) of the Royals.

Pitching continued to dominate the Mets' season after the All-Star break. Under the heading of strange but true was a 3-0 shutout Jim McAndrew posted against the Padres on July 21 in San Diego. It wasn't so much what the Mets did that made the game unusual but what they didn't do. For eight innings, they had no hits and a 1-0 lead.

But San Diego manager Preston Gomez chose to pinch-hit for his pitcher, 22-year-old Clay Kirby, in the eighth inning, thereby denying him the opportunity of his first no-hit game and denying the Mets the opportunity of being held hitless for the fifth time. Kirby had yielded a run in the first inning on walks to Tommie Agee and Ken Singleton, a strapping rookie, a double steal, and a groundout by Art Shamsky. Although the Padres were solidly entrenched in the Western Division cellar, Gomez played for the win and was roundly booed for his decision. The Mets collected three hits and two runs off relief pitcher Jack Baldschun in the ninth.

That game represented one of the few breaks the Mets got in 1970. Although the pitching still was good and the team was scoring runs at the best rate in its history, there was a missing ingredient. Things were happening to them, not for them.

The Mets had a 61-54 record and trailed the division-leading Pirates by two games entering a series against the Braves in Atlanta. Ron Reed bested Nolan Ryan, 10-2, in the first game, but Koosman came back to defeat the Braves, 4-2, in the second game. Then, on Aug. 15, came the game that demonstrated this was not to be the Mets' year.

Seaver brought a 17-6 record into the game. His counterpart, Phil Niekro, a 20-game winner in 1969, was struggling along at 10-14. Seaver was sharp that night and, given a 2-1 lead in the sixth by Clendenon's 17th home run, seemed a certain winner as he prepared to pitch the ninth.

Tony Gonzalez led off the inning with a single, but Seaver

retired Orlando Cepeda on a fly ball. Rico Carty then hit a pop which Wayne Garrett failed to handle, and pinch-hitter Hank Aaron drew a walk to load the bases. Seaver needed a strikeout. He got it, and lost the game.

Bob Tillman swung at a 1-2 pitch, an inside fastball, and failed to nick it. Jerry Grote didn't have any better success attempting to catch it. The ball rolled to the backstop as Gonzalez scored, and Grote's hurried throw to Seaver covering the plate got through the pitcher, allowing Carty to score the winning run in a galling 3-2 defeat for the Mets.

They did manage to gain a share of the lead on Sept. 10 and, after falling back, still had a chance to catch the Pirates as they moved into Pittsburgh for a late-season three-game series. Pittsburgh led, 4-2, in the ninth inning of the first game when Ron Swoboda drew a leadoff walk and scored on Agee's double. Garrett then walked to put the potential tying and winning runs on base. Jones flied deep to right, but Agee, halfway between second and third, did not tag up. With Shamsky up, however, Agee attempted to steal third. He was thrown out, and Shamsky then struck out to end the game. The Pirates went on to sweep the series, and the Mets were ex-champions.

Their final record of 83-79 left them six games from the top. Agee set a club record with 182 hits, and Clendenon's 97 runs batted in also was a high for a Met player. Ken Boswell, who had worked hard to become a better second baseman, set a league record of 85 consecutive errorless games, and Seaver's 283 strikeouts were a record for a NL right-hander. His earned-run average, 2.81, also was the lowest among league pitchers, but his record sagged to 18-12.

Perhaps the most remarkable aspect of 1970 was the attendance. The Mets drew 2,697,479 to Shea, the second-largest total in major-league history at the time. The fans had retaken the lead from the players.

There was no hangover of success to carry the Mets through spring training in 1971. The excitement of 1969 had worn off. It was time for a fresh start.

The annual third-base search turned up Bob Aspromonte. The Mets had given up on Joe Foy when his .236 average failed to hide a poor aptitude for defense. Aspromonte had enjoyed several fine seasons with the Astros, but his acquisition from the Atlanta Braves represented something of a gamble. He was

32 and had been beset by injuries in the previous two years. However, he did have some promotional value. A native of Brooklyn, Aspromonte was the last active ballplayer to have played for the Brooklyn Dodgers. As an 18-year-old high school graduate, he went to bat once in Ebbets Field in 1956 and struck out.

The Mets enjoyed a productive spring, winning 15 and losing 12. But their record was incidental to a transaction announced on Wednesday evening, March 31, the night before the team broke camp. Swoboda, one of Casey Stengel's "Youth of America," had been traded to Montreal for Don Hahn, an outfielder with superior defensive ability.

Swoboda never had fulfilled the promise of the 19 home runs he hit in a spectacular rookie year. He had been erratic and temperamental, and his batting average with the Mets was only .242. Yet he was one of the players to grasp what the Mets were about. He hustled, he emoted, and, when the chance was there for the Mets to do the unthinkable in 1969, he came through in grand style. Swoboda had a wonderful rapport with the fans. The trade was a jolt to many.

On our radio broadcast that night, prior to the game against the St. Louis Cardinals at Al Lang Field, Swoboda said he was looking forward to playing under manager Gene Mauch at Montreal. He was only 26, and he thought he would get to play more with the Expos. He had grown disillusioned in 1970, criticizing teammates for lack of effort and chafing under Hodges's platoon system. He couldn't know it then, of course, but, before the season was over, he would again be playing in New York. Not for the Mets but for, of all teams, the Yankees.

Tom Seaver started well in 1971 and, not surprisingly, so did the Mets. The right-hander defeated the Expos, 4-2, on Opening Day and won his first four decisions. At the end of April, the Mets were 12-7 and in first place. A month later the Mets were 27-18 and in third place, three games behind the Pirates. Nolan Ryan was 6-1 and Seaver 6-2.

The Mets remained in close pursuit through June. On the last day of the month, Ryan shut out the Pirates, 4-0, lifting the club to within two games of first place. The record of 45-29 was the Mets' best ever at that stage of the season.

It was on the following day that the slide began. Dock Ellis of the Pirates bested Koosman and the Mets, 3-0, on July 1. The only game the Mets were to win of the next 11 played was an 8-0 shutout of the Expos by Sadecki. In the span of 11 days and the stretch of 12 games, the Mets fell from two games out to 10. They never recovered.

The second half of the season was a struggle as run production dropped. Only Cleon Jones (.319), Ed Kranepool (.280), and Tommie Agee (.285) hit with any consistency, and Agee spent a sizeable portion of the year on the disabled list. That the trio shared the club home-run leadership with 14 apiece was indicative of the Mets' lack of punch.

Age had eroded the skills of Clendenon and Aspromonte. The team's big hitter in 1970, Clendenon hit but 11 homers and drove in only 37 runs. Clearly, Aspromonte had run out of time, batting .225 with five home runs.

Perhaps the biggest disappointment, however, was the pitching. After his great start, Ryan had been beset with control problems and finished with a 10-14 record; Jerry Koosman suffered from arm miseries and staggered to a 6-11 mark; and Gary Gentry, who threw his second one-hitter in two years early in the season, failed to carry the extra burden. He was 12-11.

What kept the team respectable were the performances of Tug McGraw and Tom Seaver. McGraw pitched brilliantly in relief, compiling an 11-4 record and a remarkable 1.70 earned-run average. Seaver pitched a one-hitter against the division champion Pirates on Sept. 26, then closed out the season by beating the Cards, 6-1, in the final game. It was his 20th victory against 10 defeats.

In addition to attaining the 20-victory plateau for the second time, Seaver led major-league starters with a 1.76 ERA. And he surpassed the National League strikeout record for a right-hander, the one he had established in 1970 with 283. In 1971, Seaver fanned 289 batters.

The Mets' 37-39 record after the All-Star game enabled the team to finish with an overall mark of 83-79, identical to the previous year. It also left them tied for third place, 14 games behind the Pirates. The Mets were on a treadmill, and some wholesale changes had to be made.

Al Weis, the mighty mite of 1969, had been released during the season. On Oct. 22, Clendenon and Aspromonte also were cut. Art Shamsky, limited to pinch-hitting duty by back trouble, was traded to the Cards along with pitching prospects Jim

Bibby, Rich Folkers, and Charlie Hudson for pitchers Chuck Taylor and Harry Parker, first baseman Jim Beauchamp, and outfielder Tom Coulter.

The big shakeup was saved for the winter meetings. On Dec. 10, Bob Scheffing completed his first major transaction as general manager. The Mets obtained the services of Jim Fregosi, a six-time all-star shortstop with the California Angels. In return, the Mets sent Nolan Ryan and three minor-league prospects—outfielder Leroy Stanton, catcher Francisco Estrada, and pitcher Don Rose. The Mets despaired of Ryan ever achieving the control necessary to transform him into a big winner, and Ryan had grown frustrated with his role on the staff. He had asked to be traded.

In Fregosi, the Mets were getting a proven performer who would not be 30 until the first month of the season. However, they did not want Fregosi to play shortstop. They had an all-star of their own at that position in Bud Harrelson. Fregosi, Scheffing said, would become the Mets' 46th third baseman. It was expected that a 47th would not be needed for some time.

Naturally, Fregosi became a focal point of spring training. He had never played a game at third base, but the Mets were confident he could do the job. The first exhibition game was scheduled against the White Sox in Sarasota. Everyone was hopeful Fregosi would get off to a good start. Instead, he reached to field a ground ball in infield practice and broke his right thumb. It was the first in a series of injuries that would shorten his career with the Mets.

Despite the bad break, the Mets enjoyed a fine spring. When they broke camp on March 30 and flew to the east coast of Florida for games against the Yankees and the Expos, they had a record of 15-8. In Jon Matlack, they had an outstanding pitching prospect capable of moving into the starting rotation. In John Milner, they had a powerful young hitter who could play first base and the outfield. Gil Hodges said this was the best team he had ever managed.

But after the Mets checked into the Ramada Inn in West Palm Beach on March 31, there occurred two stunning events that altered the course of the season and the overall future of the club. One was temporary in nature, the other very final.

On the night of the Mets' arrival, representatives of the Players Association convened in Dallas and voted unanimously to stage the first strike in modern major-league history over the matter of pension benefits. The exhibition games scheduled for that weekend were canceled and the start of the regular season was placed in jeopardy.

Players began scattering on Saturday, some to their homes, others back to St. Pete to await further developments. The official Mets' party remained at the Ramada Inn. The chartered flight which was to ferry the Mets and Yankees to exhibition games in Kinston, N.C., and Norfolk, Va., on Monday simply would pick up the manager, coaches, and other club officials and transport them directly to New York.

On Easter Sunday, with no game now scheduled, Yogi Berra and his wife drove to Miami for the day. Hodges and his other coaches—Joe Pignatano, Rube Walker, and Eddie Yost—decided to play a round of golf on the course adjacent to the hotel. Gil had not felt better nor looked healthier than at any time since his heart attack in 1968. The foursome completed 18 holes, played a few more for good measure, then walked back to the hotel about 5 P.M.

They stood around chatting for a time before making arrangements to meet for dinner. As Hodges turned away from the group, he suddenly fell backwards. He was unconscious before his head hit the stone walk. He had been felled by a massive heart attack. There was no chance to revive him. Gil Hodges, the man who hit the Mets' very first homer, the man who led the Mets to the World Championship, the man who was one of the most popular sports figures in New York history, was dead two days shy of his 48th birthday.

The chartered flight left Monday morning as scheduled. Yankee officials and several players had boarded in Fort Lauderdale. Numbly, the Met contingent joined them. The body of Hodges was placed aboard. On Thursday, April 6, the scheduled date of the season opener, a requiem mass was celebrated in Brooklyn for the man who, two decades earlier, inspired a priest to ask his parishioners to pray that Hodges might break his slump. He would be missed terribly.

Following the funeral, the Mets called a press conference to make two major announcements. Yogi Berra had been appointed as the new manager and outfielder Rusty Staub had been acquired from Montreal for three promising youngsters. The trade had been sanctioned by Hodges, who reasoned that the hard-hitting Staub would give the team enough punch to put it over the top, but had not been announced earlier because of the strike.

At the request of the Mets, I had spent the previous winter working with three of their outstanding prospects in the instructional league. The three had potential but had not demonstrated the needed consistency at the plate. By the end of the instructional league season, they had made considerable progress and appeared ready to take on major-league pitching. The trio was Ken Singleton, Tim Foli, and Mike Jorgensen. To obtain Staub, the Mets sent Singleton, Foli, and Jorgensen to the Expos. I had spent the winter helping a Met opponent without realizing it.

Yogi Berra is an original. There are in circulation literally hundreds of stories regarding Yogi's baseball career. Some of them are even true.

One of my favorites was a story told by Whitey Ford, the pitching star of the Yankees in the years Berra was the most celebrated catcher in the game. Ford was having difficulty with the circulation in his fingers and, in order to get a better grip on the ball, had devised a clear, sticky substance which he applied by means of an aerosal spray can. This was done without the knowledge of the umpires and, apparently, without Yogi's knowledge as well.

On this particular day, Whitey left the unmarked can atop his locker. Wandering out of the shower, Yogi spied the can and, assuming that it contained deodorant, applied two short blasts to the underarms. The spray having solidified on the spot, Berra had to be led back to the shower and freed from his imprisonment with liberal amounts of soap and hot water.

Yogi was accomplished in the art of borrowing. I can verify that. At the winter meetings in Hawaii, Yogi, Stan Musial, Red Schoendienst and I decided to play a round of golf. As I recall, we didn't have to pay any greens fees, and golf carts also were at our disposal. Yogi, however, had neglected to bring his clubs.

"You can rent a set for five dollars," I told him, pointing in the direction of the pro shop.

"That's okay," he said. "I'll play out of your bags."

And so Berra, who drives and hits long irons from the right side and pitches and putts from the left, spent the round walking back and forth across the fairway, alternating clubs from my bag and from that of Musial, a left-hander. I don't remember what he shot, but, as always, Yogi drove a hard bargain.

With the Mets, Yogi added to the legend shaped by Joe Garagiola, a friend from his childhood days on The Hill in St. Louis. There was the time he attempted to reach his wife while on a road trip. He tried for four hours before Carmen answered the telephone at their home in New Jersey.

"Where have you been?" Yogi asked.

"I went to see *Doctor Zhivago*," she replied.

"What's wrong with you *now?*" Yogi inquired.

One day, Berra was in the outfield when Tom Seaver was doing his running. Seaver had intended to work out for a specified number of minutes, and, when he saw Yogi, he asked him the time. "You mean now?" Yogi asked.

There were many baseball people who considered Berra among the luckiest men alive. His business investments reaped amazing dividends. Yankee teammates had no fear of flying anywhere on any plane as long as Yogi was aboard. If he had cause to miss a flight, however, the fear did not cease until the plane had landed safely.

In the spring of 1969, the spring in which Gil Hodges had walked his way back to health, the Mets' coaches and officials habitually used a dry-cleaning establishment that offered one-day service. They would drop the clothes off on the way to the ball park and pick them up on the way back to the Mets' hotel on St. Petersburg Beach.

The cleaners, in an effort to promote business, offered free service to any customer who had the good fortune to receive a ticket with a star. That spring only one member of the Met family had his clothes cleaned free of charge. It was, of course, Yogi Berra.

The 1972 season was an emotional roller coaster for Yogi. Not only was there the shock of Hodges's death and his sudden succession to the manager's job, but in August he received the greatest honor that can befall a baseball man. He was inducted into the Hall of Fame at Cooperstown.

Two other men associated with the Mets had preceded him. In 1966, a year after the fractured hip forced him into retirement, Casey Stengel limped into the Hall. "I'm thankful I have baseball knuckles," he told the assembled gathering, "and I couldn't become a dentist." Five years later, his great friend, George Weiss, who had appointed him manager of the Yankees and the Mets, was similarly honored.

And now it was the turn of another ex-Yankee who had been restored to prominence by the National League expansion franchise in New York. In his remarks, Yogi alluded to perhaps his most famous malaprop, the speech he had made on the occasion of Yogi Berra Night in his hometown of St. Louis, when he said, "I guess the first thing I should do is thank everyone who made this day necessary." It was a grabber.

Then Yogi Berra pulled out his reading glasses and a speech typed by Carmen on the back of a sheet of business stationery. "Since I guess this is the most important day of my life," he said, "I'm gonna get it right. I better read it."

He asked Carmen and his three sons—Larry, Timmy, and Dale—to rise. And then his voice cracked. "I only regret," he said, struggling to continue, "the people who didn't live to see this day. My mother, my father, my brother John, and Gil Hodges."

In the crowd around the steps of the National Baseball Library, men cried. Cooperstown is like that.

"You Gotta Believe!"

It was April 14, eight days after the scheduled start of the 1972 season, when the Mets reassembled at Shea Stadium. They would play their opening game the following day.

The first six dates had already been lost, and, according to the terms of the settlement between the players and owners, those games would not be rescheduled. Each team would pick up the schedule in progress on Saturday, April 15. The Mets' first opponent would be the Pirates.

There was a sad tone to the ceremonies that day, a tone not associated with the first day of a new season. The flag behind the center-field fence flew at half staff, the crowd was asked to observe a moment of silence, and the Mets' uniforms bore mourning bands, all in honor of Gil Hodges.

The Mets won their first game, 4-0, lost their next two, and then embarked on a seven-game winning streak, taking three from the Cubs, three in San Diego, and beating the Dodgers, 6-1, behind Jon Matlack in Los Angeles.

After scoring only one run against the Dodgers in their next two games, both losses, the Mets swept a series from the Giants in San Francisco as Tom Seaver gained his fourth victory, Gary Gentry his second, and Matlack, the splendid rookie, his third. At the conclusion of the road trip, they were a first-place team.

The interest generated by the Mets in the first month of the season mushroomed on May 11 when, at a press conference preceding a doubleheader against the Dodgers, they announced the fulfillment of a fan's fantasy and an owner's fondest wish. Willie Mays was returning to New York.

Willie had been Mrs. Payson's favorite ball player when he wore the uniform of the New York Giants in the 1950s. He had made some of the most memorable catches in baseball history in the Polo Grounds and had led the Giants to a World Championship in 1954. His years in San Francisco had merely confirmed his greatness. But now Willie was 41 and a part-time player, and Horace Stoneham, the Giants' financially beleaguered owner, could no longer afford his salary or future commitments.

"I think we owe it to our fans," said M. Donald Grant, who engineered the trade and who, like Mrs. Payson, was an unabashed admirer of Mays. "I think our fans deserve to have Willie wind up in the city which loved him. We have magnificent fan support, and we feel a lot of sentiment, a lot of pride in this. We feel New York City will be happy Mr. Stoneham has given us this opportunity."

A few years earlier, when Mays still was near the top of his game, the Mets had offered $1 million to Stoneham for his star. Stoneham had declined. This time the Mets had offered Charlie Williams, a spare pitcher, and a considerably smaller amount of cash, and Stoneham accepted. As part of the agreement, the Mets signed Mays to a long-term contract, guaranteeing him a lucrative position after his retirement as an active player.

Jim Beauchamp, who never had been a star, graciously consented to give up uniform number 24, which Willie had worn in 21 seasons with the Giants. The following evening, Mays dressed in pinstripes for the first time. The scene was recorded for posterity by a battery of photographers.

When Mays walked onto the field in his new uniform, it was to endure the kidding of his teammates. "Hello, rookie," Jerry Koosman said, in greeting. Seaver guided him to the batting cage and tried to help him solve the baffling delivery of Sheriff Robinson, the portly coach and batting-practice pitcher. "You were my idol, Willie," claimed coach Joe Pignatano, 42. "My father used to take me to see you play."

Mays, at home among all ball players, relished the attention.

Ironically, the Giants were in town for a weekend series, and, when manager Yogi Berra decided not to start Mays on Friday night, I and others assumed there was an unwritten agreement that Willie would not play against San Francisco. In a pinch-hitting situation that night, Berra chose John Milner over Mays, and the crowd, which had chanted "We want Willie" throughout the game, booed the rookie for no other reason than he was not Willie Mays. Milner drew a walk and the Mets won the game, 2-1. They also won the following day, 1-0, again without Mays's help.

On Sunday, however, Giants' manager Charlie Fox selected left-hander Sam McDowell to start the final game of the series. Berra, who said he wanted to play Mays against left-handers, placed Willie in the leadoff slot in his batting order. It was May 14, Mother's Day, a day with a chilling drizzle which held down the crowd to 35,505.

Mays drew a walk in the first inning and scored on Rusty Staub's grand-slam homer. He struck out in the third. When he came to bat in the fifth, the score was tied, 4-4. It was then he proved he had not lost his flair for drama.

Don Carrithers, a right-hander, was pitching in relief for the Giants. The count went to 3-2. Then Mays drilled a pitch on a line over the left-field fence and into the visitors' bullpen. Jim McAndrew pitched four shutout innings of relief, and the Mets won, 5-4. "You couldn't have written a better script," said Eddie Yost, the third-base coach.

It was a marvelous occasion, one which could have happened only to a player of Mays's stature. The home run was his first of the season, his first in a New York uniform since 1957, and the 647th of his storied career. The people stood and cheered for several minutes, and his teammates did the same. "It was super," Staub said. "I was ecstatic over my own home run, but I can't tell you how I felt when Willie hit his."

Mays didn't know what to think. "I had feelings for both sides," he said. "I wanted to help the Mets, but, at the same time, I had certain feelings for the Giants . . . I didn't think I would do anything today to win a ball game. I thought I would be so nervous I wouldn't hit the ball at all."

The Mets won their next eight games, running their record

to 25-7 and opening a six-game lead. At the end of May, on the strength of a 6-0 shutout by Matlack, the Mets were 29-11 and led by four games. Then came June and problems no one could have foreseen.

The first blow landed on June 3 when, in the course of a 5-2 victory over the Braves, Staub was hit on the hand by a pitched ball. Six days later, at Wrigley Field, Jim Fregosi injured his shoulder. On June 16, at Cincinnati, the Reds' Joe Morgan collided with Cleon Jones, playing first base, and the Met suffered elbow damage. Later in the same series, Staub swung at a pitch and dropped the bat in pain. A second series of x-rays revealed a broken hand, the result of the Atlanta incident.

Although the Mets left Cincinnati in first place, they lost two of three games in Houston, all three in St. Louis, and began sinking slowly under the weight of their injuries. Beauchamp was added to the disabled list on July 10 followed by Bud Harrelson (Aug. 3). Jerry Grote, another player whose season was interrupted by injury, underwent surgery for bone chips in his elbow in September.

There were occasional flashes of light amid the gloom. On July 4, Seaver flirted with another no-hit, no-run game. But, as had been the case against the Cubs three years earlier, the no-hitter eluded him with two outs remaining. Leron Lee singled for the Padres' only hit of the game.

Mays made a triumphant return to San Francisco later in the month, his two-run, fifth-inning homer lifting the Mets to a 3-1 victory over his former teammates. Mays had done it twice to the Giants in as many starts. At 41, his ability to rise to the occasion was as remarkable as ever.

Staub returned in mid-September, but it was too late for the Mets. With him in the lineup, the team had won 36 games and lost 20. Without him, the Mets were 36-47.

At the time he was sidelined, Staub led the Mets in hits, home runs, and runs batted in and had a .301 average. He finished the season with a .293 average, and his 38 RBIs in 66 games was not far behind the 52 of Jones, the club leader who had been limited to 106 games. Mays did as well as could be expected, batting .267 with eight homers in 69 games.

As usual, the pitching had held up its end. Matlack won 15 of 25 decisions, compiling a 2.32 earned-run average, and took Rookie-of-the-Year honors. McAndrew, 11-8, enjoyed his first winning campaign. And Tug McGraw set a team record with 27 saves and received credit for the National League's victory in the All-Star Game, where he struck out four and yielded only one hit in two innings. The big man, of course, continued to be Seaver. He struck out 249 batters, his fifth consecutive season with 200 or more strikeouts, and fashioned a 21-12 record.

The team's overall record of 83-73, which left them 13½ games behind the division-champion Pirates, was a disappointment. But in view of all the injuries, the Mets were convinced they could win the division in 1973 if they remained healthy.

Obviously, they were a better team with a healthy Staub, Grote, and Harrelson. And they made a significant trade over the winter, acquiring a solid hitter and an accomplished second baseman in Felix Millan. In exchange for Millan and left-handed pitcher George Stone, the man who had broken Staub's hand, the Mets sent pitchers Gary Gentry, 7-10 in 1972, and Danny Frisella to the Braves.

Although they managed only an 11-13 record in spring training, they started fast in the regular season. Seaver shut out the Phillies, 3-0, on Opening Day, and Matlack followed with a 3-2 decision a day later. The Mets then defeated the Cardinals twice behind Jerry Koosman and Seaver. Never before had they begun a season with such positive results.

But before they could make it through April, the ailments began anew. John Milner, leading the club with five homers and 13 runs batted in after 14 games, pulled a hamstring muscle on April 25. He was placed on the disabled list three days later. Before the season was over, the DL was to claim eight Mets, an unofficial major-league record.

One injury seemed to lead to another as the Mets dropped in the standings. Cleon Jones, whose two homers had provided Seaver with all the Mets' runs on Opening Day, damaged his right wrist and forearm diving for a ball. After attempting to play, with little success, he was disabled on June 1.

By that time, the Mets also had lost Grote and Willie Mays, and Staub had been rendered ineffective. Grote and Staub were injured in the same game at Three Rivers Stadium in Pittsburgh. A pitch by the Pirates' Ramon Hernandez struck Staub, whose right hand still troubled him, on the left hand. Later in the inning, a Hernandez pitch drilled Grote on the right wrist.

He suffered a fracture and was placed on the 60-day disabled list the following day. "I think I'm going to quit," Yogi Berra grumbled after the game. "Maybe if I give some other guy a chance, our luck will change."

But Berra stayed on and the Mets' luck got worse. As a result of the Grote incident, the Mets purchased veteran catcher Jerry May from Kansas City. In May's first game as a Met, he sprained his left wrist. Returning from that injury, he pulled a hamstring and was disabled.

Fortunately, what appeared to be the most frightening injury of all had no lingering effect. On May 8, at Shea Stadium, Matlack was struck in the forehead by a line drive off the bat of Atlanta's Marty Perez. The force of the blow was such that the ball caromed all the way to the Mets' dugout.

X-rays disclosed a linear fracture of the frontal bone of the skull. Matlack made an amazing recovery. Eleven days after being felled, he was back on the mound. Not only was he not gun shy, but he pitched six scoreless innings against the Pirates in a game the Mets lost, 4-1, in 10 innings.

No sooner was he back in the rotation than other regulars began departing. Following Jones onto the disabled list was Harrelson, who fractured his left wrist on a double-play pivot against Cinncinnati. George Theodore, the rookie outfielder playing in place of Jones, returned from an eye injury only to fracture his hip in a collision with Don Hahn. Harrelson came back from his wrist injury in July, cracked a bone in his chest and went back on the disabled list. Grote was activated on July 11 and suffered a broken finger on July 15.

The Mets were under siege. "For two years, I haven't had a full team yet," Berra said. "It's getting so I got to laugh."

Reeling from the injuries, the Mets fell into last place on June 25. By July 4, they were 12 games out of first place. Between then and the All-Star break they managed to win nine of 17 games and, much to their surprise, inch within 7½ games of the top.

"That's pretty damn close for a last-place club," Berra decided. A strange thing was happening. No team in the Eastern Division was playing well. The National League Least, outsiders called it.

For all their injuries, the Mets' most significant failure had been their relief pitching, specifically Tug McGraw. A year after setting a club record for saves, he was blowing games at every opportunity. "If you ain't got a bullpen," the manager noted, "you ain't got nothin'."

Without McGraw, the Mets did not have a bullpen. There was nothing wrong with him from a physical standpoint. He just appeared to have lost confidence in himself. Berra gave him a start on July 17 in the hope that might get him untracked, but Ralph Garr of the Braves hit his first pitch over the center-field fence and McGraw withdrew farther into his shell. On Aug. 20, he lost for the sixth time. He was still without a victory, and his earned-run average swelled to 5.45. The Mets were 56-67 and still occupied last place.

It was in the 124th game of the season that the transformation began. McGraw entered a game against the Dodgers in the eighth inning with the Mets trailing, 3-2. He held Los Angeles hitless for two innings, and the Mets rallied in the ninth for a 4-3 victory as Jones, Millan, Staub, and Milner singled.

It coincided with a post-game appearance by Donald Grant, who told the team that he and Mrs. Payson were still confident that the Mets could win. After Grant's speech, McGraw shouted, "You gotta believe!"

The Mets closed the month of August by beating the Cards, 6-4, in 10 innings. The winning pitcher, for the second time in the season, was McGraw. The victory boosted the Mets out of last place for the first time since June. They were only 5½ games behind the Cards, the division leaders, and their key players were healthy for a change. "You gotta believe!" McGraw repeated. By then it had become a rallying cry for the entire team.

In winning 7 of their first 10 in September, the Mets skipped into fourth place, only three games from the top. The Cards still led the division. Then came the Pirates, who had fired manager Bill Virdon and replaced him with Danny Murtaugh. The Expos were third, 2½ games out, followed by the Mets and the Cubs (3½ games back). Only the Phillies appeared to be out of the race.

On Sept. 17, the Mets began a five-game confrontation with the Pirates which, in all likelihood, would determine the order of finish. The first two games were to be played in Pittsburgh, the last three in New York. The Pirates had won seven of 10 under Murtaugh and supplanted the Cards in first place. The

Mets, still fourth, were 2½ games back. They needed to win at least three of the five to stand a reasonable chance.

Berra had his rotation ready. The Mets would open with Seaver, who was 17-9 for the year and who had enjoyed extraordinary success against Pittsburgh throughout his career. The planning was perfect; the execution was not. Seaver was routed, and the Pirates breezed to a 10-3 victory.

The Pirates also dismissed Matlack early the following night and carried a 4-1 lead into the ninth inning. The Mets were down to their final three outs. Implausibly, they rallied, tying the score on a hit by Ron Hodges—a reserve catcher who had earned a place on the roster during Grote's convalescence —and taking a 6-4 lead on a two-run single by Don Hahn. McGraw had been lifted for a pinch-hitter in the top of the ninth, and now Berra had only two youngsters in the bullpen, Buzz Capra and Bob Apodaca. He chose the latter.

Apodaca had never appeared in a major-league game. He joined the team nine days after the end of the International League season, following a hand injury to Harry Parker. He had not pitched anywhere in almost two weeks and he was entering the most important game of the season for the Mets. Understandably, he was nervous. Understandably, he was wild. Understandably, he walked the first two batters on eight pitches.

Berra now summoned Capra, in his second major-league season. The runners were sacrificed to second and third, and Al Oliver followed with a hard smash on which first baseman Jim Beauchamp made a fine play to record the second out while a run scored. Berra ordered Capra to walk slugger Willie Stargell intentionally, an unorthodox move considering he represented the potential winning run. Capra then walked Bob Robertson unintentionally, loading the bases. The Mets were facing a moment of desperation.

The count went to 3-1 on Manny Sanguillen. Capra's fifth pitch was in the vicinity of the knees. It might have been ball four, but Sanguillen, a notorious bad-ball hitter, swung and lifted a fly to left field. The Mets had produced an amazing victory, but it was to be just the beginning of a chain of events that wouldn't be topped for 13 years.

At Shea Stadium, on Sept. 19, the Mets scored a relatively easy 7-3 victory behind Stone as Cleon Jones hit his first and second homers in a home uniform since Opening Day. The Pittsburgh lead was cut to 1½ games with two more games to play in the series. Belief now was widespread and the following night erased all doubt.

It began with a news conference called to announce Willie Mays's retirement, effective at the end of the season. "These kids are going for a pennant," he said, "and the best thing I can do for them is to step aside. But if they get in a World Series, I'll be there to help." The Mets were not only thinking about the possibility of a pennant, they were talking openly about it.

The game that followed was tense throughout. The Pirates held leads of 1-0 and 2-1. On each occasion, the Mets rallied to tie. A double by Dave Cash, however, gave Pittsburgh a 3-2 lead in the ninth. Once again, the Mets were down to their last three outs. But pinch-hitter Ken Boswell blooped a leadoff single, reached second on a sacrifice bunt, and, with two out, scored the tying run on a clutch double by pinch-hitter Duffy Dyer.

Ray Sadecki retired nine Pirates in a row through the 12th, but the Mets also neglected to score. Then, in the 13th, Richie Zisk singled for Pittsburgh with one out. Sanguillen was retired on a fly, but rookie Dave Augustine blasted a pitch far over the head of Jones. It appeared destined to sail over the left-field fence, but, instead, it struck the very top, at the point.

The strange angle at which the ball hit produced a high carom directly into Jones's glove. "The ball said, 'Here I am, get me,'" Jones recalled. "I've never seen that happen before."

Jones whirled and threw to the cutoff man, Wayne Garrett. He, in turn, threw a perfect one-bounce strike to Ron Hodges, and Zisk, running with the hit, was cut down at the plate. It was a moment of sorcery that left the Pirates, the Mets, and the fans equally stunned.

The Mets put the game away in the bottom of the inning when Milner and Boswell walked and, with one out, Hodges singled. That meant first place was at stake on Sept. 21, and the Mets were not to be denied. Jones and Grote doubled in the first inning to stake Seaver to a 4-0 lead. Milner hit his 23rd homer, Garrett his 14th, and Staub his 15th later in the game, and the Mets breezed, 10-2. In three weeks, they had rushed from last to first.

A two-game sweep of the Cards and a split in a two-game series with the Expos preceded the final series of the season, a four-game set with the Cubs in Chicago. Single games were scheduled for Friday and Saturday, with a doubleheader Sunday. But it rained on Friday, the Pirates lost, and the Cards won. When the Mets reported to Wrigley on Saturday, five teams were still in contention.

The Mets and Cubs waited for the rain to end Saturday. They waited and waited until, finally, it grew too late to start a game. Wrigley Field, the only park in the majors without lights, was dark and foreboding. The postponement necessitated a doubleheader Sunday and a doubleheader Monday. The Pirates lost to Montreal Saturday and the Cards defeated the Phillies, taking over second place.

At the start of Sunday's action, a five-way tie remained a possibility. The Cards trailed by 1½ games with one left to play, the Pirates by two games with two left to play, the Expos by 2½ with one game left and the Cubs by four with four left, all against the Mets. Only the Mets, at 80-78, had a chance to finish above .500.

In the first game of the doubleheader, Matlack and Rich Reuschel staged a torrid pitching duel. Both teams were scoreless through seven innings, but, in the eighth, a single by Dave Rosello, a sacrifice, and a single by Ron Santo gave the Cubs a 1-0 lead. Bob Locker preserved the Cubs' victory with a scoreless ninth. The Cubs, however, learned of their elimination between games. By virtue of a victory over Philadelphia, the Cardinals had finished their season with a record of 81-81.

Montreal also was eliminated, by losing to Pittsburgh. The Mets' lead was a half game as they started the second game. However, Jones hit a two-run homer and Staub drove in three runs in a 9-2 victory behind Jerry Koosman, and the Mets clinched a tie for the division title.

According to the official schedule, the season was over. Yet the Mets still had two games to play and the Pirates one, a makeup against the Padres, who had to fly from California because the game might have a bearing on the outcome of the race. Seaver was rested. The only question was whether to pitch him in the first game or save him for the second, if needed. "If you got to get beat," Berra decided, "get beat with your best."

Monday was another day of rain and gloom, but the teams played anyway. Jones, who had been sensational down the stretch, homered off Burt Hooton in the second inning for a 1-0 lead. The Mets added a pair of runs in the fourth on Grote's bases-loaded single and scored two more in the fifth on hits by Garrett, Millan, and Staub and on Milner's sacrifice fly. The Cubs rallied for two in the fifth, and, after the Mets increased their lead to 6-2 in the top of the seventh, Rick Monday hit a two-run homer off Seaver. The score was 6-4. Time for McGraw.

It was only fitting. McGraw had gotten them this far. Starting with that game against the Dodgers on Aug. 22, he had appeared in 18 games, amassing 5 wins and 11 saves. Now he had a chance to wrap up the division title. He didn't fail. When Glenn Beckert lined into a double play in the ninth inning, the Mets were champions. McGraw had his 12th save in six weeks. His earned-run average for the period was 0.88.

"You gotta believe!" he shouted over and over again in the clubhouse. By now, everyone did. The celebration was relatively mild until the announcement by umpire Augie Donatelli that the second game had been cancelled because of wet grounds. The Mets had made the final game superfluous.

The championship series was next. While the Mets had struggled to an 82-79 record, the Cincinnati Reds had won 99 games to outdistance the Dodgers in the Western Division. Furthermore, the Reds had defeated the Mets 8 times in their 12 meetings. "Yeah, but we weren't always healthy then," Berra said. "When we had all our fellas, we did all right with them."

All their fellas were accounted for on the Wednesday before the start of the best-of-five playoffs in Cincinnati when Seaver, who had been troubled by a sore shoulder, threw without pain. He was given the starting assignment on Saturday against the Reds' Jack Billingham.

Seaver provided the Mets with a 1-0 lead in the second inning by following a walk to Bud Harrelson with a double. He protected the slim margin until the eighth when Pete Rose homered over the right-center-field fence. Johnny Bench then homered in the ninth for a 2-1 Cincinnati victory, nullifying a 13-strikeout effort by the Mets' ace.

As good as Seaver was on Saturday, Matlack was even sharper on Sunday. He limited the Reds to two singles. Staub's fourth-inning homer off Don Gullett was the only run of the game until the ninth when the Mets scored four times in a 5-0 triumph.

The third game was played at Shea Stadium, and the Mets quickly turned it into a rout as Staub homered in each of the first two innings. But the rout became a riot and then a near-forfeit in the fifth when Rose and Harrelson tangled at second base with the Reds trailing, 9-2.

Rose was running from first when John Milner fielded Morgan's ground ball and threw to second for the force. Harrelson's return throw was in time for the double play. The inning was over, but Harrelson and Rose were too busy arguing about the latter's hard slide to notice. Words led to action, and soon the two men were rolling on the ground. Not surprisingly, the 200-pound Rose was on top, the 150-pound Harrelson on the bottom. Players charged out of the dugouts and the bullpens. While Wayne Garrett jumped Rose and others attempted to settle that dispute, another front was formed around Pedro Borbon, the Cincinnati relief pitcher, who took wild swings at anyone wearing a Mets' uniform. Order finally was restored, but only temporarily.

When Rose took his position in left field, he was bombarded by missiles, including bottles of various shapes, sizes, and liquid contents. The shelling continued with such intensity that Cincinnati manager Sparky Anderson pulled his team off the field rather than risk the players' safety. The fans were warned over the public-address system that there was the possibility of a forfeit if they continued in their actions, but that appeal had little effect.

Finally, National League president Chub Feeney asked Berra and Mays to go to left field and plead with the fans to desist. They were joined by Seaver, Jones, and Staub as they walked across the diamond to the left-field corner. It worked. The Reds returned to the field and the teams played out the Mets' 9-2 victory.

The Mets threatened to clinch the pennant the following day, taking a 1-0 lead into the seventh inning. But George Stone, who had enjoyed a remarkable 12-3 season, yielded a homer to Tony Perez in the seventh. The teams battled into the ninth, where McGraw escaped from a bases-loaded situation, only to create another in the 10th. Again, he survived. In the 11th, with two Cincinnati runners on base and two out, Dan Driessen drove a McGraw pitch deep to right field. Staub overtook it on the warning track, crashing into the fence. He held the ball for the third out but injured his right shoulder in the process.

McGraw left the game for a pinch-hitter in the Mets' 11th, and Rose, the target of garbage and abuse the previous day, promptly homered off Harry Parker. He raced around the bases, pumping his right fist in the air. The Mets went out quietly in their half of the 12th, and the series was even at two games apiece.

Seaver and Billingham staged a rematch in Game Five. Neither pitcher was as sharp as he had been in the first game. With the score tied at 2-2 in the Mets' fifth, Garrett doubled. Millan then attempted to bunt Garrett to third. Billingham's throw arrived in plenty of time. However, third baseman Driessen, in a costly mental lapse, merely tagged the bag thinking there was a force play involved. Garrett slid in safely.

A double by Jones, a walk to Milner, an infield single by pinch-hitter Mays, a fielder's choice, and Harrelson's single produced four runs. The Mets added another run in the sixth on Seaver's double and Jones's single. It fell to McGraw, of course, to preserve the victory. He replaced Seaver in the ninth with the bases loaded and one out, retired Morgan on a pop, and then got Driessen on a grounder. The Mets had beaten the mighty Reds. The Mets, a last-place club in August, were National League champions.

The accomplishment wasn't so stunning as in 1969, but it may have been more satisfying. "To keep fighting back through all those disappointments and injuries," Harrelson said, "that's what we're proud of. To win when you're expected to win, as we were when the year started, that's the greatest satisfaction of all. We showed everyone, finally, what we knew we were, a good grown-up ball club."

Only one challenge remained, the World Series. The Oakland A's, defending World Champions, had won 94 games in breezing to the Western Division title and had defeated the Baltimore Orioles in five games for the American League pennant.

Since Seaver and Jim (Catfish) Hunter of the A's had been required to work in the playoff finals, neither team had its best pitcher ready for the Series opener. Matlack got the call for the Mets, opposing Ken Holtzman, the former Cub who was one of Oakland's three 20-game winners. Staub, still troubled by the shoulder injury suffered in the fourth game of the playoffs, was unable to play, so Willie Mays started in center field, flanked by Jones and Hahn.

Holtzman had batted only once all season because of the AL's designated-hitter rule and had drawn a walk on that singular occasion. But, in the third inning, he doubled down the left-field line, triggering a two-run rally. A ground ball by Bert Campaneris skipped through the legs of the dependable Millan, and Holtzman scored. Campaneris then stole second and scored on Joe Rudi's single.

The Mets scored one run in the fourth on a double by Jones and a single by Milner. But Reggie Jackson, forced to move from right field to center field because of an injury to Bill North, ran down Grote's drive on the warning track, curtailing the damage. Rollie Fingers held the Mets scoreless in the sixth, seventh, and eighth, and Darold Knowles came on to get the final two outs of the game. The Mets were in a familiar position. They were behind.

The second game produced a batch of records and some of the sloppiest play in Series history. Before the game ended 4 hours and 13 minutes after the first pitch (a record), the two teams had employed 38 players (a record), including 21 by the A's (a record). They had also committed six errors, including five by the A's. The Mets won, 10-7, in 12 innings.

It was the A's who made necessary the extra innings. They scored two runs off McGraw after two were out in the ninth to tie the score at 6-6. But a leadoff double by Harrelson triggered a four-run outburst by the Mets in the 12th. The tie-breaking run was driven in by Willie Mays, who singled up the middle in what was to be his last at-bat in the major leagues. A pair of errors by reserve second baseman Mike Andrews enabled the Mets to score their final three runs.

At the conclusion of the game, Charles O. Finley, the A's controversial owner, induced Andrews to sign a statement that he had suffered a disabling injury in the game, enabling Finley to activate infielder Manny Trillo in his place. Andrews did have a chronic back condition but had played with it the entire season. When they learned of the development the following day, Andrews's teammates were incensed, and threatened some sort of action in the third game scheduled for Tuesday night in New York. That became unnecessary, however, when

Commissioner Bowie Kuhn ordered Andrews to be reactivated and levied a $7,000 fine on Finley.

There was more turmoil to come. Before the start of the third game, Oakland manager Dick Williams informed his players that, no matter what the result of the Series, he would resign at its conclusion. He had served three years on the job, a record for peaceful coexistence with Finley. Although saddened, the A's had been through too much to be shaken.

Hunter, the A's money pitcher, drew the starting assignment. Garrett, a standout in the Mets' stretch drive, hit Hunter's second pitch for a homer. Millan and Staub followed with singles and Hunter uncorked a wild pitch. The Mets led, 2-0, before a batter was retired. Those were all the runs they were to get.

Seaver blew away the A's over the first five innings, striking out nine. In the sixth, however, doubles by Sal Bando and Gene Tenace produced the first Oakland run. The A's tied the score, 2-2, in the eighth when Campaneris singled, stole second, and raced home on Joe Rudi's single. A walk, a passed ball, and a single by Campaneris off Parker in the 11th provided the A's with a 3-2 lead, and Fingers, the fourth Oakland pitcher, retired the Mets in order.

Staub, changing his batting style to offset the shoulder injury, dominated the fourth game. He hit a three-run homer in the first inning off Holtzman, added three singles and a walk, and drove in five runs in the Mets' 6-1 victory. Matlack received credit for the win with relief help from Sadecki in the ninth.

The balance swung in favor of the Mets in the fifth game, and the catalyst, as ever, was McGraw. Jerry Koosman was protecting a 2-0 lead in the seventh inning when a walk to Tenace and a one-out double by Ray Fosse put the tying run in scoring position. When Berra walked to the mound, there were 54,817 who knew what had to be done and who had to do it. McGraw entered to a tumultuous ovation.

He walked Deron Johnson, heightening the drama, then got Angel Mangual on a pop, and struck out the dangerous Campaneris. McGraw wriggled out of another jam in the eighth, then set the A's down in order in the ninth, striking out Billy Conigliaro for the final out. As McGraw pranced to the Mets' dugout, the veins popping in his neck, the Mayor of New York held aloft a placard that read, "You gotta believe!"

It was to be the high point of a remarkable season. The Mets needed only to play .500 ball to win their second World Series, but the A's were too formidable and resilient. Reggie Jackson doubled across runs against Seaver in the first and third innings of the sixth game, and Hunter, with help from Knowles and Fingers, checked the Mets, 3-1.

The A's put the seventh game away early on two-run homers off Matlack by Campaneris and Jackson in the third inning. Knowles retired Garrett on a pop fly with two runners on base for the final out in a 5-2 decision.

I was in the Mets' clubhouse during the final at-bats, dispatched there by the National Broadcasting Company for television interviews in the unlikely event they rallied to win the championship. In the room when I arrived were the camera crew and Willie Mays. He was sitting at his locker in the corner, watching the final minutes of his major-league career on a television set.

It reminded me of *The Picture of Dorian Gray.* As an active player, he had seemed perpetually young, his body hard, his manner spirited, as if he didn't have a care in the world. Now, as he faced the end, the years seemed to grow on him. His face appeared drained beyond its years, his brow furrowed by deep lines, as he sat motionless, uttering no sound and displaying no emotion. The laughter so familiar to all who followed baseball through the 1950s and 1960s was stilled.

I had difficulty relating this Willie Mays to the man who had played such a prominent role in the lives of Americans for 22 summers, the man who had hit 660 home runs and thrilled millions, the man who had been the greatest player of his generation. For a moment, I felt older myself.

Home Runs

I always had the ability to hit a baseball great distances. From the moment I learned to time Bob Bodkin's delivery in a vacant lot in Alhambra until the end of my career, mine was a power game. And yet, as much satisfaction as I took in hitting home runs, I remember very few of them.

I do know the first major-league home run I ever hit was against Howie Pollet in St. Louis. What was surprising about the drive was that the ball landed on the right-field roof in Sportsman's Park, and, in my entire life, I don't think I hit more than seven or eight homers to the opposite field. Throughout my career, I was a dead pull hitter.

That worked against me as far as my batting average was concerned. During spring training in 1948, we played the Cleveland Indians in Tucson. Lou Boudreau was the player-manager of the Indians, and he had devised a shift to combat Ted Williams whenever his club played the Boston Red Sox. Since Williams was a left-handed batter, Boudreau (playing shortstop) positioned himself alongside the second baseman on the right side of the infield and invited Williams to stroke the ball to the opposite field. In my case, he motioned the second baseman to the shortstop side of the bag.

After that experience, every National League club began to

employ the shift against me. It probably cost me a .300 lifetime average. I lost a lot of base hits. I talked to Williams about hitting against the shift before an exhibition game between our clubs in Pittsburgh in 1948. Rather than foul up his swing trying to hit singles to the opposite field, he determined he would continue to pull the ball with power whenever possible. It confirmed my own thinking on the subject.

So I hit away. And it really was the only sensible thing for me to do. I had hit 23 home runs as a rookie and led the National League, in part because Johnny Mize of the Giants suffered a broken arm and missed a month of the season. With the help of Greenberg, I really blossomed the following year. I hit 51 homers in 1947, 40 in 1948, and my career high of 54 in 1949. The latter total might have been higher, but a 55th homer was erased by a rainout and I hit five other balls that struck the tops of fences around the league and went for doubles.

Although I never did threaten Babe Ruth's one-season record of 60, or even Greenberg's 58, the 168 homers in my first four seasons were more than Ruth, Greenberg, Williams, Lou Gehrig, or Mel Ott had managed at that stage of their careers. Twice in that period I hit four home runs in consecutive at-bats. And yet, there aren't many drives that stand out in my mind, perhaps because the Pirates were rarely playing for more than their salaries.

One notable exception occurred in early September 1948. The Pirates were engaged in their one and only pennant race during my tenure. We had won our last five games and trailed the first-place Boston Braves by three games as we prepared to open a series against the Cubs in Chicago.

Red Ruffing, the great former Yankee pitcher (later to be a member of the first Mets' coaching staff), and I had been good friends for many years. Well, Red invited Max West and me to his house in Chicago for dinner the night before the first game. Ruth had died a few weeks earlier, and we got to talking about Ruffing's famous teammate.

Pauline, Red's wife, opened a bottle of champagne and, in the course of several toasts, Red decided to break out films he had of the old Yankees. It was fascinating to watch Ruth, Gehrig, and others hit the ball, and we stayed later and drank more than we had intended.

I woke up sick the following morning. My stomach felt terrible. I couldn't eat breakfast. I didn't feel any better at Wrigley Field. They took my temperature and I was running a high fever. Billy Meyer, our manager, told me to stay in the clubhouse, and he'd send for me if he needed me to hit. I lay down on the trainer's table and tried to rest.

In the sixth inning, the batboy climbed the stairs to the small visiting clubhouse and told me to get out to the dugout. By the time I arrived, however, we had scored three runs and led, 8-5. Meyer sent me back inside, just before the Cubs rallied for five runs.

Neither team scored in the seventh, and Meyer sent for me again in the eighth. As I reached the dugout, we scored a run and had the bases loaded. I batted for Mel Queen. My legs were rubbery, my eyes were watering. Hank Borowy, the Chicago pitcher, got two quick strikes. The next pitch was a fastball, low and on the outside corner.

I'm still not sure just how I did it, but I hit that ball about as hard as it is possible to hit a ball. It was a line drive that started so low Roy Smalley, the shortstop, made a leap to grab it. It kept rising and rising and, finally, cleared the brick wall in left-center field for a pinch-hit grand-slam home run. We needed all the runs, too, winning the game, 13-12. No, we did not win the pennant. We finished fourth, the high-water mark of my National League career.

Probably the homer with which I have been most closely identified took place at the 1950 All-Star Game in Chicago's Comiskey Park. It happened in the ninth inning and it tied the score. Red Schoendienst of the St. Louis Cardinals won the game for the National League with a homer in the 14th. The game might have been the best in the history of the event.

It was a scorching day. The temperature reached 103 degrees. Art Houtteman was the pitcher in the ninth, and I hit the ball nine miles into the air, which was the way I hit most of my home runs. This one looked like a routine fly ball to left field, but it kept carrying and carrying until it landed in the upper deck. What people may not recall is that I also hit a long drive to left in my first at-bat. Williams made a great play to catch the ball against the fence but banged his elbow in the process. He played nine innings with what later was diagnosed as a broken elbow and was lost to the Red Sox until the end of the season.

We staged a lot of home-run contests before exhibition

games in those days in an effort to increase attendance. I don't think I ever lost one, including the contest against Williams and the Red Sox before that '48 game. In fact, Williams finished third, behind teammate Walt Dropo.

I'll never forget the night in Cleveland's Municipal Stadium. We were scheduled to play an exhibition game against the Indians, and, naturally, they set up a home-run contest between me and Luke Easter. Now Easter was a massive man who hit awesome home runs. I had first seen him play in California and I was impressed.

The rule for this contest was that I, as the visitor, was to hit 10 balls, and then he would hit 10 balls. Well, I hit nine out of 10 over the fence, including six into the upper deck. And Easter wouldn't come out to hit. I won the trophy by default, and I still have it at home. Now, of course, they give players money for their participation. In those days, you performed for the glory.

I set a major-league record with my seventh consecutive NL home-run title in 1952, the year the Pirates set a record for futility later exceeded by the 1962 Mets. We had Dick Groat, the All-American basketball player out of Duke, at shortstop and the O'Brien twins from Seattle University. In fact, we may have had the best basketball team in the major leagues. But we were less skilled when it came to baseball. Two of our regulars, first baseman Tony Bartirome and center fielder Bobby Del Greco, were local kids shanghaied into Pittsburgh uniforms shortly after their high school graduations. Alas, youth was no match for experience and talent.

Going into the final series of the season, against the Reds, I trailed Hank Sauer of the Cubs by one homer, 37-36. Although the Pirates were taking the train, I paid my own way to fly to Cincinnati. I never slept well on the train and I wanted to be rested.

Despite taking extra batting practice against Groat the next afternoon, I didn't hit any homers on Friday night. But I did get one on Saturday to tie Sauer. I remember the Reds made a big production of my going for another home-run title. Since they were well out of the pennant race, they geared their advertising to me in hopes that I might draw a significant crowd. So, after all that buildup, Ken Raffensberger walked me three or four times. I never got a chance to hit.

I didn't know what Sauer had done. We took the train back

to Pittsburgh, and at every station I ran inside to the telegrapher to see if he could find out whether Sauer had hit a home run. It wasn't until about 2 A.M., at some cowtown, that I learned Sauer hadn't homered. By sharing the title with Sauer, I had broken the mark I had shared at six in a row with Babe Ruth, who did it in the American League from 1926 through 1931. Just as I was tied by Sauer, Ruth was tied by Lou Gehrig in 1931.

I'm frequently asked about the last of my 369 home runs. All I can say is that I was wearing a Cleveland uniform when I hit it. I didn't give it much thought at the time because I didn't know at the time it was going to be my last. I wouldn't have had any trouble remembering if it had occurred on my final major-league at-bat. But like Casey of Mudville, I, too, struck out.

The End of an Era

It took the Mets nine years to win an opener. Once they learned how, they made it look easy, sweeping four in succession. But in 1974, in Philadelphia, they reverted to an old habit.

The Mets lost, 5-4, to the Phillies on April 6. Tug McGraw was provided with a lead and failed. Months later, people would have cause to look back and find significance in that development.

As it was, the Mets rebounded to win their next two games, then embarked on a seven-game losing streak. A 2-1 defeat by the Phillies in 11 innings, a defeat charged to McGraw, was the most unsettling of the seven.

After 15 games, the Mets were 4-11 and tied for last place. There was no alarm, because Jerry Koosman (3-0) had been pitching better than at any time since 1970, Jon Matlack figured to improve with age and experience, and Tom Seaver was sure to find himself at any moment. The very next day, in fact, Seaver set down the Giants, 6-0.

Two days later, Matlack pitched his first shutout, also 6-0 and also against the Giants. There were knowing looks in the clubhouse. The Mets hit well on the West Coast, averaging nearly five runs in splitting the 10 games, and there was genuine optimism as the team returned home only 4½ games out of first place.

No ground was gained on the home stand, which the Mets split. Seaver had another poor outing and was charged with his third defeat in four decisions. But the major cause for concern was McGraw. By then, it was clear something was seriously wrong with the hero of '73. He was throwing without velocity. At times, he wasn't even throwing with his normal motion. The problem, it was agreed, was a muscle under the left shoulder blade, which had been bothering him since spring training. Rest was prescribed.

McGraw didn't pick up a baseball from May 5 until May 13, when he warmed up in the bullpen in St. Louis. Two nights later, in a lost cause, Yogi Berra decided to conduct a test. It was 6-0 when McGraw entered the game in the eighth inning. It was 9-0 when he left and it was still the eighth inning.

"He's not throwing good," Berra observed. "He had nothing." McGraw was placed on the disabled list the following day.

A victory by George Stone, his first of the season, preceded consecutive shutouts by Seaver and Matlack against Montreal as the Mets climbed to within 2½ games of the top. That was as close as they would get in 1974. They lost five of their next six games and tumbled in the standings.

By the end of June, the Mets were 30-44 and occupied the basement. A 5-3 loss to the Cards on the final day of the month was charged to McGraw, recently activated. The Mets were 10 games in arrears.

On June 21, the Mets defeated the Phillies, 3-1. The winning pitcher was Seaver. It was his fourth victory against six losses, and even his success was disquieting. He had pitched only five innings before leaving the game with a pain in his left hip.

Seaver evened his record at 6-6 before the All-Star break, but, for the first time in his eight major-league seasons, he failed to be selected for the National League squad. The Mets were represented by Matlack and Grote.

They began the second stage of the season with a 40-52 record. The offense had not lived up to its potential. Rusty Staub, after his spectacular finish in 1973, was struggling to regain his form. John Milner, the club's top home-run threat, was nagged by injuries, although Ed Kranepool had performed exceptionally well in his place. Neither Don Hahn nor Dave

Schneck adequately filled the vacancy in center field, and Bud Harrelson was sidelined at various times with a pulled groin muscle, a bruised finger, and a fractured hand.

A four-game winning streak, featuring a 3-0 shutout of the Cards by Seaver, and McGraw's first victory in relief, sparked some hope. August had been a special time for the Mets, the time they had begun their drives to the pennant in 1969 and 1973. It was not yet out of the question that they could recover in 1974.

On Aug. 5 in Montreal, McGraw relieved Seaver after six innings with the Mets trailing, pitched three scoreless innings, and broke open the game with a bases-loaded double. He said he was encouraged. He was not ready to say he believed. "I've been struggling," he said. "It's too early for me to get excited about one ball game."

He was right not to get excited. The following night, in Pittsburgh, the Mets blew leads of 4-0, 7-3, and 8-5. And, with the score tied in the 11th, McGraw threw a ball over third baseman Wayne Garrett's head after fielding a bunt. The result was a 9-8 defeat.

Although they never joined the pennant race, the Mets did make some news in the final five weeks of the season. Benny Ayala, a powerful outfielder, was promoted from the Mets' Triple A farm club at Tidewater on Aug. 27, arrived at Shea Stadium hours before game time, and, in his very first appearance, homered off Tom Griffin of the Astros. He became the first Met to hit a home run in his first at-bat, the first National Leaguer to do so in 13 years, and only the 40th player in the history of the game to make such a showy debut.

The long season grew even longer on Sept. 11 when the Mets and the Cards met in a night game at Shea. Koosman carried a 3-1 lead into the ninth inning. There were two outs and Larry Herndon, a pinch-runner, was on base when Ken Reitz drove a pitch over the left-field fence. The game went on . . . and on . . . and on.

Before it ended, at 3:12 A.M., the Cards employed seven pitchers, the Mets six. The teams went through 15 dozen baseballs. They played for 25 innings, and they played their way into the record book.

The longest night game ever played in time (7 hours 4 minutes) and innings finally ended because Hank Webb, a rookie pitcher, attempted to pick Bake McBride off first base in the 25th inning. The errant toss sailed down the right-field line, and by the time first baseman Milner could retrieve the ball and deliver it to the plate, the dashing McBride had crossed with the winning run in a 4-3 decision.

To a club history that included a 23-inning game and a 24-inning game, the Mets had added a 25-inning game. And they had lost all three. Webb was charged with the defeat, his first decision in the major leagues.

The 50 players used by both clubs was a league record, as was the 26 used by the Cards. The big question for the broad-casting team at the end of the game, the longest ever played to a decision in point of innings, was whether we should conduct a post-game show. We had done some late shows in the past, but nothing this late. Finally, we got the go-ahead, and McBride agreed to appear. It was almost 3:30 A.M. when "Kiner's Korner" went off the air.

Oh, yes, the home plate umpire was none other than Ed Sudol, the man who had called balls and strikes in the 23-inning game against the Giants in 1964 and the 24-inning game against the Astros in 1968. "What is it about the Mets?" a weary Sudol asked after the game. It was a question that had intrigued people for years.

On Sept. 25, at Philadelphia, Seaver was forced to leave a game after six innings. It marked the fifth occasion on which he had to depart because of a recurring spasm of the sciatic nerve. He was concerned about the possibility of permanent injury. He appeared to be finished for the season with a record of 11-10.

Seaver had struck out 187 batters, 13 shy of his goal. Only two pitchers, American League immortals Walter Johnson and Rube Waddell, had managed to strike out 200 or more in seven consecutive seasons. The opportunity to become the first Na-tional Leaguer to achieve that milestone apparently vanished with the recurrence of the pain.

But just when the pitcher was ready to call it a season, he was persuaded by M. Donald Grant to consult Dr. Kenneth Ri-land, a noted osteopath whose patients included Nelson Rocke-feller. Seaver underwent two treatments over a five-day period and reported such improvement that he requested one more start. He made the most of it, striking out 14 Phillies in a 2-1 defeat on Oct. 1.

The additional start enabled him to gain a share of the record held by Johnson and Waddell. It also eased his mind about the future. On my post-game show, he said he felt no pain and he threw the ball as well as he ever had. The season ended the following day with a 3-2 loss, lowering the Mets' final record to 71-91.

The 1974 season brought to an end the stewardship of Bob Scheffing. Longing to spend more time at his Arizona home, Scheffing voluntarily relinquished his position as general manager. The Mets had a willing replacement. He was Joseph Anthony McDonald, the same Joe McDonald who had been the statistician for our broadcasts in the 1962 season and who had spent so many years in the minor-league department.

Joe had grown up in baseball. His father, Jim, had been a ticket-taker at Ebbets Field starting the day the park opened in 1913. Joe had worked for the Dodgers as a 13-year-old schoolboy with doctored papers. "It's the happiest day of my life," said McDonald, whose career as a first baseman had ended on the Brooklyn sandlots. "I just wish my father could have been here to share it with me. Pop would have been proud." Jim McDonald had died two years earlier.

In making the announcement, Grant said the Mets had not considered any other candidates for the job. "We believe in developing our own people," he said. "We believe in Joe McDonald. He must have had something to do with producing the talent which won a world championship and two pennants in the 12 years he's been here."

McDonald said he would actively pursue trades to strengthen the Mets, and it didn't take long for him to prove he was as good as his word. In the midst of the World Series, he sent pitchers Ray Sadecki and Tommy Moore to the Cardinals for Joe Torre, the Brooklyn native the Mets had coveted as far back as 1969. Within the next two weeks, McDonald initiated trades that sent catcher Duffy Dyer to the Pirates for outfielder Gene Clines and infielder Ken Boswell to the Astros for outfielder Bob Gallagher.

Torre joined the team in time for a scheduled tour of Japan and led all hitters with a .437 average and 18 runs batted in, in 18 games. Ed Kranepool, who had enjoyed his first .300 season in 1974, continued his surge with a .386 average and seven home runs. Perhaps the most significant development of the trip, however, was the progress of Seaver. Although he had but a 1-2 record, he struck out 28 batters in 29 innings and pitched without pain.

McDonald wasn't finished dealing. On Dec. 3, he stunned New York fans with the announcement that Tug McGraw had been traded to the Phillies, along with outfielders Hahn and Schneck, for outfielder Del Unser, catcher John Stearns, and relief pitcher Mac Scarce. McDonald had been one of McGraw's biggest boosters with the Mets, and the decision was not an easy one. But the Mets needed a professional center fielder, one who hit as well. Unser appeared to answer their needs.

McGraw reacted emotionally. So, too, did McDonald. "After I told him I traded him," the general manager reported, "we both broke down. It figured. We're both left-handers."

Eight days later, in a trade that drew little attention at the time but would gain in prominence, utility infielder Teddy Martinez was shipped to the Cards for Jack Heidemann, also a utility infielder, and Mike Vail, an outfield prospect whom the Mets assigned to their Tidewater club.

The splurge of trading left only Kranepool, Seaver, Jerry Koosman, Jerry Grote, Wayne Garrett, Cleon Jones, and Bud Harrelson from the World Championship club of 1969. And the Mets were concerned about the futures of Jones and Harrelson as they reported for spring training in 1975. Jones had undergone surgery on his left knee in October, and Harrelson's right knee was unstable.

Jones's progress in Florida was painfully slow. McDonald, seeking additional right-handed hitting, was able to purchase Dave Kingman from the Giants for a reported $100,000. Kingman had been a disappointment in San Francisco, but he was only 26 and had awesome power. He quickly demonstrated his capabilities with eight home runs in exhibition play.

The Mets' 8-18 Grapefruit League record was the worst in their history. Jones had to be left behind for further conditioning, and pitcher George Stone also remained in Florida, suffering from a torn rotator cuff in his left shoulder. But Seaver was throwing well again, and the additions of Kingman, Unser, and Torre promised greater run production.

All the elements of a fine season were evident on Opening Day. Seaver pitched nine innings, allowing only six hits, Kingman hit a mammoth home run, and the Mets defeated the Phillies, 2-1, on Torre's line single in the ninth.

One major concern as the season began was the bullpen. In McGraw's absence, the only experienced relief pitchers were Harry Parker and Bob Apodaca. And Apodaca had an inflamed elbow which earned him a spot on the disabled list.

The concern quickly was justified as the Mets lost their next five games, the bullpen failing on four separate occasions. McDonald reacted by trading Scarce, one of the offenders, to Cincinnati for veteran left-hander Tom Hall. Apodaca was reactivated on April 18 and recorded his first save two days later as the Mets swept a doubleheader from the Cubs.

That was the start of a seven-game winning streak that propelled the Mets into second place in the Eastern Division. They finished April with a record of 9-7, 2½ games behind the front-running Cubs. They had scored 69 runs in their previous 10 games, and Seaver once again was a dominant pitcher.

Harrelson's knee, however, continued to be a problem. On May 3, McDonald acquired Mike Phillips, a young shortstop, from the Giants for the $20,000 waiver price. Now they had insurance at that position.

On the following night, Jones was discovered with a young lady in the back of a van parked on a St. Petersburg street. He was charged with indecent exposure, a charge that became public the next day. After a wait of 10 days, the Florida state attorney's office decided not to prosecute. For his indiscretion, Jones was fined $2,000 by the Mets. He rejoined the team, but only after reading a public apology, at Grant's insistence, to his teammates and fans.

Jones made the road trip with the Mets, taking private batting practice and running hard. On May 27, at Shea Stadium, he was activated and he singled as a pinch-hitter against the Dodgers. That same night Harrelson was placed on the disabled list, preparatory to an operation on his right knee. Garrett also had to be disabled when he suffered an ankle joint infection.

Seaver raised his record to 7-4 with a 7-2 decision over the Padres on May 31. On the team's first West Coast trip, Seaver pitched consecutive shutouts over the Giants and Padres, and

George Stone, returning from an injury many thought final, pitched seven strong innings for his first major-league victory in 13 months.

Three losses in four games at Montreal took some luster off the trip, and the Mets returned to Shea to lose a three-game set to the Pirates, now in first place. After eight meetings with the team they had to beat, the Mets had yet to win their first.

A four-game winning streak preceded the first encounter with Tug McGraw. The ebullient relief pitcher had undergone minor surgery before the start of the season, but he was back in form during the June 29 doubleheader in New York. He appeared to a thunderous ovation in the seventh inning of the first game, retired the side, and then, puckishly, bounced off the mound in the direction of the Mets' dugout. It delighted the crowd. He pitched seven scoreless innings that day, gained a save in the first game, and was credited with his fifth victory in the nightcap.

As painful to the Mets as these two defeats was an incident in the second game. Apodaca, in relief of Seaver, was struck by a ball off the bat of Johnny Oates. He suffered a broken nose and a mild concussion and was placed on the disabled list, joining Parker who had tendinitis in his right shoulder. With the bullpen almost bare, McDonald purchased the contract of veteran Ken Sanders and recalled Nino Espinosa from Tidewater.

Trouble lay ahead. Jones was growing increasingly restless sitting on the bench. When Bob Murphy had asked him the previous week in Philadelphia how his knee reacted to the artificial surface, Cleon replied, "I ain't never had the pleasure." Yogi Berra said there was no place to play him since Kingman, who had hit 15 homers, had won the left-field job and Kranepool was batting well above .300 at first base.

The Mets lost all four games in Cincinnati prior to the All-Star Game. They remained in third place, 10½ games behind the Pirates. The worst was yet to come.

On July 18, after defeating the Braves in the first game after the break, Berra sent up Jones as a pinch-hitter in the seventh inning, then told him to report to left field. Jones declined the latter order, stormed into the clubhouse, and left the stadium before the Mets' 4-3 defeat was official. Berra, McDonald, and Grant huddled in the manager's office following the game but failed to come to a decision on a course of action.

Jones returned to uniform the next day. He claimed his knee had not been wrapped, thereby making it dangerous for him to play the field. McDonald sounded out other clubs in preparation for a possible trade, which Jones, as a 10-year veteran, would have to approve. Kingman hit two home runs, his 17th and 18th, on Sunday, July 20, in a dramatic 10-9 victory over the Astros, and Jones's fate was sealed.

The Astros defeated the Mets, 6-2, the following night as Torre set a dubious National League record by bouncing into four double plays. "When I retire," he said, "I'm going to put a shortstop in my den, and, whenever I get lonely, I can go hit him grounders." Although he was able to manage a laugh at his own expense, Torre was thoroughly disappointed in his overall performance. A productive hitter all his career and a former Most Valuable Player, he had driven in only 21 runs in the first 15 weeks of the season.

Jones did not accompany the Mets on a 13-game road trip, which began in Chicago. Cleon, it was announced, had been suspended. Two days later, after the final trade possibility had been exhausted and Grant's attempt at a reconciliation between the player and the manager had failed, McDonald reluctantly placed Jones on waivers for the purpose of giving him his unconditional release. Cleon Jones, the all-time club leader in hits, home runs, and runs batted in, no longer was a Met.

Berra had made his stand. Now it was time for the Mets to make their move. They won five of the first eight games on the trip and had a chance to jump into contention as they opened a five-game series in Pittsburgh. They trailed the Pirates by nine games.

The Mets won the first game, 6-2, behind Koosman. Stone turned back the Pirates, 4-2, the following night, and Matlack overpowered the Bucs, 6-0, on Saturday afternoon, Aug. 2, for his 13th victory. A doubleheader sweep on Sunday would cut the deficit to four games, and Seaver was pitching the opener.

The season turned for the Mets in the first game on Aug. 3. They broke a 3-3 tie in the seventh inning on Rusty Staub's sacrifice fly, but the Pirates tied it again in their half of the inning on Al Oliver's bloop double. Seaver left the game in the 11th, and Apodaca, reactivated the previous week, yielded a 15th-inning home run to Manny Sanguillen. The Pirates defeated Webb, 4-3, in the second game, and the Mets slid back-wards.

It marked the beginning of the end for Yogi Berra. The Expos rallied to beat the Mets, 4-3, at Shea Stadium, and in a twi-night doubleheader the following night, Banner Night, the Mets absorbed beatings by identical 7-0 scores. In an early-morning conference after those defeats, it was decided to re-place the popular Berra on an interim basis with Roy McMil-lan, the quiet first-base coach who had played such a majestic shortstop for the club a decade earlier. Grant said he felt that McMillan had the same qualities as the late Gil Hodges, but whereas Hodges was the strong, silent type, McMillan turned out to be merely silent.

The Mets made some progress in August. They won 7 of their next 12 games on the home stand and had an 8-6 record on an extended West Coast trip. They came home to a three-game series against the Pirates, still within striking distance. When Seaver went to the mound on Labor Day, the Mets trailed Pittsburgh by five games.

Seaver began the game with 194 strikeouts for the season. Through the first six innings, he struck out five. He was one strikeout away from becoming the first major-league pitcher in history to strike out 200 or more batters in eight consecutive years. Dave Parker led off the Pittsburgh seventh with a single, the Pirates' fourth hit, and advanced to second on a groundout. The batter was Sanguillen, a free swinger. Seaver went to his power and threw three successive fastballs. Strike one. Strike two. Strike three. The crowd roared. Seaver had his record, and, two innings later, he had a 3-0 shutout and his 20th victory in a marvelous comeback season.

The Pirates' lead was reduced to four games. Koosman, the starter in the second game of the series, had a cumulative re-cord of 20-3 in the stretch drives of 1969 and 1973. Surely, the Mets had an outstanding chance. But Pittsburgh knocked out Koosman and rolled to an 8-4 victory. And Jerry Reuss out-dueled Matlack, 3-1, in the series finale. The race was over for the Mets.

One significant item of interest remained. On Aug. 17, Mc-Donald had reached down to Tidewater and purchased the contract of the International League's leading hitter. He was Mike Vail, a throw-in in a trade of utility infielders eight

months earlier. Vail singled in his first major-league appearance as a pinch-hitter in Houston, failed to hit safely in his next
game, and then went on a tear the likes of which had rarely
been seen.

Vail batted safely in 23 consecutive games. It was one game
longer than the best streak of any major-league player in 1975,
and it enabled him to tie a National League record for rookies
set by Joe Rapp in 1921 and equaled by Richie Ashburn in 1948.
The streak ended with finality on Sept. 16 when, in an 18-inning
triumph over the Expos, Vail went hitless in eight at-bats.

In the final game of the season, Seaver defeated the Phillies,
5-4, for his 22nd victory against 9 losses. He had come all the
way back, a point acknowledged when he was honored with his
third Cy Young Award as the outstanding pitcher in the National League. Kingman, who hit a club-record 36 home runs,
and Unser, who batted .294 and was a dependable center
fielder, were welcome additions, as was Vail, the late-blooming
rookie, who batted .302, second best on the team behind Kranepool's .323.

And yet, the year produced a bitter aftertaste. The Mets had
won 26 and lost 27 under McMillan, who was not considered as
a managerial candidate for 1976. They had barely finished
above .500, they had waived Cleon Jones and fired the likeable
Berra in midseason, and, within a week of the season's conclusion, they lost two of the major figures associated with the franchise.

Casey Stengel died of cancer at Glendale Memorial Hospital in California on Sept. 29. He was 85, and his final days were
filled with loneliness and pain. Edna, his wife of 51 years, had
suffered a stroke the previous year and was in a Glendale nursing home.

Stengel's record indicates he was the greatest manager who
ever lived. He ranked among America's most famous people.
Certainly, he contributed to the language of the country's sporting life.

"Casey Stengel proved himself to be the most romantic
figure in the history of baseball," Grant said in tribute. "It is a
great personal loss to everyone associated with the Mets, from
the grounds-keepers to the ticket-takers up to Mrs. Payson, and,
in fact, to everyone who ever saw a baseball game."

Ironically, the woman who persuaded Stengel to return to

New York 13 years earlier lost her own battle for life five days later. Joan Payson, confined to a wheelchair in her latter days, died at New York Hospital–Cornell Medical Center.

I first heard of her death upon entering Cincinnati's Riverfront Stadium to broadcast a playoff game between the Reds and the Pittsburgh Pirates for the Mutual Radio Network. The previous day, I had stopped at Shea Stadium to pick up mail and had encountered Mrs. Payson's granddaughter, who worked in the group sales department. I inquired about Mrs. Payson's health and was told her condition was grave. I wondered if she knew about Casey's death. I decided not to ask.

She had loved life so and derived so much pleasure from baseball. I can remember a time in the club's early days when she threw a party in Florida and we all gathered around the piano and sang song after song after song. Despite her wealth, she was an unpretentious and warm woman.

On Oct. 6, at the Church of the Recessional in Forest Lawn Cemetery, Glendale, funeral services were held for Stengel. The organist played "Take Me Out to the Ball Game," and baseball officials gathered from throughout the country to pay final respects to the man who lay with a Met uniform and a Yankee uniform folded beside him.

One day later, a continent away, Joan Payson was remembered in services at Christ Episcopal Church in Manhasset, N.Y. I attended with club executives Jim Thomson and Arthur Richman. We were seated by Ed Kranepool, the only man who played for the Mets in each of their 14 seasons and who had been a personal favorite of Mrs. Payson. Admittance was by invitation only, and the list of "her boys" included Tom Seaver, Willie Mays, Rusty Staub, Bud Harrelson, Wayne Garrett, and Joe Torre.

As had been the case at the Stengel funeral, the organist, Robert L. Mahaffey, played a light rendition of "Take Me Out to the Ball Game." In his eulogy, the Reverend Frank Johnston credited Mrs. Payson with ministering to him and said he could look down and still see the image of her sitting alongside the Mets' dugout, wearing a floppy hat, with a hot dog in one hand and a scorecard in the other. "Ownership meant very little to her," he said. "Friendship meant everything."

At the eulogy, a choir sang "The Battle Hymn of the Republic." It had been played at Gil Hodges's funeral in April 1972, and Mrs. Payson thought it so appropriate she requested its inclusion in her own service.

Now so many who had done so much for the Mets were gone: George Weiss, Johnny Murphy, Gil Hodges, Casey Stengel, and Joan Payson, the president of the club since its inception. An era had ended. The Mets would not recover for some time.

Making the Hall of Fame

It is said a tourist once stopped a New Yorker on the street and asked him, "How do you get to Carnegie Hall?" The New Yorker looked at the man and said simply, "Practice."

I had a similar response ready when it came to the Baseball Hall of Fame. If anyone had asked me how to get to Cooperstown, I would have told him, "Wait." That's what I had been doing for 15 years.

I was in my final year of eligibility for election under the rules of the Baseball Writers Association of America. I had come close to receiving the required 75 percent of the vote on several occasions, but now I was down to the final ballot. If I didn't get the necessary number of votes in January 1975, I would have to wait a minimum of five more years for consideration by the Veterans Committee. God, I wanted it. I'd been knocking on the door for so long.

In my mind, I had earned it. It wasn't an ego thing. I started to think of it as a degree, a doctorate. I had excelled in what I did. Yet, I steeled myself for the worst on the day the votes were tabulated. I was in St. Petersburg at the time, and I didn't dare pack for the trip to New York, where the official announcement would be made.

Jack Lang, the secretary of the BBWAA, was to call with the

results between 3:30 and 5 P.M. Five o'clock came and went. At about 5:25, I figured, well, that's it. Jack doesn't want to give me the bad news.

Then the phone rang. I let it ring four times. Four was my uniform number. I'm not generally superstitious, but in this case I couldn't help myself. It was Jack's voice, all right, and he said, "Ralph, how does it feel to be a member of the Hall of Fame?" I said, "You're kidding!" And he said he wasn't kidding. Then I said something clever, like "Wow!"

The reason for the delay, it developed, was that of the 362 votes cast, I needed 272. I received 273. That was all right with me. I would gladly have settled for 272. I flew to New York that night and appeared at a press conference in the Americana Hotel the following morning. Hank Greenberg joined me there, making the day complete.

Induction ceremonies at Cooperstown were scheduled for Monday, Aug. 18. Since festivities were planned for the previous day, I flew out of New York on Saturday evening following the Mets' game. I soon found out Cooperstown was almost as difficult to reach as enshrinement there was to achieve.

Most of my family had driven to Cooperstown earlier that day. My daughter K.C. was with me on a chartered two-engine airplane that was to carry us to Oneonta, the nearest town to Cooperstown with an airfield. The day was overcast, and we flew on instruments the entire way. Since I had flying experience in the Navy, I was familiar with instrument procedure. I was not familiar with the mountains in the area or the condition of the airport.

We descended from 8,000 to 2,000 feet over Oneonta, and there was still no sign of the ground. Suddenly, the pilot climbed sharply and thought better of the landing. He considered Westchester, but that was where I lived at the time and almost the starting point of our flight. Syracuse also was fogged in. We tried Albany, where I had begun my professional baseball career, as a last resort and finally landed after dusk. Not only was the sky dark, but so was the terminal. It had suffered a blackout.

With great difficulty, we groped our way to a rental car counter. I dismissed the problem we had in reading the map. I was sure I knew the way, so we set out on what I thought was the New York Thruway, stopped for dinner, then continued on.

At Exit 20, I spotted a sign for Montreal. We were on the North-way, headed out of the country. I turned the car around and started back. We finally reached Cooperstown at 2 A.M., some nine hours late.

The experience of the ceremony was everything I was told it would be, and more. The setting, a small tree-shaded park adjacent to the National Baseball Library, was perfect. Bowie Kuhn, the Commissioner of Baseball, introduced the electees in alphabetical order. I was the last to speak, following Earl Averill, Stanley Harris (accepting for his ill father, Bucky Harris), Billy Herman, my manager of the 1947 Pirates, and William (Judy) Johnson. This was one time when I didn't mind being dropped from the cleanup position.

As calm as I was speaking to millions on radio and television, the thought of an acceptance speech in a small village named for James Fenimore Cooper left me shaking. Still, I struggled through it, recounting some of the standout moments in my life. These included the backyard burial of the magazines in Alhambra, the embarrassing date with Liz Taylor, and memories of Pittsburgh, where the laughs certainly outnumbered the victories.

One story I told was about an event that was no joke when it happened. I was sitting in the Pirates' clubhouse one day, sorting fan mail and chatting with Les Biederman, who worked for the *Pittsburgh Press.* I opened an envelope and started reading a letter that consisted of words cut from a newspaper and pasted on a page. It demanded I come up with an odd amount of money, something like $4,755, and gave explicit details as to when and where it should be left. If I didn't do as the letter said, I would be shot. I read it aloud, then made a comment to the effect that there were all kinds of nuts around and tossed the letter into a wastebasket.

Biederman asked me if he could see it. I said yes, and he dug it out of the basket and examined it closely. "You know," he said, "this guy might be serious." And he took it to Branch Rickey, who turned it over to the Federal Bureau of Investigation.

Well, the FBI certainly took it seriously. The bureau issued me a license to carry a gun, and it assigned an agent to me. He moved into my apartment, accompanied me to the ballpark, and even caddied for me when I played golf. I wasn't scared because I still thought the note was a hoax.

Finally, the day arrived when the directions were to be carried out. I was supposed to get into a People's Cab about a block from Forbes Field after a night game, leave the money in a package under the seat, and get out two blocks later. Well, the FBI told me to get into cab No. 23 and no other. When I did, I found an agent about my size and wearing my clothes lying down in the back of the taxi. The driver was also an FBI agent.

I was told that the FBI had staked out the building across the street from where I hailed the cab and they were armed. The driver took evasive action to make sure we weren't being followed, then let me out and continued to a town called Ambridge, where the cab company had its terminal. Meanwhile, they had rigged the package containing the money with a homing device.

Well, nothing happened. No one picked up the package. I thought my original instinct was correct, and I told the FBI to please move its agent out of my apartment.

But a day later the ball club got a telephone call, and a voice said, "You tricked me." The man also said he was going to kill Ralph Kiner during Sunday's doubleheader. Now even *I'm* a little worried.

So they put a bunch of FBI guys in the stands, swelling attendance. This was just before the Fourth of July and, naturally, people were entertaining themselves by setting off firecrackers in the stands. Every time one went off, my heart jumped a little. Nobody on the team wanted to sit next to me in the dugout.

This was probably the longest day I ever spent in baseball. But we finished the doubleheader without incident. As I came jogging in from left field alongside George Metkovich, the center fielder, he said to me, "Am I glad this day is over."

"George," I said, "it's nice of you to worry about me."

And he said, "I wasn't worried about *you*. I was worried about *me*."

I asked him why and he said, "What's your number?" I said, "Four." Then he asked, "What's my number?" And I said, "Forty-four."

"Well," he said, "what if that guy had double vision?"

The FBI finally did track down the guy. It turned out to be the visiting batboy. He had gambling debts, and I guess he figured I was a most logical source of financial stability because of my large salary. I was supposed to fly in from California to testify at his trial the following February, but bad weather delayed my flight. In my absence, Rickey pleaded for leniency on behalf of the poor batboy, and they let the kid off. Naturally, Rickey was honored with headlines praising his charity and humanitarianism. Can you beat that?

The story wasn't included on the bronze plaque with which I posed for photographers after the Hall-of-Fame ceremony. This is how the plaque read:

RALPH McPHERRAN KINER. PITTSBURGH, NATIONAL LEAGUE. CHICAGO, NATIONAL LEAGUE. CLEVELAND, AMERICAN LEAGUE, 1946–55. HE HIT 369 HOME RUNS AND AVERAGED BETTER THAN 100 RUNS BATTED IN PER SEASON IN HIS TEN-YEAR CAREER. HE WAS THE ONLY PLAYER TO LEAD HIS LEAGUE OR SHARE LEAD IN HOMERS SEVEN YEARS IN A ROW, 1946 THROUGH 1952. HE TWICE HAD MORE THAN 50 HOME RUNS IN A SEASON. HE SET NATIONAL LEAGUE MARK OF 101 HOME RUNS IN TWO SUCCESSIVE YEARS WITH 54 IN 1949 AND 47 IN 1950. HE LED THE NATIONAL LEAGUE IN SLUGGING PERCENTAGE THREE TIMES.

It wasn't poetic, like "Casey at the Bat." But it summarized my accomplishments in baseball and it left me feeling honored and proud.

"Welcome to Grant's Tomb"

Among the people who took up residence at Shea Stadium in the early years of the franchise was a commercial artist from Queens named Karl Ehrhardt. One night, in 1964, he brought along a friend and an irreverent sign poking fun at the incompetence of the team that occupied the new stadium and at the stuffy manner of the club's chairman. "Welcome to Grant's Tomb," the sign said.

That particular sign was confiscated by a Met employee. However, Ehrhardt would return again and again over the years, bringing boxes of signs appropriate to almost every occasion that he would display from his seat near the visitors' dugout. Working from under a black cardboard derby with an orange band, he became "The Sign Man" and as much of a celebrity as some of the players he praised or, more frequently, lampooned.

The sign that offended Donald Grant was more amusing than telling in 1964 because the Mets, for all their inadequacies, were in the process of drawing 1,732,597, the second-highest attendance in the majors and a remarkable figure for a last-place team. But in the late 1970s, as attendance began to drop precipitously, it would have been right on target.

Grant had assumed almost total responsibility for running

the ball club. Upon the death of Murphy and, later, Hodges, whose strength he respected and perhaps even feared, he took greater interest in personnel decisions. Although Bob Scheffing was an experienced baseball man, his reluctance to spend more time in New York than necessary played into Grant's hands. With the appointment of McDonald, the chairman had his own handpicked general manager, one beholden to him.

The death of Joan Payson only solidified Grant's leadership. Under the terms of her will, the ball club passed to her husband, Charles Shipman Payson. He was not a baseball fan, and he designated his daughter, Lorinda de Roulet, to take his wife's place on the board of directors. She, in turn, deferred most decisions to Grant.

Those decisions would lead the Mets to ruin in short order. The problems between players and management began with Seaver's negotiations for a long-term contract. Seaver and McDonald waged a war of words in the newspapers throughout spring training, and McDonald even talked to the Dodgers about a trade that would send the Mets' greatest star to Los Angeles for Don Sutton. Seaver finally signed a three-year contract containing a base salary of $225,000 and many performance bonuses. At the time, it was the most lucrative contract ever awarded a pitcher, but it would be totally eclipsed by the advent of free agency later in the year.

The Mets experienced other problems before the start of the 1976 regular season. During the winter meetings, they had traded Rusty Staub to Detroit, receiving left-handed pitcher Mickey Lolich in return. Staub's contract had expired in 1975, and Grant was irritated by some of the demands made by his most productive hitter. Management viewed Mike Vail as an ideal replacement for Staub, but Vail dislocated his right ankle while playing basketball in February, was sidelined until the middle of June, and never again was a force at the plate.

Still, the Mets got off to a strong start under new manager Joe Frazier, who had been McDonald's choice after doing an excellent job at Tidewater. A strike, precipitated by a delay in the new basic agreement between the Players Association and the owners, held back the opening of training camps until mid-March. But the Mets' pitchers, conditioned by their own workouts supervised by Seaver near the Mets' complex in St. Petersburg, were ready to go when the season started.

They won 13 of 20 games in April and remained tied for first place in the Eastern Division as late as May 13. But the Mets lost five of their next six games, with two of the losses charged to Seaver, and began to slip out of contention. By the end of the month, they were a .500 team and they trailed the Phillies by 9½ games. They remained mired in mediocrity until a late-season surge at a time when they were out of the race.

What excitement there was in 1976 was attributed to the presence of Kingman, the brooding slugger. By mid-July, he had hit 32 home runs, placing him seven games ahead of the pace set by Hack Wilson when the Chicago outfielder set the National League record of 56 in 1930. He had also driven in 69 runs. But on the night of July 19, while diving for a ball in left field, Kingman tore ligaments in his left thumb. He didn't return to the lineup until the end of August and, playing with pain, added only five more homers to his total.

Del Unser got off to a slow start, and, two days after Kingman's injury, he was sent with Garrett to Montreal for outfielders Pepe Mangual and Jim Dwyer in a trade that bombed. Additionally, Bud Harrelson was limited at shortstop following knee surgery. The Mets' defense, once so dependable, was as much to blame as the offense for the team's lackluster season.

Once again, it was pitching that kept the Mets afloat. The staff led both major leagues with 1,025 strikeouts and an earned-run average of 2.94. Jerry Koosman achieved his career high of 21 victories and Jon Matlack won 17. Also, the Mets uncovered a consistent reliever in Skip Lockwood, whom they had acquired the previous year from the Oakland organization in a cash transaction. A decade earlier, he had been a $100,000 bonus baby as an infielder. Converted to pitcher in 1967 and to a reliever in 1974, he emerged as the main man in the Mets' bullpen in 1976 with 10 victories and 19 saves.

Among the disappointments of the season was Lolich, the portly left-hander who had been the star of the 1968 World Series with Detroit. He didn't pitch badly, as his 3.22 ERA attested, but he didn't have much success, and he retired after the season. His 8-13 record contrasted sharply with Staub's contribution to the Tigers. Staub batted .299, with 15 homers and 96 runs batted in, in his first American League season.

Seaver's 14-11 record did not accurately reflect the way he pitched. He had five shutouts and a 2.59 ERA while striking out

235, extending his major-league record for consecutive 200-strikeout seasons to nine. Still, he collected little of the bonus money written into his contract.

A truly ominous sign was the falloff at the box office. The Mets had drawn 1,730,566 in 1975, but only 1,468,754 paid their way into Shea Stadium a year later. Money would become a major consideration for the Mets in the months ahead.

The first free-agent draft was conducted that winter. This meant the Mets could buy the hitter they needed to make them contenders rather than deal one of their front-line pitchers. Those pitchers, particularly Seaver, publicly urged Grant to go after one of the available players. The Mets showed interest in Gary Matthews, an outfielder who had hit 20 homers and batted .279 for the Giants in 1975, but they were outbid by the Atlanta Braves.

Furthermore, Kingman was entering his option year, and negotiations between him and the Mets, played out in the papers, were even more disagreeable than had been the negotiations with Seaver. Certainly, the pitcher wasn't pleased with his own situation, now that inferior pitchers who had taken the free-agent route had become millionaires overnight.

Spring training was not a happy time for the Mets. The players thought they still needed a hitter to make a run at the pennant. Grant thought otherwise. "We will be competitive," he said. "We have a splendid bunch of boys."

The high-toned chairman had been fooled by the Mets' surge in September, when they won 20 and lost 9, beating indifferent ball clubs who were marking time until the end of the season. It was no time to judge the strength of a baseball team, but Grant persisted in his view and the team opened the 1977 season in a foul mood. On Opening Day, after the Mets beat the Cubs behind Seaver, 5-3, Kingman announced he was playing out his option and would be leaving the Mets at the end of the season.

After winning three of their first four games (with two victories credited to Seaver), the Mets sagged. Despite plucking the versatile Lenny Randle off the waiver wire where he had been placed after punching manager Frank Lucchesi in Texas, the offense was not of major-league quality. It was Frazier who took the fall. Frazier, McDonald's managerial choice, was replaced by Joe Torre on May 31. The Mets were 15-30 and in sole possession of last place.

Torre did not have managerial experience, but he was perceptive, articulate, and popular with the other players, the press, and the fans. Also, his baseball skills were deteriorating. Two weeks after the 36-year-old Torre accepted the job of player-manager (he retired as a player the following month), the bottom dropped out of the franchise.

In an action that came to be identified as the "Midnight Massacre," both Seaver and Kingman were traded on June 15. The feud between Seaver and Grant had heated up during the season, with the chairman referring to the pitcher at one point as an "ingrate." Feeling grossly underpaid, Seaver contacted Lorinda de Roulet about his contract. Over the course of several conversations, they worked out a proposal whereby Seaver's contract would remain as it was but he would receive an extension with escalating salaries.

The agreement, which had yet to be put to paper, collapsed when Seaver learned of a column written by Dick Young of the *New York Daily News* in which Young accused Seaver's wife of being jealous of Ruth Ryan because Ruth's husband, Nolan Ryan, a former teammate on the Mets, had signed a bigger contract with the California Angels. Seaver said the attack on his family by Young, a confidante of Grant, was the last straw, and he demanded to be traded.

Grant acted swiftly. While the Mets were playing the Braves in Atlanta, Seaver flew home to New York. After the game, the club announced that the man who had been dubbed "The Franchise" had been traded to Cincinnati for four players —pitcher Pat Zachry, infielder Doug Flynn, and outfielders Steve Henderson and Dan Norman. Two other deals were announced on the team's flight to New York. Reserve infielder Mike Phillips had been sent to St. Louis for Joel Youngblood. And, finally, Dave Kingman was headed for San Diego in exchange for Bobby Valentine, a utility player, and pitcher Paul Siebert.

It was a stunning series of developments. The Mets had banished the greatest pitcher and most charismatic figure in their history and, on the same night, exiled their only power hitter. Seaver cleaned out his locker the following day and cried as he spoke of his relationship with the New York fans. The switchboard was besieged by angry callers. Torre went along with the party line and said that although he was sorry to see them go, he didn't want unhappy players on the team.

Henderson, an excellent athlete, took Kingman's place in left field. Flynn, a smooth fielder, shared shortstop with Harrelson while awaiting full-time employment at second base. Zachry, a gangling right-hander who had won 14 games for the World Champion Reds the previous season, was moved into Seaver's spot in the rotation. Of all the players in the trade, Zachry suffered the most. Attempting to replace Seaver was an exercise in frustration.

While Seaver pitched a shutout against Montreal in his first start for the Reds and became a 20-game winner for the fifth time, the new Mets had mixed results. Henderson, a top prospect, hit for average (.297) but not for power, which would be the story of his career. Flynn carried a Gold Glove but a plastic bat. And Zachry was a mediocre 7-6 in 19 starts.

John Stearns, acquired in the McGraw deal, became the everyday catcher in 1977, which made Grote expendable. Another part of Met history was expunged when Grote was sent to the Dodgers for cash and a minor-league player on Aug. 31.

Randle led the Mets with a .304 average, Henderson looked like a player, and Lee Mazzilli, a handsome Brooklyn native who had been the team's number-one draft choice in 1973, caused a stir in center field, especially among female fans. But nothing could stem the Mets' slide on the field and at the gate.

Torre did well to win 49 and lose 68 with the club. Jerry Koosman, a 21-game winner the previous season, lost 20 for lack of support in 1977. Jon Matlack, troubled by a sore shoulder, was 7-15. Only Nino Espinosa won as many as 10 games, and he lost 13. Lockwood's 20 saves were welcome, but the Mets still finished in last place, 37 games behind the Phillies, for the first time in 10 years.

The traumatized fans stayed away from Shea in droves. The box-office tally at the end of the 1977 season was 1,066,825, the Mets' lowest home attendance since that first season at the Polo Grounds. Seven years earlier, they had attracted almost 2.7 million customers. Nor was the downward spiral at an end.

No quick fix, such as buying a hitter in the free-agent market, could bolster the Mets now. The club did sign two free agents, but neither Elliott Maddox, a former Yankee who had injured his knee while playing center field at Shea in 1975 and responded with a law suit against the city, nor pitcher Tom Hausman was a blue-chip acquisition.

During the winter, they also added Tim Foli, a first-round draft choice of the Mets many years earlier, from the Giants. He was brought in to play shortstop, pushing Flynn to second base. This left Bud Harrelson without a job, and the veteran was traded to the Phillies for cash and a minor-leaguer during spring training.

Jon Matlack and John Milner also were traded. They were involved in a complicated four-team swap in which the Mets obtained first baseman Willie Montanez, who would play regularly, and outfielders Ken Henderson and Tom Grieve, who were on their way out of the major leagues. With the exception of Kranepool and Koosman, this was a club that resembled the 1969 and 1973 champions in uniform only.

The collection of strangers began reasonably well in 1978 but dropped under .500 on April 26 and never again saw daylight. Randle, who had been grateful for the opportunity to play a year earlier, attempted without success to renegotiate his contract in spring training, and he stumbled through a dreadful season. Henderson's average dropped to .266, and Maddox, who played the outfield and third base, hit only .257 with two home runs.

Montanez, a showboat, produced 17 home runs and 96 runs batted in. Stearns displayed power (15 homers) and tenacity behind the plate. And Mazzilli continued to blossom in center field, batting .273 with 16 homers and 20 stolen bases. Still, individual achievements were not enough to keep the Mets out of last place or to renew interest among fans.

It was an opponent who was responsible for the only "big" series of the year. In July, Pete Rose arrived in town with the Cincinnati Reds, seeking to equal the modern National League record of batting safely in 37 consecutive games. The record belonged to Tommy Holmes of the old Boston Braves, who happened to work for the Mets in their community relations department.

A crowd of 40,065 saw Rose go hitless in his first three at-bats on July 14 before he singled to left field in the seventh inning against former teammate Pat Zachry to tie the record.

Removed from the game later in the inning, an incensed Zachry kicked the dugout step, broke a bone in his foot, and was disabled for the season. At the time of the accident, Zachry was the Mets' biggest winner with 10. Although there were two months left in the season, only Nino Espinosa was able to exceed that figure, and he won just 11 games.

Skip Lockwood remained the key man in the bullpen, but it was an impossible task. Before the season was over, he found himself seated alongside Koosman. Once the best left-handed starter in the National League, Koosman was dragged down by the drudgery of a last-place team. He won only three times, suffered 15 defeats, and finished the campaign as a reliever. Grant publicly questioned whether or not Koosman was trying to win, a slap in the face to one of the most popular Mets. Koosman requested a trade to the Minnesota Twins so he could be near his home and threatened to retire if his request was not honored.

Although the team won two more games than the 1977 Mets, it still finished last and failed to make a dent on the public consciousness. Once again, Rose or no Rose, the attendance declined, to 1,007,328.

Finally, Lorinda de Roulet took a major step on her own. She forced out the 74-year-old Grant and was elected to fill his position as chairman of the board. The announcement was made on Nov. 8, 1978.

It might have signaled a turnaround for the ball club, but, rather than hire an astute baseball man to take charge, she decided to do the work herself, aided and abetted by her daughters, Whitney and Bebe. It was a major mistake.

Before the year was out, Koosman's wish was granted. He was traded to the Twins for two minor-league pitchers. McDonald saw something he liked in one, a left-handed reliever. His name was Jesse Orosco.

The new management team promised a change in the Mets' approach to the free-agent market. The Yankees, bolstered by expensive free-agent acquisitions, had just won the second of two consecutive championships in the Bronx, and the Mets' inaction had been particularly embarrassing by comparison. Charles Payson himself indicated the Mets would open the treasury, and the team did consider signing Pete Rose, whose long association with the Reds had been terminated. Rose, however, said he wanted no part of a last-place team in New York.

Among the additions to the club in 1979 were third baseman Richie Hebner, obtained from the Phillies for Espinosa, and left-handed pitcher Pete Falcone who was, like Torre, a Brooklyn native. Without Koosman and Espinosa, the Mets were desperately short of experienced pitchers. Torre had no choice but to take three rookies north with the club, although two of them —Orosco and Mike Scott, the same man who would bedevil the club in the 1986 playoffs—were returned to the minors as soon as the club signed some relatively undistinguished veterans.

In addition, Zachry damaged a nerve in his elbow and was sidelined in early June. Only Craig Swan, a homegrown talent whose earned-run average had led the National League the previous year, won as many as 10 games. He was 14-13 in 35 starts. Falcone started 31 games and won only 6 while losing 14.

Lockwood experienced shoulder trouble but his place in the pen was taken by Neil Allen, a rookie with an outstanding curve ball who won six games and saved eight. In all, the Mets employed 22 pitchers in 1979, reminiscent of the Bing Devine years.

After his fine 1978 season, Montanez slumped and was traded back to Texas, from whence he came, for Mike Jorgensen, the former Met who had been dealt away in the Rusty Staub transaction seven years earlier. Hebner's 79 runs batted in tied him with Mazzilli for the club lead, but he was an indifferent fielder and certainly was not motivated by the Mets' inability to win more than one out of every three games.

A six-game losing streak which began 10 days after the start of the season was all the people had to see. The Mets sank into last place after 24 games and stayed there. Shea was virtually abandoned by the fans. One solution of the de Roulet women was to run a name-that-mule contest for an animal they inexplicably presented as the team mascot. The winning entry was "Mettle" and before each game Bebe de Roulet would sit in a sulky and drive Mettle around the warning track. It was embarrassing.

The money that Payson had said would be available for free agents was barely enough to cover expenses. Lorinda de Roulet did not have her mother's fortune to work with, and her father was not about to write blank checks for a baseball team. Upkeep and routine day-to-day operations were cut back as the

Mets ran at a loss. Not once during the long, long season did they draw as many as 30,000 fans to the park. Fan support dwindled to a precious few after the All-Star break, creating the perfect atmosphere for a team going through the motions. Of the final 38 games played at Shea that season, the Mets won six.

Not even the emergence of Mazzilli as an All-Star as well as a matinee idol could forestall the desertion of the fans. Only 778,905 passed through the gates in the nation's largest city. It was clear something would have to be done.

There had been rumors of a sale throughout the season, rumors denied by Payson. But on Nov. 8, 1979, one year to the day after Lorinda de Roulet had pushed Grant out the door, the family confirmed that the club was for sale.

The Mets needed fresh leadership and they needed fresh money. They would get both in a matter of months.

Three for the Show

It was the Mets who brought us together and the Mets who drove us apart, at least in a manner of speaking. Lindsey Nelson, Bob Murphy, and I worked together for 17 years, from that first spring training to the final game of the 1978 season. The longest-running association of a trio in baseball broadcasting ended with Lindsey's departure for San Francisco.

The demise of the Mets precipitated the demise of the trio. By 1978, it was clear to all of us that the organization was collapsing. The team was in the cellar, the farm system had dried up, and the Mets weren't participating in the free-agent draft. Worst of all, there was no professional baseball man at the top. At least in 1962, there was George Weiss.

I also considered leaving during that depressing period. Peter O'Malley, who had inherited the Dodgers from his father, asked M. Donald Grant for permission to talk to me about a broadcasting job in Los Angeles, my hometown. At the time, Vin Scully was doing network television on the "Game of the Week" and the Dodgers wanted an experienced man to team with Jerry Doggett when Vin was away.

The Dodgers pared their list of candidates to two, me and Ross Porter, who was working in Los Angeles. I didn't get the call. I don't know whether or not I would have gone, but it wouldn't even have occurred to me if the Mets weren't in such dire straits.

Well, Murphy and I stayed on to another championship in our 25th year. It supports the old baseball adage that sometimes the best trades are the ones you don't make.

Lindsey, Bob, and I were only casual acquaintances when we arrived in St. Petersburg in the spring of 1962. My first contact with Bob had occurred during the 1961 season when I was broadcasting for the White Sox and he was working for the Baltimore Orioles. I had become friendly with his brother during my years in San Diego. Jack Murphy was a nationally prominent columnist for the *San Diego Union* and a man who was instrumental in convincing the American Football League and later the major leagues to establish a franchise there. After his death, San Diego Stadium was renamed in his memory.

Of the unholy trio, Lindsey enjoyed the greatest stature in the business. He had been a celebrated network broadcaster for a decade and had handled all the major sports events, with particular emphasis on college and professional football. Yet, for a man of his reputation, he had no ego. He never pulled rank. If there was one reason the three of us worked so well together, it was that. To meet Lindsey was to like him.

We did a lot of socializing that first spring. We did radio only from Florida in 1962, and we'd drive back from the ballpark to the Colonial Inn, which had been chosen as team headquarters because it accepted black players. There we'd take another lesson in Stengelese from the Old Professor in the press room and then go to dinner together. More often than not, we'd wind up in a piano bar. Lindsey and Al Moore, the Rheingold Beer executive, knew the words to all the songs.

Rheingold was the primary sponsor of Mets' broadcasts and was spending $6 million over five years for the privilege. Remember, the total expenditure for the team was $3 million. That led Lou Niss, the team's traveling secretary, to make the caustic comment in later years: "The Mets never paid a nickel and they never spent a dime."

We also had a cigarette sponsor in the early years. Neither Lindsey nor I smoked. That left Bob to do all the on-camera commercials.

Murphy had a passion for cars, especially for fast cars. It was he who talked me into buying a Porsche 356C, an experience I thoroughly enjoyed. It was also he who introduced me to my second wife, an experience I did not enjoy. But whenever I'd needle him about it, he would say: "Hell, I just introduced you to her. I didn't say you had to marry her."

At the start of one spring training, Bob drove nonstop from New York to St. Petersburg. I don't know how fast he was traveling, but he certainly left some of his faculties behind. Lindsey and I were at the bar, preparing to go out to dinner, when Bob arrived at the hotel and checked in. After he went to his room, the desk clerk asked us who that man was. We told him, and he then showed us the register. He had signed in as "Robert A. Mets."

M. Donald Grant was constantly critical of Murphy. He just didn't like his broadcasting style. After five years in New York, Bob got an offer to return to Boston, where he had first broadcast major-league games from 1954–59. He went to George Weiss, told him about the contact, and said he didn't want to leave the Mets. He just wanted Grant off his back. Weiss, who had the power, said he would handle Grant and kept his word.

Bob probably was the least recognizable of our trio. Lindsey had his network affiliation plus a wardrobe of outrageous sports jackets. And I had been a major-league player. But there was this one day when Bob received more attention than he would have liked.

We had driven to the ballpark together and had arrived about 2½ hours before the game. As we were getting out of the car, a young couple called to Bob, completely ignoring me. The woman said, "Bob? Are you Bob Murphy? We'd love to have your autograph?"

Flattered by the attention, he said he'd be happy to sign. The woman—she was very attractive—handed him a piece of paper and said, "Please sign here." It was only after he finished that he realized he had just acknowledged receipt of a summons. He went wild, but it was too late. The couple was walking away, melting into the crowd. But the woman did turn around and say, "I always did like the way you broadcast. Good luck in court."

Lindsey's jackets, if you will pardon the pun, went from the sub-lime to the red-iculous. When our telecasts were switched from black-and-white to color, he decided to create an identity by wearing the most outrageous coats he could find.

He had served in the Army during World War II and had been befriended by, among others, Ernest Hemingway, famed correspondent Ernie Pyle, and Andy Rooney, who would become a prominent television commentator. Of Nelson, Rooney once said, "He's the only friend from my Army days who dressed better then than he does now."

On road trips, I would frequently browse through men's stores when I had nothing to do. And if I came upon a particularly outlandish item, I would recommend it to Lindsey. Invariably, he would buy it.

His outfits always reminded me of the story about the worst sports jacket ever made. It sat in the window of this store until one day the manager could stand it no longer. On the way out to lunch he told the salesman, "When I come back, I want it gone or else you're out of a job." Upon returning from lunch, the manager was pleased to see the jacket was not in its accustomed spot. The salesman, however, was battered and bleeding.

"What happened to you?" the manager said.

"Well, I sold the jacket to a blind man," the salesman said. "But his seeing-eye dog almost killed me."

Suddenly, in 1978, Lindsey and his wonderfully awful jackets were gone. His decision to leave caught me by surprise. He never said anything to indicate he was prepared to take the step when he did, not even in the press room following what would be his final Mets' broadcast. But then, that was Lindsey. In all the years I had worked with him and as friendly as we had been, I never felt I really knew him.

I would learn about Lindsey's new job with the Giants from a most unlikely source. It happened at a cocktail party, and the messenger was George Steinbrenner.

Tom Seaver was the Mets' greatest pitcher. Manager Yogi Berra watches him warm up during a workout prior to the opening game of the National League playoffs in 1973. *(UPI)*

You gotta believe! Reliever Tug McGraw (left) and Ed Kranepool celebrate after the Mets beat the Reds, 7-2, to clinch the National League pennant in 1973. *(UPI)*

Willie Mays argues with umpire Augie Donatelli after Bud Harrelson was called out at the plate in the second game of the 1973 World Series. The Mets won the game, 4-1, in 12 innings, but lost the Series in seven games to Oakland. *(top right)* (UPI)

Joe Torre clinched the first National League championship for the Mets in 1969 when he played for the Cardinals and grounded into a double-play for the final out. He was later a player-manager and then manager of the Mets. *(bottom right)* (New York Mets)

The Mets greet Rusty Staub after his three-run homer in the first inning of the fourth game of the 1973 World Series against Oakland. The Mets won, 6-1. Rusty was one of the Mets' few bonafide power hitters. *(below)* (UPI)

Two of my best friends, Hall-of-Famers Monte Irvin and Hank Green-berg, were with me when I was notified of my election to the Hall of Fame in 1975. *(Wide World)*

Hall-of-Fame material: My wife DiAnn. *(Kiner Collection)*

(Vic Milton)

Dwight Gooden is the
greatest young pitcher
I've ever seen.

(Dennis Burke)

Lenny Dykstra rounds the bases after his game-winning homer off Bob Knepper in Game 3 of the National League Championship Series. "Nails" is the perfect nickname for him. *(Wide World)*

Darryl Strawberry watches his three-run homer off Houston's Bob Knepper in Game 3 of the National League Championship Series. *(Wide World)*

(Dennis Burke)

(George Gojkovich)

Keith Hernandez: the best fielding first baseman I've come across.

(Wide World)

(Dennis Burke)

Ron Darling makes his third World Series start in Game 7 against the Red Sox. He's an intellectual who can pitch.

The picture says it all after Jesse Orosco
strikes out Marty Barrett to win the World
Series. *(left)* *(Wide World)*

Nice guys don't finish last. That's how I view Gary Carter, celebrating with
World Series MVP Ray Knight after the Mets did it.
(below) *(Wide World)*

Davey Johnson treasures the World Series trophy. Mets' general manager Frank Cashen is on the left. Team president Fred Wilpon is on the right in front of Baseball Commissioner Peter Ueberroth.

(Wide World)

World Series MVP Ray Knight arrives for the ticker-tape parade with his wife, golfer Nancy Lopez. *(Wide World)*

The 1986 World Champion Mets: **Front row** (from left)—Trainer Steve Garland, coaches Mel Stottlemyre, Bill Robinson, Bud Harrelson, Vern Hoscheit and Greg Pavlick, assistant trainer Bob Sikes. **Second row**—Wally Backman, Mookie Wilson, Lee Mazzilli, Keith Hernandez, Dwight Gooden, Manager Davey Johnson, Gary Carter, Ron Darling, Darryl Strawberry, Lenny Dykstra. **Third row**—assistant to the general manager and travel director Arthur Richman, Rafael Santana, Howard Johnson, Kevin Mitchell, Tim Teufel, Roger McDowell, Doug Sisk, Ray Knight, Sid Fernandez, Randy Myers. **Back row**—batboy Paul Greco, equipment manager Charlie Samuels, Rick Anderson, Kevin Elster, Ed Hearn, Randy Niemann, Rick Aguilera, Bob Ojeda, Danny Heep, John Gibbons, assistant equipment manager John Rufino, batboy Mike Rufino. **Absent from photo:** Jesse Orosco. (New York Mets)

Mr. Baseball

There was no shortage of wealthy suitors for the Mets. The team may have hit bottom and the fan support may have eroded, but this still was a National League franchise in New York. The potential was enormous if the organization could be rebuilt.

In the two months following the sale announcement, prospective owners or sets of owners appeared almost daily in the newspapers. Whether all had bothered to tender offers to the Mets' law firm for screening by a three-man committee was uncertain. But the names that appeared in print certainly had financial clout. They included Robert Abplanalp, a friend of former President Nixon; Earl Smith, a former ambassador to Cuba, and Sonny Werblin on behalf of his employers, Gulf + Western.

It was very late in the process, so late in fact that the original deadline for bids had passed, when a very prominent name entered the negotiations. It happened to be one of the most famous names in baseball even though the man who had made it so never had anything to do with the sport. The name was Doubleday.

Perhaps the single greatest myth associated with baseball involved its roots. In the early years of the century, 1907 to be exact, Albert Spalding proclaimed Abner Doubleday as the inventor of baseball. A powerful figure in the game, Spalding had appointed a select seven-man commission to study the evolution of baseball with the suggestion that it discover an American origin. This was in response to the challenge of Henry Chadwick, a famous British-born baseball writer and the man who invented the box score. Chadwick insisted baseball was a derivation of rounders, a game played by English schoolboys.

According to Robert W. Henderson, a New York librarian who traced the origin of baseball back to ancient times in his authoritative book, *Ball, Bat and Bishop,* Spalding charged his committee of cronies this way: "I claim baseball owes its prestige as our National Game to the fact that as no other form of sport it is the exponent of American courage, confidence, combativeness; American energy, eagerness, enthusiasm; American pluck, persistency, performance; American spirit, sagacity, success; American vim, vigor, virility."

To no one's surprise, the commission found baseball to be a purely American invention. Actually, all the commission did was rubber-stamp the declaration of Spalding, who received, among thousands of communications, one letter purporting that Abner Doubleday had conceived the game in Cooperstown, N.Y. It was signed by Abner Graves, an octogenarian mining engineer raised in upstate New York. Spalding quickly embraced the idea and stressed its appropriateness.

"The tea episode in Boston Harbor had not been sufficiently forgotten in 1840 for anyone to be deluded into the idea that our national prejudices would permit us to look with favor, much less adopt, any sport or game of an English flavor," Spalding told the commission. He then brought up the Doubleday theory. "In this connection it is of interest to know that this Abner Doubleday was a graduate of West Point in 1842 and afterward became famous in the Civil War . . . It certainly appeals to an American's pride to have had the great national game of baseball created and named by a major general in the United States Army."

And so it was duly sworn and attested that Abner Doubleday marked off a diamond in a cow pasture adjoining Cooperstown in the spring of 1839, after which he proclaimed a set of rules to the eager youths gathered about him and called the creation (trumpets please) "baseball." So comfortable were baseball officials with this tale that, 100 years after the great moment, they opened the doors of the National Baseball Hall of Fame and Museum in the upstate village.

By all accounts, Abner Doubleday led an interesting and rewarding life. As captain of artillery at the federal garrison in Fort Sumter in the spring of 1861, he aimed the first gun fired at the Confederates in the Civil War. He fought at Antietam and Fredericksburg, Chancellorsville and Gettysburg, and published memoirs of those battles. Trained in engineering, he advised the city of San Francisco on a cable-car system while he was stationed there.

Yet there exists no evidence that Doubleday ever mentioned his "creation" to a soul outside Cooperstown. Strange behavior, indeed, for the father of the national pastime. By the time Spalding made his proclamation in 1907, Doubleday was powerless to protest. He had died in 1893.

The Doubleday who emerged suddenly on the New York baseball scene, Nelson Doubleday, was said to be a great-grand-nephew of the man who invented baseball. Nelson, however, owed his wealth not to the baseball industry, but rather to the family publishing business, Doubleday & Company, founded by his grandfather—Abner's nephew—in 1897.

Doubleday became involved only at the suggestion of a friend, John Pickett. Pickett, the owner of the New York Islanders, a hockey club, had made a bid for the Mets in conjunction with Fred Wilpon, a real-estate developer. They did not have enough capital to satisfy the Paysons. Pickett bowed out, but not before bringing together Wilpon, president of Sterling Equities Inc., and Doubleday.

On Jan. 24, 1980, it was announced that the Mets had been purchased by Doubleday, Wilpon, and the City Investing Company. The price paid for the club, a reported $21 million, was the largest sum ever paid for a baseball franchise at the time.

"We had a feeling we had gone as far as we could in the book business," Doubleday said. "The Mets are here. The Mets obviously are down. We felt it was not that much different from selling entertainment. We are always dealing with stars, with authors and agents. It's not all that different from selling a seat at the ballpark as it is selling books to our three million book-club members. Sure, what we paid is a great deal more than anyone had paid for a baseball team. But this is New York, and New York is a bigger deal than any other city.

"This is a National League city just waiting to be tapped. We regard this as a long-term investment. It will eventually be profitable. It is a business, and we feel we are going to do very well with it."

Doubleday, the majority stockholder, was appointed chairman of the board. Wilpon, a minority owner, became president.

Unlike Doubleday, Wilpon had a genuine background in the game. He had been a star left-handed pitcher on the Lafayette High School team in Brooklyn, a team whose first baseman—Sandy Koufax—would become a Hall-of-Fame pitcher with the Dodgers. Wilpon had earned a baseball scholarship to the University of Michigan, but there he suffered an arm injury and turned his thoughts to business.

With only a month before the start of spring training, Doubleday and Wilpon had no time to waste in forming an organization. After talking to a number of baseball officials, they decided the man they wanted to run the baseball operation was working as an administrative assistant to Commissioner Bowie Kuhn. It required only a 10-cent local call to reach Frank Cashen.

Cashen had served as chief operating officer of the Baltimore Orioles. A former newspaperman who favored bow ties and conservative clothing, he had resigned from the Orioles in 1975 to serve as senior vice president of Carling National Breweries Inc., then taken a job with Kuhn's office in January 1979 in order to get back into baseball.

On Feb. 21, 1980, Cashen was signed to a five-year contract as executive vice president and general manager. In the next 12 months, relying heavily on his contacts in Baltimore, he hired most of the front-office staff needed to replenish the bankrupt farm system. It was too late in the year to do much about the major-league club. He said he would spend the season "observing."

The 1980 Mets were not a pretty sight. They had a small nucleus of good players—Lee Mazzilli, John Stearns, shortstop Frank Taveras—under long-term contract. They had one dependable starting pitcher in Craig Swan, whom Cashen quickly signed to the most lucrative contract in club history. Swan was eligible for free agency after the season, and the owners couldn't afford to let him walk if they were to have any credibility with the fans.

Alas, Swan tore a rotator cuff in his shoulder, spent the second half of the season on the sidelines, and never again was the pitcher the Mets had counted upon. He won only five games in 1980 and lost nine. Pat Zachry's elbow problems continued, and he was able to win only 6 of 16 decisions. That placed a burden on Pete Falcone (7-10) and Ray Burris, a retread who had been picked up on waivers from the Yankees in 1979. Burris started more games than anyone on the staff, yet could do no better than 7-13.

The only pitcher to win as many as 10 games was Mark Bomback, acquired in a minor trade with Milwaukee in September 1979. Bomback didn't throw hard and he had never been envisioned as an ace, but he did win 9 of his first 12 decisions before finishing at 10-8.

At least the bullpen was solid. Neil Allen had another good year, with 7 wins and 22 saves in 59 appearances, and he was joined by a promising youngster named Jeff Reardon, who saved an additional six games.

Joe Torre, who had signed a contract for another year as manager before the club was put on the market, had to scratch for runs. Although Cashen did obtain Claudell Washington from the Chicago White Sox on June 7 at the cost of a minor-league pitcher, the Mets were almost powerless at the plate. In fact, Washington's 10 home runs in less than four months was the second-highest figure on the club, behind the 16 hit by Mazzilli.

The Mets did what they could, which was run. They stole a club-record 158 bases, topped by Mazzilli's 41. And they were competitive for a time, inching to within 2½ games of third place by mid-August. But a five-game sweep by the Phillies sent them into a tailspin from which they never recovered. They lost 23 of 26 games and settled into fifth place. Still, they finished at 67-95, three games ahead of the Cubs, and that was enough to convince the fans that the new regime was at least trying. The attendance of 1,178,659 represented the first gain in five years.

There was one major personnel move that wouldn't help the Mets on the field for several seasons but that certainly raised hopes. For only the third time in their history, the Mets held the number-one pick in the June draft. They had bungled the first one, selecting catcher Steve Chilcott over Reggie Jackson in 1966. They couldn't afford a mistake here, not with their talent gap.

The most publicized high school player in the country was Darryl Strawberry, a tall, lean outfielder from Los Angeles. He was a marvelous athlete who excelled in basketball as well as baseball. He was swift, he had outstanding power (he had hit a home run at Dodger Stadium), and he had led Crenshaw High School to the city championship. Even the name had star quality.

Cashen and his assistants vacillated between Strawberry and another outfielder, Billy Beane, before making their decision. Seventeen years after the Mets said goodbye to Throneberry, they said hello to Strawberry. (They also were able to land Beane with a later pick in the first round.) They sent Strawberry to Kingsport of the Appalachian League and awaited developments.

In that same year, they got their first look at the players who had been chosen on the first and second rounds of the 1977 draft. Wally Backman, an infielder from Oregon, and William Hayward (Mookie) Wilson, an outfielder from South Carolina, each appeared in 27 games for the Mets after their minor-league seasons ended. They would be back.

In fact, Wilson opened the 1981 season in right field as the Mets presented a vastly different lineup than the one with which they began the 1980 campaign. Cashen's first move after the season was to obtain Bob Bailor, a versatile utility player who had once been Orioles' property, from the Toronto Blue Jays for pitcher Roy Lee Jackson. On Dec. 15, he added left-handed pitcher Randy Jones, a former Cy Young Award winner who had undergone arm surgery, from the San Diego Padres. Because of his medical history, Jones represented a gamble, but the cost, pitcher John Pacella and infielder Jose Moreno, was low and the potential gain great.

Then the general manager signed two free agents, a major step for the organization after Grant's policies. The two were Rusty Staub, the hero of 1973 who no longer was capable of playing every day but who could still hit, and third baseman Mike Cubbage. Staub not only provided the Mets with a professional pinch-hitter but his return didn't hurt the club's standing with the public.

At the outset of spring training, Cashen also made one more acquisition. He sent Steve Henderson and cash to the Cubs for Dave Kingman, the slugger who had been banished in the Midnight Massacre of 1977. The hope was that Kingman's power would cover some of the team's deficiencies while the Mets continued to restock the farm system. Kingman had hit a league-leading 48 homers for Chicago in 1979, but, slowed by injuries, he had managed only 18 homers in 1980 and had alienated teammates and club officials.

Both Staub and Kingman were in the Mets' lineup on Opening Day in Chicago. So was Hubie Brooks, a rookie third baseman who had been selected by the club in the first round of the 1978 June draft. The Mets won the game, 2-0, behind Zachry, but it didn't take long for the optimism of spring to sour.

During that first series, Tim Leary was chosen to make his major-league debut. Leary, who had been the club's top pick in the 1979 draft after a stellar career at UCLA, had pitched brilliantly in spring training. In fact, he appeared to be the Mets' finest young pitching prospect since Tom Seaver. Hence the nickname Tim Terrific.

It was the belief of Cashen, conservative by nature, that Leary needed at least a half-season in Triple A before he was prepared to face major-league hitters. But he allowed himself to be persuaded by Joe Torre and his pitching coach, former Cardinal great Bob Gibson, that Leary was ready now. Besides, the condition of the staff was such that the Mets needed all the good arms they could muster.

So Leary went north with the team and started against the Cubs in Wrigley Field on April 12. He pitched two hitless innings, striking out three, and then pitched no more because his elbow stiffened. A later examination identified the problem as a muscle strain. Leary was placed on the disabled list, didn't throw again all season, and never was the same pitcher thereafter.

This not only was a serious setback for the Mets but proved divisive in the relationship between Cashen and Torre, who, since he had done such an admirable job the previous season, had been rewarded with a two-year contract. It didn't take long for the rest of the staff to follow Leary into oblivion. In all, the

Mets used 19 pitchers in 1981 although they played only 103 games because of a players' strike at midseason. Of those 19, only reliever Neil Allen was an unqualified success. He had 7 wins and 18 saves, which meant he had a hand in 25 of the club's 41 victories.

Swan was able to pitch in only five games. Jones won only one of nine decisions and didn't pitch in the final month. Mike Scott, the hard-throwing youngster whose future was elsewhere, was 5-10. Zachry (7-14) also lost twice as many games as he won. Falcone, who spent most of the season in the bullpen, pitched the Mets' only shutout.

As for Bomback, the surprise of 1980, he had been traded before the start of the season for Charlie Puleo, a right-handed pitcher who was assigned to Tidewater. Cashen continued to seek proven talent for the patchwork team. In late May, he traded Jeff Reardon and Dan Norman to Montreal for Ellis Valentine, a superb outfielder whose stock had fallen after difficulties with Expo management. It so happened there was a vacancy in right field because Torre had moved Kingman to first base, placed Mookie Wilson in center, and shifted Lee Mazzilli to left.

This was a blow to Mazzilli's ego. To be a center fielder in New York was to be someone special, particularly if you had grown up in the area as Maz had. But Wilson was the better outfielder, and Mazzilli was suffering from back problems as well as a season-long slump. He hit only .228 with 17 stolen bases, well below Wilson's figures of .271 and 24 steals.

The Mets dropped into fifth place before April had run its course, and they were a sorry 17-34, 15 games behind the first-place Phillies but 2½ games ahead of the last-place Cubs, when the players walked out on June 12. The strike and then the decision to conduct a "split season" upon the players' return in August gave the Mets, and especially Torre, a second chance to salvage the year.

And, for two weeks, they hovered around first place. With 12 games left, they remained only 2½ games back of the Expos, but they lost 8 of those contests and finished fourth, with a record of 24-28. Considering that Valentine batted .207 and Kingman hit only .221 and struck out 105 times in 353 at-bats (he hit 22 homers), it wasn't bad. But it wasn't good enough to save the manager's job.

Cashen wanted his own man to supervise the rebuilding process. He wanted someone who could work with young players, particularly pitchers. He knew just such a man from his Baltimore days. His name was George Bamberger, and he had been a celebrated Orioles' pitching coach before managing the Milwaukee Brewers.

Bamberger was available because he had suffered a heart attack early in 1980, returned to manage for three months, and then retired to his home in Redington Beach, Fla., adjacent to St. Petersburg. There were several reasons why Bamberger, after refusing the first offer, was persuaded to return to uniform. Cashen was a friend, Bamberger was a native of Staten Island, and the money was terrific.

The managerial shift, however, paled in comparison to the announcement made on Feb. 10, 1982. The Mets were sending catcher Alex Trevino and pitchers Greg Harris and Jim Kern (who had been acquired only two months earlier from Texas for Doug Flynn and Dan Boitano) to the Cincinnati Reds for slugger George Foster. The man had been a home-run champion and a Most Valuable Player in the National League, and the Mets rewarded him with a $1 million signing bonus and a contract that would make him the highest-paid player in the game. It was proof positive that Doubleday and Wilpon, who had promised they would spend the money necessary to revive the franchise, were men of their word.

Pitching still was in short supply, not only on the major-league level but in the farm system. Foster's arrival made Mazzilli expendable, and the onetime star and poster boy was traded to the Texas Rangers on April 1 for right-handed pitchers Ron Darling and Walt Terrell. Not only was Mazzilli wounded by the thought of leaving New York, he was offended that he had been dealt for two minor-leaguers.

It's true Darling and Terrell were minor-leaguers, but they were outstanding prospects. Terrell had been the leading winner in the Texas League and Darling had been a first-round draft choice out of Yale. They were exactly what Cashen was looking for, and the trade would prove to be one of the best the Mets ever made. But the pitchers needed additional seasoning. Bamberger would have to make do with what he had, and it wasn't much.

The staff was such that Randy Jones, 1-8 the previous season, drew the Opening Day assignment against the Phillies and Steve Carlton. The Mets managed to win, 7-2. They won more often than they lost throughout April and May. They were in third place as late as June 21, and it was a tribute to the manager.

Outside of Neil Allen, who was enjoying another outstanding season in relief, the only other pitcher to make a positive impression was Craig Swan. Bamberger had nursed him back from his rotator cuff injury, and, with careful handling, Swan managed to win 11 of 18 decisions. He was the only starter to win 10 or more games.

Nor did the offense produce the fireworks that had been anticipated with Foster added to the lineup. The pressure of living up to his well-publicized contract appeared to make Foster uncomfortable and tentative. After hitting 22 homers in the strike-shortened 1981 season, he managed only 13 in 151 games for the Mets and his average dropped from .295 to .247.

I had my own opinion on the reason for Foster's slide. Although he kept himself in great shape, he was 33, and at that age the reflexes just aren't as sharp. George's stance and bat position were ideal for a power hitter, but his long swing required too much time for him to get around on a good fastball. If he would move closer to the plate and lower his bat, as players like Carl Yastrzemski had learned to do, I thought he could continue to be an effective hitter.

It has always been my policy never to offer suggestions without being asked. I hung around the batting cage before games, hoping Foster would solicit my opinion as a former home-run hitter. The opening came one day when he asked me if I had a picture of myself standing at the plate. I brought one to the ballpark the next day and gave it to him in the belief this would lead to a conversation about hitting. Instead, he studied the picture for about 30 seconds, handed it back, said "Thanks" and walked away. George never changed.

Although Kingman hit for power (37 home runs) in 1982, he batted only .203 and struck out 156 times. Since Foster struck out 123 times, the middle of the order did not make contact nearly enough to sustain an attack.

Mookie Wilson continued to develop as an everyday player. He batted .279 and stole 58 bases in 1982. For John Stearns, who worked so hard to make himself a better baseball player, the season represented both the peak of achievement and the beginning of the end. He was in the midst of his finest year, batting .293 with 17 stolen bases (remarkable for a catcher), when a sore elbow he had played with for two months became so painful he had to be sidelined and then placed on the disabled list. The injury effectively ended his career although he continued his comeback efforts for years thereafter.

The loss of Stearns was bad enough, but the Mets also lost Allen for a month at about the same time. Shortly thereafter, they lost 15 consecutive games and dropped into the basement, where they would stay for the remainder of the season. At year's end, Ellis Valentine filed for free agency. The Mets did not even attempt to re-sign him. He batted .288 but displayed limited power and almost no enthusiasm.

Despite their disappearing act in the second half of the year, the Mets drew 1,320,055. And it appeared the team's popularity was on the upswing when Cashen announced on Dec. 16 that Tom Seaver was returning home. The Reds, who believed Seaver was at the end of his career after a 5-13 season complicated by injuries, sent him back to New York for Charlie Puleo and two minor-leaguers. Cashen followed that move by obtaining veteran Mike Torrez from Boston.

Now Bamberger would have some experience on which to build a pitching staff. When Seaver completed his warmup tosses in the bullpen on Opening Day in 1983 and walked across the outfield to the mound at Shea Stadium, he was accorded a long standing ovation which produced chills and more than a few tears in the crowd. He responded by pitching six shutout innings against the Phillies, and Doug Sisk was credited with the victory in relief.

The aura of the good old days didn't last very long. The Mets struggled to win 6 of their first 21 games. Allen was the biggest offender. After four fine seasons, he suddenly lost his touch and his confidence. He called the ballpark one day to say that he couldn't make the game because his wife was sick and he had to rush her to a hospital. A reporter who drove to his house found both Neil and his wife at home. He confessed to a drinking problem.

He underwent tests at a rehabilitation clinic at a New York hospital. According to the results, he was not an alcoholic. Hell, my good friend Phil Harris spilled more than Allen drank. But his cry for help was the symptom of someone who had lost control. His pitching suffered, and so did the Mets.

They looked so ragged and inept that Cashen felt the need to reach into the farm system and promote Darryl Strawberry on May 4. The future star had led the Texas League with 34 homers in 1982, and the general manager had hoped to let him play a full season in the International League in 1983. But the Mets could wait no longer.

So Strawberry brought his immense potential to the Big Apple, and he didn't disappoint. Only 21, Strawberry hit 26 home runs and drove in 74 in 122 games. He also stole 19 bases. Those figures were such that he became the third Met in history (after Seaver and Jon Matlack) to win Rookie-of-the-Year honors.

And yet the Mets still floundered. They made too many mistakes on the field, and Bamberger wasn't willing to spend the time correcting them during their numerous days-off during the first month. He was flying back to Florida, to be with his wife and relax on his boat, at every opportunity. It was becoming clear that he had lost his stomach for the job.

Finally, on June 2, the manager called Cashen from the West Coast and told him he planned to quit. He was concerned about his health, or at least what the Mets were doing to it. Unable to convince his former Baltimore manager Earl Weaver to come out of retirement on an instant's notice, Cashen appointed coach Frank Howard to serve out the year.

It would be another long season, one in which the Mets showed a one-game improvement (68-94) over 1982 and still finished a distant last. But their future took a dramatic turn on June 15 when Cashen announced the club had received Keith Hernandez from the St. Louis Cardinals in exchange for Allen and pitcher Rick Ownbey. Not only was Hernandez a superb hitter and former batting champion but he was the best-fielding first baseman I'd ever seen. In addition, he was an intense competitor who had been the main man on a championship club. On the surface, it looked like the biggest steal since the Brinks' Robbery.

It was the Cards who sought the deal, and the reason, we would later learn, was Hernandez's previous involvement with drugs while a member of the team. If Cashen knew about his personal history, he certainly kept it secret. As crestfallen as

Hernandez appeared to be after the trade, he was a true professional and responded to his new surroundings with a .306 average. Furthermore, he gave the younger players direction. Hernandez was a natural leader.

Since he would be eligible for free agency, it was essential that Cashen sign Hernandez to a long-term contract. It took a strong selling job by the general manager, as well as Wilpon and Doubleday, but he finally agreed that there was considerable talent in the farm system, that the Mets were about to make a great leap upward, that he would be playing for a contender in New York before the end of his career. It was a breakthrough for the Mets. Now they had what Cashen called a foundation player.

In the midst of the 1983 World Series, Cashen introduced another positive factor. He was Davey Johnson, and he would be the new manager. Johnson had been with the organization for three years as a minor-league manager and roving instructor, but Met fans were familiar with him for another reason. He had made the final out for the Orioles in the 1969 World Series.

Johnson said he hoped to view a World Series at Shea from the home-team dugout. Yes, the man was an optimist.

"Git on Your Mule, Son"

From the time I first dreamed of the major leagues through my playing career with the Pirates to my association with the Mets, baseball has undergone significant change. All around the National League there are modern symmetrical stadiums, many with artificial surfaces. The game I knew was one of power. By the 1960s, it had evolved into one of speed.

As great as has been that change, however, it is minimal compared to what has taken place in the field of broadcasting. I grew up in the era of re-created games on radio. The Mets broadcast live every game on the schedule, from coast to coast, and rare is the game that is not telecast as well. No longer is baseball left to the imagination.

Since I was raised in Southern California at a time when the sport's westernmost outpost was St. Louis, major-league baseball to me was the voice of Hal Berger operating out of a studio in Los Angeles. It seemed so vivid and immediate when Berger would read the notation "HR" on the Western Union ticker and say into the microphone, "Git on your mule, son." No one had to tell me or thousands of other youngsters in the area what that meant. The batter had just hit a home run.

Berger was one of a legion of baseball re-creators around the country. One of his peers, who deciphered Chicago Cub games for a station in Des Moines, was an ambitious young man named Ronald Reagan. Each re-creator had his own expressions, and the excitement of a broadcast varied with the individual's resourcefulness, for he worked with the barest of information supplied from the ballparks.

An operator in the press box would send a play-by-play report of the game in progress by Morse code to a Western Union relay station. There it would be translated onto tape and sent to radio stations. The announcer would receive the starting lineups and the facts, nothing more. F7, the designation for a fly ball to left field, might become a leaping grab against the wall or a sensational shoestring catch. Because of such poetic license, re-created games rarely were dull.

Many re-creators dressed their broadcasts with renditions of the national anthem, crowd noises, and other sound effects to indulge the listeners' fantasy. Berger's technique included rapping two sticks together to simulate the sound of bat against ball. To me, as I sat by the radio 1,500 miles from the nearest big-league ballpark, it was spellbinding.

The system was still in use when I reached the majors after the war. And it had lost none of its charm, especially not in the imaginative interpretations of Albert K. (Rosy) Rowswell, the colorful Pittsburgh broadcaster.

Rowswell didn't adhere to the usual sound effects. There was no crowd noise in the background, only the unmistakable click made by the Western Union ticker as it fed him reports from Forbes Field and other parks. What set Rowswell apart was his language.

There was no such thing as a strikeout in a Pittsburgh game. It was a "dipsy doodle." No Pirate was credited with an extra-base hit; it was a "doozey marooney." His most famous expression, of course, came to be associated largely with my efforts. It involved home runs.

"Open the window, Aunt Minnie," Rowswell would say whenever I homered. "Here comes another one." Then, after a slight delay, he would signal an assistant to drop a tray loaded with nuts, bolts, cowbells, broken glass, and ball bearings to the studio floor. It made a terrible racket. "She never made it," Rosy would tell his audience. "She tripped over the garden hose."

Rosy had a style all his own, one which was incomprehensible to the first-time listener. When he was managing the Dodgers, Leo Durocher was ejected from a game at Forbes Field and set about to run his team from the clubhouse. He turned on the radio and periodically sent messengers bearing his strategy to Herman Franks in the dugout. After two innings, however, he gave up. Not understanding Rosy's special code, Durocher didn't have the foggiest notion of what was transpiring on the field.

One of Rowswell's assistants, who later succeeded him as the top man on Pirate broadcasts, was a colorful announcer in his own right. Bob Prince could stir things up nicely.

Once, Prince got so excited after Whitey Lockman homered for the Giants against the Pirates, he shouted into the microphone, "That sunofabitch just hit a grand-slam homer." Rowswell, who was catnapping on the studio couch while Prince completed the inning, quickly jumped to his feet, grabbed the mike and said, "We have some painters working in the studio today and you'll have to excuse their language." He was something special, all right.

Lindsey Nelson, my colleague on the Mets' broadcasts for 17 years, once worked for the Liberty Network founded by the renowned Gordon MacLendon. Always searching for more realistic effects, MacLendon wanted to simulate the sound of a public-address announcer in the background, the way it would be heard at the ballpark. An echo chamber was needed, but the only place that fulfilled the requirements in the network's Dallas studio was the men's room.

So when you tuned into a Liberty re-creation of a Dodgers' game, you heard a muffled voice in the background saying, "Welcome to Ebbets Field for today's game." Occasionally, however, you might have heard the announcer say, "The game is held up because of a downpour." More than likely, it had been the flush of a toilet by someone who failed to notice the off-limits sign posted during broadcasts.

I got my chance to do re-created games while I was teaming with Bob Elson on Chicago White Sox broadcasts in 1961. Whenever the Sox played at night, I would be required to go to the studio and re-create another American League game played in the afternoon. It taught me more about broadcasting than did anything else. I learned to invent rain delays, fights, unusual plays, and to make a host of other split-second decisions whenever the telephone lines went dead or the Western Union operator failed to get his message across or made a mistake.

On the spot, I created plays that I thought could not be topped. I found out otherwise in 1962 when I observed the Mets. They operated beyond the bounds of anyone's imagination. Indeed, truth was stranger than fiction.

A Tale of Two Pitchers

With apologies to Charles Dickens, a slugger in the literary league, it was the worst of times, it was the best of times. In 1984, the Mets misplaced the greatest pitcher in their history. It was a public relations blunder that might have done permanent damage to the image of a struggling franchise but for the sudden arrival of a spectacular talent. Goodbye Tom Seaver, hello Dwight Gooden.

Perhaps if Seaver had remained for at least one more season, there might have been a formal ceremony, a passing of the torch. But by the time Gooden started his first major-league game, Seaver was getting his initial look at the American League. That Seaver's appearance in a Chicago White Sox uniform was not intentional on the part of the Mets only served to make them appear foolish.

Seaver had not been a great success in his comeback year at Shea Stadium, losing 14 of 23 decisions. Yet he did not pitch badly. He led the staff in innings, posted two shutouts, and his 3.55 earned-run average was the best of any starter. The Mets wanted him back for another season.

But Cashen also wanted to protect some of the young prospects from the free-agent compensation pool. He left Seaver off the protected list in the belief that no other major-league club would want a 40-year-old pitcher with a high salary whose value now was based as much on sentiment as practicality. As reasonable as that position seemed, it didn't take into consideration the needs of the Chicago White Sox.

After losing Dennis Lamp to the Toronto Blue Jays through free agency, the White Sox had a pick in the compensation pool. They saw Seaver's name and envisioned a man still capable of winning 15 games with offensive support. Cashen and the Mets were shattered by the White Sox' action, and the bridge to the public they had painstakingly rebuilt in the wake of the Grant regime was undermined.

As it developed, Seaver still had a lot left. He would win 15 games in 1984, leading the Chicago staff in virtually every category, and among his 16 victories in 1985 would be the 300th of his career. Ironically, number 300 occurred in New York, against the Yankees.

All this would have been difficult for Met fans to swallow if not for the emergence of Gooden as the premier pitcher in the game. Gooden had been the Mets' choice in the first round of the June 1982 draft. The Mets really would have preferred to take shortstop Shawon Dunston from Brooklyn, acknowledged by most scouts as the number-one amateur player in the country, but he went to the Cubs, who had the first pick. The Mets were fifth in the order of selection and thrilled that Gooden still was available when it was their turn.

Gooden had been an outstanding athlete at Hillsborough High School in Tampa. He had the makings of a good hitter, and he played other positions when he wasn't pitching. But it was his pitching that captivated Joe McIlvaine, a former pitcher whom Cashen had lured to New York in the fall of 1980 to be his director of scouting. Gooden was long limbed and threw with a free and easy motion. He threw hard and he had amazing poise and control for someone so young.

The Mets knew they had a terrific prospect in Gooden, but even they didn't realize at first how special he was going to be. After signing with the Mets, Gooden reported to Kingsport of the Appalachian Rookie League, where he struck out 66 batters in 66 innings, pitched two shutouts, and fashioned a 2.47 earned-run average, sixth best in the league. Among the Mets' officials who marveled at Gooden's command of the game was

Davey Johnson, who spent that year touring the minor-league clubs.

It was in 1983 that the rest of baseball suddenly became aware of a new force. At Lynchburg, in the Class A Carolina League, Gooden won 19 of 23 decisions, pitched six shutouts, and struck out an astounding 300 batters in 191 innings. At the end of Lynchburg's season, Gooden was promoted to the Triple A club at Tidewater, managed by Johnson. At that rarified level, he split two playoff decisions and then pitched a complete game in a 4-2 victory over Denver in the Little World Series. At 18, he was proclaimed minor-league player of the year by one publication.

When Johnson was appointed manager of the Mets on Oct. 13, 1983, he had every intention of taking Gooden north with him at the start of the 1984 season. Naturally, Cashen had other ideas. He thought a full season in Triple A would be beneficial for someone so young. And there was the lesson of Tim Leary, still struggling to regain his form after two long stretches on the disabled list.

Cashen and Johnson were polar opposites in terms of personality. Unlike the contemplative and scholarly Cashen, a lawyer by training although he never practiced, Johnson was outspoken and blunt. He had attended two colleges and held a degree in mathematics from Trinity University in Texas. He also had built his own real-estate empire in Florida. He was a licensed pilot and a demon on computers, which he used to assess strengths and weaknesses and plan baseball strategy.

The two men had had some dandy arguments when it was time to negotiate Johnson's contracts with the Orioles. Even then, the future manager had come armed with sheafs of statistics and data supporting his value to the club. Johnson had played on two World Championship teams in Baltimore, had tied a major-league record for second basemen by hitting 42 homers in one season while playing that position for the Atlanta Braves, and had even spent two years in Japan batting behind the legendary Sadaharu Oh.

Johnson was a forceful man, as sure of himself as Hodges had been, although much quicker to verbalize his opinions. And it was the manager who prevailed in the spring-training tussle over where Gooden should start the season. He would be a Met, a starting pitcher on a major-league team at the tender age of 19. Walt Terrell and Ron Darling, obtained at the cost of Lee Mazzilli two years earlier, also made the final squad and moved into the starting rotation after Johnson determined the veterans would be of little help.

The Mets began the season with a staff that included Craig Swan, Mike Torrez, and Dick Tidrow, a former Yankee who had been signed as a free agent the previous winter. Torrez was given the starting assignment on Opening Day in Cincinnati but failed to last two innings in an 8-1 defeat. He would start seven more games before being released in mid-June. By then, Tidrow and Swan had been waived after 21 combined relief appearances, mostly ineffective.

It was the kiddie corps that got the Mets rolling. Darling and Doug Sisk combined to shut out the Reds, 2-0, in the second game of the season; Terrell was credited with an 8-1 triumph in Houston; and Gooden pitched five strong innings in the Astrodome, allowing three hits and striking out five, as the Mets defeated the Astros, 3-2.

Johnson had made some other changes. He was an aggressive manager, always looking for ways to score more runs. To that end, he selected Wally Backman as his second baseman over Brian Giles, a smoother defensive player. Backman had spent most of the 1983 season at Tidewater under Johnson and had responded with a .316 average. He was a player who wasn't afraid to get his uniform dirty, and Johnson loved his spirit. Although a switch-hitter, Backman didn't hit very well right-handed, so the manager promoted Kelvin Chapman to handle second base against left-handed pitching, and the platoon system was an unqualified success in 1984.

The manager was not enamored with the incumbent shortstop, Jose Oquendo. Before the season was over, Johnson had demoted him to Tidewater and used Ron Gardenhire, the recently acquired Rafael Santana, and even Hubie Brooks, the third baseman who had the range to play the position. Catching was a problem all season. Stearns still was attempting to rehabilitate his elbow, and veteran Ron Hodges, who had spent his career as a reserve, was not capable of playing every day at age 35. No sooner had the Mets decided to go with rookie John Gibbons than he was hurt and placed on the disabled list. Another rookie, Mike Fitzgerald, shouldered much of the burden for the remainder of the season.

Meanwhile, the focus of public attention was directed not to the catching but to the pitching. After being shelled in Chicago in his second start and getting no decision in his Shea Stadium debut, Gooden struck out 10 Expos in a 2-1 Met victory at Montreal. In his next start, against the Cubs, he again struck out 10. New York began to buzz about the phenom in its midst. Soon thereafter, a group of young fans arrived at the ballpark with a group of "K" signs which they posted in the upper left-field stands after each Gooden strikeout.

In time the so-called "K Korner" became a craze not only at Shea but at ballparks throughout the major leagues. And, before long, Gooden was dubbed "Dr. K," a play on basketball star Julius Erving's designation as "Dr. J." From a local phenomenon, Gooden went national on July 10. Appearing in the All-Star Game at San Francisco, he struck out the side—Lance Parrish, Chet Lemon, and Alvin Davis—in the first of two innings he worked.

Meanwhile, Darling and Terrell also were pitching well, and the Mets, to the surprise of all but Cashen and Johnson, who had preached in spring training that the Mets were capable of winning the Eastern Division, occupied first place. Darling was 10-3 at the All-Star break, Terrell had won six games, and Bruce Berenyi, acquired from the Reds on June 15, already had won three starts. The rotation was strengthened and balanced by the promotion of Sid Fernandez, a young left-hander whom the Mets had received from the Dodgers' organization in exchange for Bob Bailor and relief pitcher Carlos Diaz at the winter meetings in late 1983.

They appeared to hold the balance of power in the division until the Cubs, their immediate pursuers, added starting pitchers Dennis Eckersley and Rick Sutcliffe in midseason. Now the race was joined.

On July 27, Gooden struck out eight Cubs in eight innings and beat Chicago, 2-1, with relief help from Jesse Orosco, boosting the Mets' lead to 4½ games. That was to be the high point of the season. Inheriting a 3-3 tie from Darling on the following day, Doug Sisk was victimized by two hits, a walk, an error, and shoulder soreness in an 11-4 loss. The Cubs swept a doubleheader by scores of 3-0 and 5-1 the next afternoon.

Within a week, the Mets fell out of first place, never to return. In a four-game rematch at Wrigley Field in early August, Gooden and Darling both were shelled, as was veteran starter Ed Lynch. Chicago won all four games.

The teams met in two more series that season. Gooden produced a one-hit, 11-strikeout gem at Shea Stadium in early September, and the Mets won two of three games. But the Cubs won two of three the following week in a Wrigley Field series that featured beanballs.

Although the Mets were not mathematically eliminated until the final week of the season, they didn't seriously threaten Chicago in the final month. Still, the season was a huge success. The Mets' record of 90-72 was the second best in club history, exceeded only by the 100-62 mark of the 1969 World Champions. And attendance shot up to 1,829,482.

Keith Hernandez enjoyed a superlative season, batting .311 and driving in 94 runs. Hubie Brooks not only hit a career-high 16 home runs to go with a .283 average but he played a professional shortstop after Johnson moved him there in September. That position shift would be one of the key ingredients in a major off-season trade. Surrounded by better hitters, George Foster tagged 24 homers, although he still wasn't the force he had been with Cincinnati.

The only negative reviews, from the press, manager, and players alike, were reserved for Darryl Strawberry. It wasn't a matter of numbers, because, in his first full major-league season, Strawberry hit 26 home runs and led the club with 97 RBI. Yet he struggled through protracted slumps, occasionally arrived late at the park, and appeared to miss his personal guru, Jim Frey. Frey had been the batting coach in 1983 when Strawberry reported to the big leagues, and the two had spent many hours talking baseball. Now Frey was managing the Cubs, quite successfully.

Without Frey, Strawberry seemed adrift. It didn't help that he had proclaimed himself a team leader in spring training. He was anything but, which led to an unusual public criticism by Hernandez late in the season.

"He quit on himself," Hernandez said. "He gave in on certain tough situations. When things got tough, he gave in. In August, I didn't think he was giving it a one-hundred-percent effort. He was down on himself. The second year is the toughest for any player. I know how tough it was for me. There were certain situations where he gave up. He has got to toughen up. He couldn't handle things when they went bad."

Homerless in August, Strawberry finished with a flourish, hitting three home runs in the final series of the season. He vowed to bear down in 1985.

There was much to celebrate after the season. Gooden had led the National League with 276 strikeouts, surpassing the previous rookie record of 245 set by Herb Score of Cleveland. His 11.39 strikeouts per nine innings was a major-league record. So was his 32 strikeouts in two consecutive games. For the second successive year, the league's Rookie-of-the-Year award went to a Met.

Certainly, the Mets were well stocked for starting pitchers with Gooden (17-9), Darling (12-9), Terrell (11-12), and Fernandez (6-6). Orosco had been brilliant in relief with 10 victories and 31 saves. The team, however, had two apparent weak spots—third base and catcher. Ray Knight had been obtained from Houston in midseason, but, because of his history of injuries, they weren't sure what they had. To bolster third base, they traded Terrell to Detroit on Dec. 7 for Howard Johnson, a young switch-hitter with power.

That was only the appetizer on Cashen's menu. Three days later, he sent Hubie Brooks, Mike Fitzgerald, outfielder Herm Winningham, and minor-league pitching prospect Floyd Youmans to Montreal for Gary Carter. Cashen placed Carter in the same class as Hernandez. He was a foundation player.

Carter had been the ranking catcher in the National League since the retirement of Johnny Bench. At 30, he had just completed his 10th season with the Expos. He was a slugger and top RBI man as well as a fine receiver.

The Kid, as he called himself, was expendable because the Expos were in a transition stage. They had failed by the margin of an extra-inning home run to win the 1981 National League pennant, and the stars of that team were aging. Although popular with the Montreal fans for his accommodating nature, Carter was not a favorite in the clubhouse. His teammates perceived his ready smile and availability to reporters as a hunger for publicity, a form of selfishness. The way they spoke after the trade, they were not sorry to see him go.

But the Mets were delighted by his presence. He provided them with precisely what they needed, an experienced catcher to handle one of the youngest pitching staffs in baseball and a dangerous right-handed cleanup hitter, a role that Foster no longer could fulfill. For its part, Montreal wanted a hard-hitting shortstop, and the Mets had the most productive hitter in the league at that position once Johnson decided to experiment with Brooks.

It was an eager team that began the 1985 season against the St. Louis Cardinals. The fans also were excited. On Opening Day, 46,781 paid their way into Shea Stadium, and they got their money's worth. Although neither Gooden nor Joaquin Andujar pitched well and the Mets stranded 15 baserunners, Carter hit a 10th-inning home run in his first game in a New York uniform for a melodramatic 6-5 victory. The Mets again won in extra innings in the second game of the series as Hernandez scored the winning run in the 11th inning after reaching third on Carter's single.

Carter, who relished the spotlight, homered for the only run in the third game of the season, against Cincinnati, and his homer in the fifth game broke a scoreless tie. The man's clutch hits shared the headlines with the work of the pitching staff. After nine games, the Mets had won eight, including three by shutouts.

Although they cooled considerably, the Mets were 18-8 and in first place after five weeks of the season. One of the prime reasons was Strawberry, who had hit six home runs in his first 16 games. And then, in a game against Philadelphia, the young outfielder dove for a line drive, hit the ground hard, and tore ligaments in his right thumb.

It would be seven weeks before he returned to the lineup, and in that period the Mets lost 23 of 43 games and fell into second place. During Strawberry's absence the Mets engaged in one game that might have done justice to the early ragamuffins managed by Casey Stengel.

The game was a defeat of such epic proportions that it seemed like something out of the Throneberry era. On June 11, in Philadelphia's Veterans Stadium, the Mets yielded nine runs in the first inning, seven in the second, five in the fifth, one in the sixth, and four in the seventh. They scored seven runs and lost by 19. "I've never been so embarrassed on a ballfield in my life," Wally Backman said, "and that includes Little League games."

The 26 runs were the most scored against any Met team and the most ever scored by the Phillies, who were playing their 102nd season. Von Hayes led off the game for Philadelphia with a home run off Tom Gorman and hit a grand-slam homer later in the first inning off Calvin Schiraldi. "I feel like I've been through World War III," Cashen said after the shelling stopped. "I've spent the last six innings writing headlines for the New York tabloids."

In the tabloids, the game became known as the Philly Phiasco. The loss was the Mets' sixth in their last seven games and dropped them 3½ games behind the Cubs. At least, they rebounded the next night with a season-high 18 hits and a 7-3 victory in 11 innings.

Three weeks later, in Atlanta Stadium on the night of July 4, they won a truly amazing marathon against the Braves. The 19-inning game consumed 6 hours and 10 minutes of playing time, and, because of two rain delays, it did not end until 3:55 A.M. It was followed by a fireworks display.

In the course of the game, the Mets had a club-record 28 hits, including five by Carter; Hernandez hit for the cycle; and Strawberry was ejected along with manager Davey Johnson. The Mets had the lead five times from the fourth inning on, only to lose it each time. Twice in extra innings they were one out from victory, only to have the Braves tie on home runs. The second homer, in the 18th, was hit by Rick Camp, a notoriously weak-hitting pitcher.

The Mets won the game with a five-run outburst in the 19th. Ron Darling, pitching in relief for the first time since his days at Yale, closed out the game. It was the third of nine consecutive victories which boosted the Mets from fourth place into a tie for second, 2½ games behind the Cardinals, who had sprinted to the head of the division on a combination of speed, timely hitting, and a terrific bullpen. The Mets won 12 of 13 leading up to the All-Star Game, culminating in Gooden's seventh consecutive triumph, a 1-0 shutout of the Astros.

By then, Mookie Wilson had been disabled with a shoulder injury which would require arthroscopic surgery. He was replaced in center field by Lenny Dykstra, a little hustler who dove head first into bases and ran head first into walls. Since he had a better eye at the plate, Dykstra was a more dependable leadoff hitter than Wilson. Although he didn't have Wilson's power, he could pop the ball, as the nation was to learn in the 1986 playoffs and World Series.

Carter's right knee was a more serious concern. It had given out in Houston just before the All-Star Game. He returned to the lineup a week later and played in pain for the rest of the year. Immediately after the end of the season, he underwent surgery.

Despite problems in the bullpen—Orosco was ineffective and Sisk couldn't locate home plate, much to the vocal disgust of Shea Stadium customers—the Mets remained within striking distance of the top. After losing the first of a four-game series in Chicago in early August, the Mets rebounded to defeat the Cubs three times and move into first place. Strawberry homered three times in the 7-2 finale.

A week later, after a two-day players' strike, the Mets swept a three-game series from the Cubs and the defending titlists began sinking in the East. The Mets ran their winning streak to nine, but they couldn't shake the Cardinals. Gooden continued to be virtually unhittable. On Aug. 20, he struck out 16 Giants and claimed his sixth shutout, a 3-0 victory. Five days later, against the Padres, he posted his 14th consecutive victory and became the youngest 20-game winner of the modern era. He was 20 years, 9 months, and 9 days old.

His personal winning streak ended in his next start at San Francisco, where he was beaten by the Giants, 3-2. That loss preceded one of the great games of the 1985 season, a widely publicized matchup between Gooden and Dodger ace Fernando Valenzuela in Los Angeles. Before the largest Dodger crowd of the season, both pitchers were brilliant. Gooden pitched shutout ball for nine innings, striking out 10 and working out of a bases-loaded, no-out situation. Valenzuela worked 12 scoreless innings before Strawberry's two-run double in the 13th off Tom Niedenfuer turned the game. Orosco hung on in the bottom of the inning, leaving the bases loaded in a 2-0 triumph.

In the course of the same trip, Hernandez rode an emotional roller coaster. First, he was benched in San Francisco, his hometown, because of a batting slump. But in the same game, with the Giants trying to nail down a 3-2 victory, Johnson sent Hernandez to the plate as a pinch-hitter in the ninth inning, and he delivered a game-winning two-run homer.

Later in the week, while the Mets traveled from San Diego to Los Angeles, Hernandez flew to Pittsburgh to testify in the trial of a drug dealer who had supplied many major-league baseball players. In what he later said was the hardest thing he ever had to do, the first baseman admitted he had been hooked on cocaine for a time while he was playing for the Cardinals but said he had kicked the habit by himself. Then he flew back to Los Angeles and reached Dodger Stadium in time to enter the game, started by Gooden, as an extra-inning defensive replacement.

He was concerned about what the public reaction would be to his testimony, which was splashed over all the newspapers. Hernandez needn't have worried. In his first appearance at Shea Stadium, on Sept. 10, he received a thunderous ovation.

"It gave me goosebumps," he said. "I never expected it. I haven't experienced anything like that since I returned to St. Louis after the trade and got a standing ovation."

Of course, the crowd also was turned on to a pennant race. The Cardinals were in town for a showdown, and, thanks to Howard Johnson's grand-slam homer and Roger McDowell's superb relief work, the Mets won, 5-4, edging one game in front of St. Louis. In a magnificent pitching duel the following night, John Tudor beat the Mets, 1-0, in 10 innings. Gooden once again pitched nine shutout innings to no decision, but Orosco was tagged for Cesar Cedeno's homer in the 10th. A ninth-inning single by Hernandez drove in the winning run in the final game of the series. The 7-6 victory enabled the Mets to regain a one-game lead.

However, the Cardinals rebounded with a winning streak while the Mets experienced difficulty against the division's weaker teams. They were particularly vulnerable against the last-place Pirates, who won three of the six meetings between the teams in September. By the time they reached St. Louis in the final week of the season, the Mets trailed the Cards by three games. Six games remained.

What they needed was a three-game sweep. They almost pulled it off. Although Johnson was second-guessed for not rearranging his pitching rotation so that Gooden would open against Tudor, he said he had faith in Ron Darling. And the faith was well placed. Pitching the game of his life, Darling matched the St. Louis ace through nine scoreless innings. Orosco replaced Darling in the 10th and Ken Dayley, another left-hander, replaced Tudor in the 11th. After Dayley struck out

Hernandez and Carter, however, Strawberry hit a majestic home run off the scoreboard clock in right-center field for a 1-0 New York victory.

Although not at his best, Gooden—en route to a 24-4 record and the Cy Young Award—easily turned back the Cards and 20-game winner Joaquin Andujar the following night, 5-2. Now the Mets needed only one more victory to draw even. It was up to Rick Aguilera, a rookie.

Aguilera had been a fifth-round draft choice of the Mets in 1983 after his conversion from infielder to pitcher at Brigham Young University. A 6-4 right-hander, he had enjoyed moderate success in the minors and was promoted to the major-league level when Bruce Berenyi was disabled early in the season. He responded by winning 10 games, including his previous three decisions.

But the Cards opened a 4-2 lead and used all four of their outstanding relief pitchers to post a 4-3 victory in the finale. Although Hernandez collected five hits, he was stranded at first base in the ninth as Jeff Lahti retired Carter on a fly to right field.

The defeat ended any realistic chance they had of winning the division. And yet, that series in St. Louis forged the Mets as a cohesive and mentally tough team. They had gotten their first taste of pennant pressure and responded positively. They were eliminated on the next-to-last day of the season and tossed their caps to the crowd after the final game at Shea Stadium in tribute to the support provided by the fans. The attendance of 2,751,437 was a record for a professional baseball team in New York.

Six seasons after Nelson Doubleday and Fred Wilpon inherited a bare cupboard and a largely empty stadium, the Mets were a viable force in the nation's largest city again. And no one connected with the team was satisfied with a second-place finish. The Mets fully expected to win in 1986, their silver anniversary season.

Love and Marriage

It was difficult to maintain a private life in the public arena. I could understand the fuss whenever I dated a Hollywood celebrity, but not even my proposal to tennis star Nancy Chaffee escaped notice. In fact, the media beat me to the punch.

I had met Nancy in 1950 on Tom Harmon's television sports show in Los Angeles, where she was serving as a panelist. She was among the top four women players in the world at the time. We dated a lot that winter before I went off to spring training and she began her preparation for the prestigious Wimbledon championships. I planned to present her with an engagement ring in June when the Pirates were scheduled to play the Dodgers and Giants in New York. She would be passing through en route to England.

The date I had chosen was June 10. My dramatic gesture, however, was undercut by a radio broadcast. Nancy had heard Walter Winchell announce my intentions before I told her. So much for the surprise factor. At least I received the benefit of an answer before Winchell did.

We were married in Santa Barbara, Calif., in October 1951. If we had wanted a small, quiet ceremony, we would have been out of luck. Our nuptial vows were covered by Movietone News.

After a honeymoon in Acapulco, we moved into the modern

house built for Kiner the Bachelor off the 11th green of the Thunderbird Country Club in a part of Palm Springs now called Rancho Mirage. It was the first 18-hole golf course in the area, and its members included, among others, Bing Crosby, the Phil Harrises, Bob Hope, Randolph Scott, songwriter Jimmy Van Heusen, Lucille Ball, and Desi Arnaz. I was interested in golf, but Nancy continued her tennis career.

To facilitate that career, we built the only grass court west of the Rockies on our property. The presence of that court, of course, drew some outstanding players to our front door. It also attracted some curious neighbors.

Among them was Alice Faye, the cinema star who was married to Phil Harris. She came over one day during the winter to welcome us to the Thunderbird family. The door was wide open, but no one appeared to be home. She walked inside, saw our clothes dryer running full blast, and thought to herself, she recalled later, "What a nice domesticated couple!"

About that time, Nancy came in from the pool area. Alice introduced herself, complimented her on the house, and, motioning toward the dryer, said it was nice to see that Nancy had some domestic as well as athletic skills. "Domestic?" Nancy said. With that she opened the dryer door and out bounced about two dozen tennis balls, their elasticity having been restored by the heat and spin action of the machine.

Among the wedding gifts we received was a lifetime membership in Charlie Farrell's Racquet Club. I spent a lot of time there that winter. In addition to the various social engagements on the calendar there, I was seized by the compulsion to become a competitive tennis player.

The reason was that shortly after our wedding, we got into a discussion on the relative strength of female athletes. I had played a little tennis as a youngster, and I reasoned that, as a major-league baseball player, I should be able to master what appeared to be a simple sport. I told Nancy that with practice, I would be able to beat her in a year's time. Needless to say, she did not share my perspective.

I insisted on a full year of practice because I didn't want to play tennis during the baseball season. I didn't want to mix the two sports. I began by asking her for some lessons, a request she immediately rejected. That's how I found myself at Charlie Farrell's club, working with the pro.

Before the winter was over, Nancy and I began playing sets. I didn't win so much as a game. I could serve well and I could volley well, but she had all the strokes and made me pay for my inexperience.

During the following winter, I worked to develop my second serve and my ground strokes. By the end of that vacation, I was able to win some games and make her work for her points. The scores of our sets were 6-4, 6-3, 7-5, something much closer to parity, especially if I was serving well.

Finally, in the third winter of our rivalry, I felt I had drawn almost even. And, sure enough, about two months into our own "season," I took a set off her, 8-6. Of course, two weeks later, our first son, Michael, was born.

The marriage lasted 17 years and produced three wonderful children, Michael, Scott, and Kathryn Chaffee, whom we nicknamed K.C. Nancy and I were divorced in 1968, and I'm happy to report that we remain friends.

In light of my next venture into matrimony, I should like to take the opportunity to dispute the sentiments of my friends Sammy Cahn and Jimmy Van Heusen: Love is *not* lovelier the second time around. Ironically, the wedding was held in 1969, a smashing year for the Mets.

When I was liberated in 1980, much as were the Mets by a new ownership and management team, my 1969 World Series ring was among memorabilia of my baseball career and first-family keepsakes that disappeared without a trace. But perhaps it was a small price to pay for the happiness I would find with my present wife.

I first met DiAnn Shugart at a dinner in Palm Springs, where I had returned to broadcast the Bob Hope Classic golf tournament for a local radio station. It's something I did every winter in order to spend some time with my children, who all live there. Well, DiAnn was with this group at the Indian Wells Country Club, which was the host club for the tournament at the time, and we got to talking. Neither of us had a strong first impression because I was in the process of getting divorced and wasn't particularly interested in female company at the time; and she was devoted to a new fabric protection business she had established in the desert community.

In any event, I went out to dinner with my kids that night, then rejoined the group. DiAnn and I resumed our conversation. My second impression was much stronger. She was delightful and easy to talk to, and the next night I escorted her to dinner.

Long-distance phone calls followed, we dated on my next trip to Palm Springs, and it went from there. We had a four-year courtship before our marriage in December 1982. And we're both so thankful to have experienced the love we share for each other.

An interesting sidelight was that DiAnn, who was born and raised in Texas and attended Baylor University, was not a sports fan. She knew nothing about baseball, including the identity of Ralph Kiner. So I had to teach her the subtleties of the game and fill her in on my accomplishments.

We now spend our off-seasons in Palm Desert, near Palm Springs, which not only offers us ideal winter weather conditions but enables us to see my children frequently. Scott is now the general manager of a radio station and Michael is an architect.

They were both good athletes. Scott was a fine tennis player and even spent some time as a professional, but he wasn't tour caliber and, in fact, is a better golfer. Michael specialized in baseball and was signed by the Mets' organization. After he was released, he went to architectural school. In the spring of 1986, he married Kathleen Sullivan, the ABC television personality.

And then there's K.C. She may have been the best athlete of all, but her interest in sports never equaled her talent. When I joined the Mets, Casey Stengel thought we named her after him and I never told him the truth. Every year, when she was young, we took a picture of her with Stengel. He would make a face and she would give a gap-toothed grin. Those pictures are family treasures now that she's no longer a little girl. She's married to Kenneth Schnitzler, a prominent Houston developer. He also happens to be a golf fanatic, and they spend weekends at their home in Rancho Mirage, which gives us all a chance to be together as a family.

DiAnn and I believe we know Who devised the whole scenario, and we are very grateful.

The Silver Season

The start of the 1986 season not only marked an anniversary for the Mets, their 25th in the National League, but for me as well. Opening Day was scheduled for Pittsburgh, where I had begun my major-league career 40 years earlier. Despite a shocking start—R.J. Reynolds hit Dwight Gooden's third pitch for a home run—the Mets prevailed over the Pirates, 4-2.

After a second game in Pittsburgh was snowed out, the Mets pushed on to Philadelphia, where they won the first game of a three-game series behind newcomer Bob Ojeda, then dropped the next two. A 6-2 loss in 13 innings to the Cardinals in the home opener put the Mets below .500 for the first and last time in 1986. Two rainouts gave them time to reflect on the prospect of a slow start, and the Mets responded with an 11-game winning streak which suddenly blew open the National League East.

Throughout spring training, manager Davey Johnson had stressed not just winning the division but dominating. The Mets acted like favorites even though they had fallen short the previous year. The Cardinals, they felt, had everything their way in 1985, but they had been weakened by the trade of 20-game winner Joaquin Andujar. The Mets' cocky attitude further irritated the Cards, who had complained bitterly the previous year that New York received more media attention even in defeat.

"We know they're a good team," said Ozzie Smith, the Cards' shortstop virtuoso. "But they act like they have to remind everyone all the time. Last year we won, and the way the Mets and other people acted, you'd think they beat us."

That's exactly what the Mets had in mind. Before the season even started, the Mets pointed to a four-game series in late April against the Cards. That was where they would have to make their presence felt. As it developed, that was where the title was won.

A three-game sweep at home over the Phillies preceded a significant game against the Pirates. The manager had begun the season by platooning Ray Knight and Howard Johnson at third base. Knight wasn't even assured of making the team when the Mets assembled in St. Petersburg. Davey Johnson convinced Frank Cashen that the veteran still could help the Mets after two seasons that had been ruined by injuries.

On April 21, the manager allowed Knight to stay in the game and hit against Pittsburgh's Cecilio Guante, a right-hander. Knight hit a two-run homer, providing the Mets with a 6-5 victory. It was his third homer and before the month was out he would hit six, matching his yearly total from 1985. Knight later called the homer off Guante a turning point in his career. The manager decided to discontinue the platoon and hand the job to Knight.

Three nights later, the Mets walked into Busch Stadium for the first time since their tingling series the previous September. Howard Johnson, now relegated to a reserve role and an occasional start at shortstop, stunned the Cards with a two-run homer in the ninth inning off the difficult relief pitcher Todd Worrell to tie the score. The Mets won, 5-4, in the 10th on George Foster's single.

Knight homered twice in the following game, and Gooden cruised to a 9-0 victory. Wally Backman then made a brilliant backhanded stop in the ninth inning of the third game and started a game-ending double play which preserved a 4-3 victory. The Mets completed the sweep with a 5-3 victory as rookie handyman Kevin Mitchell, making his first start at shortstop, handled eight chances flawlessly and homered off John Tudor. Suddenly, the Mets' lead was 4½ games and counting.

They closed out April with two more victories and then won seven of their first eight games in May. The Mets' top four starters had a combined record of 17-0. Ojeda, acquired from the Boston Red Sox for young relief pitchers Calvin Schiraldi and Wes Gardner, had immediately justified the trade by winning his first five decisions.

When the Mets had sought another left-handed starter, Cashen was primarily interested in Boston's Bruce Hurst. But Lou Gorman, the Sox' general manager who had worked for Cashen in both Baltimore and New York, was reluctant. Cashen had replied that he would take either Hurst or Ojeda and he would let Gorman decide. Gorman could not be faulted. Hurst had an excellent season for the Sox and would win two World Series games. Ojeda, a clever pitcher who mixed speeds and had outstanding control, became the Mets' biggest winner and most consistent pitcher.

In late May, the Mets returned from a 5-4 West Coast trip with a four-game lead. Their opponent was the Dodgers. With the score tied at 1-1, Lenny Dykstra singled in the sixth. Dykstra, a pesky left-handed hitter, had become the full-time center fielder when Mookie Wilson suffered an eye injury in spring training. The combination of Dykstra and Wally Backman at the top of the batting order—the so-called Partners in Grime—had been remarkably effective.

On this occasion, Backman followed Dykstra's single with a double and broke the tie. Keith Hernandez then singled to center, Backman moving to third. Gary Carter's single scored Backman, and a single by Danny Heep loaded the bases. It also knocked out Dodger starter Bob Welch. He was replaced by Tom Niedenfuer, who in the first two months of 1986 appeared still to be suffering the effects of yielding a pennant-clinching homer to Jack Clark of St. Louis the previous October.

Niedenfuer's first pitch was in the strike zone, and Foster drove it out of the park for a grand slam home run. Niedenfuer's second pitch struck Knight, so Knight ran to the mound and struck Niedenfuer. It was the first of four brawls to which the Mets would be a party over a two-month period, and it earned for them an image of arrogance around the league. Knight, a skilled boxer and an emotional player, would be the principal figure in two of them.

By the night of June 6, the Mets had padded their lead to

8½ games. By the end of the night, they had added to their reputation as a team spoiling for a fight. In the first game of a twi-night doubleheader at Three Rivers Stadium, the Mets were being checked by Rich Rhoden. Rhoden, they were sure, was scuffing the baseballs, an offense they had accused him of in the past. Bill Robinson, the first-base coach, had been a teammate of Rhoden's several years earlier. Passing the pitcher after an inning, he told Rhoden he was too accomplished a pitcher to cheat. The words were not graciously accepted, and they led to action. Robinson shoved Rhoden and brawl number two ensued.

Four nights later, the Mets were locked in a tie with the Phillies when Johnson told Tim Teufel to pinch-hit in the 11th inning. Teufel was the Mets' second major off-season acquisition, a right-handed-hitting second baseman they had obtained from Minnesota to platoon with Backman. The scouting reports said he had surprising power. He did on this night, connecting for a game-winning grand slam, the third pinch-hit grand slam in club history.

By the end of June, when the Mets returned to St. Louis, Cards' manager Whitey Herzog already had conceded. The Mets, he said, couldn't be caught. Certainly not by the sinking Cardinals. A three-game sweep at Busch Stadium preceded one of the memorable games of the season. At Shea Stadium, Phil Garner of the Astros broke a 3-3 tie with a two-run homer in the 10th. Darryl Strawberry then evened the score with a two-run homer in the bottom of the inning, his second homer of the game, and Knight won it with a solo homer off Frank DiPino. Knight had struck out in his first four at-bats.

The season had become one long parade, with lots of brass and percussion. Upset by losing all three games at home to Cincinnati, the Mets responded with a four-game sweep of Atlanta, outscoring the Braves 28-2. Carter drove in seven runs in the second game, with a three-run homer and a grand slam, but his curtain call after the former was not well taken by Atlanta pitcher David Palmer, who hit Strawberry with the next pitch. Strawberry charged. Brawl Three.

Meanwhile, the race had dissolved. At the All-Star break, 13 games separated the Mets from their nearest pursuers, the Montreal Expos. It stayed that way as the Mets buried the Astros in Houston, 13-2, in the first game of the second half. Later that night, Teufel, among the most soft-spoken of the Mets, and Ron Darling were charged with assaulting off-duty policemen employed as security guards at Cooter's, a Houston night spot. Ojeda and Rick Aguilera also were arrested.

The brawl of the year, however, was staged the following week in Cincinnati's Riverfront Stadium and was only a subplot among a series of bizarre developments. Dave Parker, the Reds' star right fielder, misplayed a routine fly ball by Hernandez with two out in the ninth inning, and the Mets pushed across two runs to tie the score at 3-3.

It was then that Eric Davis slid hard into third base, bumping Knight. Knight reciprocated with a hard tag. Davis made a derogatory comment. Knight landed a short right hook to the jaw. "When I feel threatened," Knight said, "I fight."

He was one of four players ejected. It left the Mets shortchanged for the rest of the game. In the emergency, Gary Carter played third base and the Mets turned an unusual 3-5-4 double play. Jesse Orosco and Roger McDowell, the Mets' bullpen aces, even got to play the outfield as Davey Johnson attempted to finesse the Reds. The Mets finally won, 6-3, in the 14th inning when Howard Johnson hit a three-run homer.

On the following night, it was disclosed, George Foster had been relegated to pinch-hitting and reserve duty as the manager contemplated the playoffs. Mookie Wilson had become the regular left fielder against right-handed pitching, moving to center field against left-handers and making room for Kevin Mitchell. The plot thickened after Lee Mazzilli, released by the Pirates, was signed to a minor-league contract by the Mets.

After a three-game sweep over Montreal boosted the Mets' lead to 17½ games, they left on a three-city road trip. The first stop was Chicago, where Foster implied to a reporter that he was being benched because of his race. Foster, a black, was being replaced by Wilson, a black, and Mitchell, a black, but the addition of the popular Mazzilli, a white player who could pinch-hit and play the outfield, apparently triggered his outburst.

The manager was furious at the suggestion and insisted upon Foster's release. Cashen obliged, leaving the Mets responsible for a $1 million option payment next season. Upon the team's return to New York, Foster appeared at a press conference and said his statements had been misinterpreted and misunderstood.

It was a graceless exit for a man who had never established any rapport with the fans. His departure opened a spot on the roster for Mazzilli, who suddenly found himself in the old clubhouse surrounded by all-stars. He said he would be happy to do whatever the manager wanted. He no longer was a star, and he was grateful just to be back in New York.

A torn ligament in his left thumb suffered during a rare start at first base sidelined Carter just as the Mets were prepared to take their second West Coast trip of the season. Because of the position he played and the Mets' lack of depth at catcher, Carter was believed to be the one player the Mets could least afford to lose. And yet, with Ed Hearn and John Gibbons behind the plate, the Mets reeled off eight victories in nine games, the most rewarding California journey in their history.

The sweep over the Dodgers, completed on Aug. 20, moved Hernandez, who chooses his words carefully, to proclaim, "The race is over. It's the gun lap already, and we've got such a big lead, the only thing we have to strive for is a world record."

It was in San Diego that the Mets completed the trip with a spectacular victory. After New York took a 6-5 lead in the top of the 11th on singles by Dykstra and Backman and a sacrifice fly by Hernandez, the Padres threatened in the bottom half. Garry Templeton was on second base with one out following a double, and Tim Flannery's base hit to center appeared to have created another tie. But Dykstra's strong throw to the plate arrived at the same instant as the runner, and Gibbons managed to hang onto the ball despite being bowled over.

Not only did Gibbons record the putout, however, he also had the presence of mind to regain his feet and fire to third. After seeing the collision at the plate, Flannery thought he could reach third without a play, but he was wrong. Gibbons's throw cut him down for a game-ending 8-2-5 double play.

Gooden had been the starting pitcher in that game for the Mets and had failed to hold a 5-1 lead. If there was anything disquieting about the 1986 season, it had been Gooden's performance. He had an excellent won-lost record, but he wasn't the dominating pitcher he had been the previous two years.

Early in the year, when the strikeouts weren't coming in

bunches, the Mets said it was all part of the plan, that he was learning to economize on his pitches. And he did win his first five decisions, including a two-hit, 4-0 victory over the Astros on May 6. That was his second shutout of the season. It also would be his last.

It soon became evident to me that something was wrong. He struggled thereafter, jeopardizing his position as the greatest pitcher in the game. The 94-mile-per-hour fastball was still there, but it didn't have the movement that had confounded hitters in 1984 and 1985. When he needed the strikeout, he couldn't get it.

The greatest fastball I ever faced was thrown by Hall of Famer Robin Roberts. It wasn't the fastest. Rex Barney of the Dodgers owned that. He threw in the vicinity of 100 miles per hour, but it was straight. However, Roberts, like Sandy Koufax, had great movement on the ball. It would literally hop over your bat. Movement is everything in a fastball, and, with Gooden, the movement suddenly wasn't there. You had to be concerned.

Still, he was good enough to win most of the time, and he still was the Mets' nominal ace. With the Mets prepared to clinch their first division title in 13 years, he got the call in the first game of a three-game series in Philadelphia. Hundreds of fans trekked down the New Jersey Turnpike to share in baseball history.

Gooden was hit hard and the Mets lost, 6-3. No problem. They would do it the next night. But the Phillies won on Saturday as well, 6-5. The Mets had brought cases of champagne with them to Pennsylvania, and they remained unopened for a third successive day as Kevin Gross bested Sid Fernandez, 6-0.

So the bubbly was loaded onto a plane and flown to St. Louis, the Mets' next stop. Now the Mets needed a victory and a Philadelphia defeat to clinch. Instead, they lost to the Cards, 1-0, in 13 innings. It was only the second time all year the Mets had lost four games in a row. "It's embarrassing," Wally Backman said. "I know what I'd be saying if this happened to some other team."

It wasn't until the following night, in the fifth and final game of the trip, that they managed to secure a 4-2 victory behind Rick Aguilera, reducing the magic number to one. The next game would be played in Shea Stadium against the Cubs.

Hernandez, Backman, and some other players had talked openly about the joy of accomplishing their first goal at home. Management had whispered of the possibility with foreboding. They were mindful of club tradition, which mandated that the field be sacked on such occasions.

Gooden got a second chance on Sept. 17, and this time he didn't fail. Hernandez was sidelined by the flu, but his replacement, rookie Dave Magadan, singled three times in his first big-league start. The final out of Gooden's 4-2, complete-game victory was a slow ground ball by Chico Walker to Backman at second base. It was so slow that Backman almost was overrun by the Mongol hordes as he made the throw to Hernandez, who asked to play the final inning as a defensive replacement so he could share in the triumph.

Players lost caps and gloves in the mad scene on the field. Someone jumped off the dugout roof and landed on Aguilera's shoulder, forcing him to miss a turn. Police reinforcements didn't chase the revelers from the field for a half hour, and by then huge chunks of sod had been removed, revealing a moonscape. Pete Flynn, the head grounds-keeper, said it was worse than either 1969 or 1973.

The ground crew worked all night and patched the field in time for a game the next afternoon. As bleary-eyed as many of them were, the Mets even won that game, 5-0, behind rookie Rick Anderson. The Mets closed out their greatest season with a five-game winning streak, including the final three at home. On Oct. 5, Darling and Fernandez combined to shut out the Pirates. Strawberry, still struggling under the burden of his superstar buildup, hit a grand slam—his sixth homer in 12 games—to silence the boos he had been hearing for a month, and Carter and Knight also homered.

The Mets finished a remarkable 21½ games ahead of the Phillies. They also finished with 108 victories, a figure that hadn't been exceeded in the National League since 1909. I thought of that first season when they set a record for incompetence with 120 defeats. And now they had tied a league record for achievement with the most victories in divisional play.

Can anybody here play this game? You bet.

Epilogue

I've been a very fortunate man. I was born in circumstances foreign to baseball and rose to center stage in our national pastime. My earliest desires to be a major-league ball player were satisfied, and the second half of my life has been even more thrilling than the first.

Broadcasting paralleled my career as a player. There was always a game and, with it, the chance to excel coupled with the ever-present opportunity to fail. That daily challenge continues, and with it the philosophy, which one develops as a player, that although I might not always be right, I'm never wrong. Those 0-for-4 days and bungled broadcasts can be erased the next day.

The one justification in sports is that there is a final result every day, a beginning and an end. The results are tabulated and recorded, and then the participants start over again. It's something I appreciate more than ever.

There are new people surrounding me in the booth now, and these changes have been as dramatic as those in my personal life. Broadcasting is a lot like being married. When you work with associates for 162 games—half of those on the road —it pays to be compatible.

Among the tasks undertaken by Frank Cashen in his role as

general manager of the Mets was restructuring the broadcast team. In 1982, he separated Bob Murphy and me and created different staffs for radio and television coverage. Bob was assigned to radio, a decision he accepted reluctantly because of the loss of exposure, and I was assigned to television.

One year later, Cashen hired Tim McCarver, a former major-league catcher who had broadcasting experience with the Phillies, to work alongside me in television. Then he added Steve Zabriskie for the 90 games we televised over station WOR. Fran Healey, another former catcher, joined Tim and me for the 60 or so cable telecasts we did for SportsChannel.

It had long been a contention of mine that putting two former players together and having them trade observations would be the basis of a good broadcast. It would be akin to sitting on the bench and eavesdropping on a game. And that's the way it has worked with Tim and me.

For a catcher, McCarver has one of the most engaging personalities I've ever encountered. I use that particular phrase for a reason. Tim has a genuine distaste for that expression, as when someone says, "He runs well, for a catcher."

It doesn't take much to get a reaction from Tim, which makes for a lively and entertaining broadcast. He has opinions on everything, and sometimes he is just off the wall, which adds a certain spontaneity to the proceedings. The reception of our broadcasts has been as positive as that accorded the team in recent years.

Much of the credit must be given to producer-director Bill Webb. Those who are familiar with our telecasts appreciate his imagination and creativity. The strength of television rests on the pictures punched up by the director. And there is no director in the business better than Bill.

He has also been an ideal companion, good natured and with an infectious joy of life. Hardly a day goes by when all of us do not meet after a game for what McCarver calls "an adult beverage" and discuss the latest telecast or whatever else merits our attention. Ours is a strong and united team in the booth.

Not that I don't miss past associations. One of the highlights of my last 25 years was a sunny Sunday in September 1984, when Lindsey Nelson, Bob Murphy, and I were reunited for our formal induction into the Mets' Hall of Fame. Lindsey and I both were guests on Bob's prerecorded radio show, and then I played host to Lindsey and Bob on a special "Kiner's Korner."

You might say we captured the market that day. Adding to the sense of occasion was the presence of producer Ralph Robbins. He had been with us since that first year in the Polo Grounds, and he was the floor manager for that inaugural edition of "Kiner's Korner" when Casey Stengel pulled the set down as he said goodbye. The entire day was like a family reunion.

In the ceremony before the game, as I stood there on the field before a sellout crowd, I couldn't help but reminisce about what had occurred during my years with the club. My children had participated in all the Family Days. I remembered my son Mike hitting a mammoth home run. I remembered the day Scott got locked in, not out of Shea, and I found him trying to climb over the bullpen fence in right field. I remembered the pictures of my daughter, K.C., taken with the original K.C., Casey Stengel. And I remembered the Banner Days in which they took part. There is a house in Pelham, N.Y., with "Let's Go Mets" on the floor in the spot where they painted their banner.

During our years together, I had gone through two divorces and Bob one, and Lindsey's wife had died. The Mets had lost and won and lost again. And now they were winning again. Hundreds of players had come and gone, as well as two great managers, Casey and Gil Hodges. They also were in the Mets' Hall of Fame, along with George Weiss and Johnny Murphy—general managers of the past—Joan Payson, a lovely woman who had brought National League baseball back to New York, and Bill Shea, who had worked so hard to make it possible.

It was quite an honor. And the pride in that moment and in the organization was underscored two years later when the Mets climbed all the way back to a position they hadn't held since 1969. They were champions of baseball again. The joy was equaled only by the sense of fulfillment.

Seated high above the field, in what pioneer baseball broadcaster Red Barber called "the catbird seat," I still felt a part of the action and excitement down below. Baseball had been good to me as a player. It has been even better to me as a broadcaster. After all, if it weren't for the camera and microphone, I never would have been involved in three World Series.

RALPH KINER'S MAJOR-LEAGUE RECORD

Born Oct. 27, 1922, Santa Rita, N.M.

Bats R, Throws R; 6'2", 195 lbs.

Year	Team	G	AB	H	2B	3B	HR*	HR* %	R	RBI	BB	SO	SB	BA	SA*	Pinch-Hit AB	H	G by POS
1946	Pitt	144	502	124	17	3	23	4.6	63	81	74	109	3	.247	.430	3	0	OF-140
1947	Pitt	152	565	177	23	4	**51**	9.0	118	**127**	98	81	1	.313	.639	0	0	OF-152
1948	Pitt	156	555	147	19	5	**40**	7.2	104	123	112	61	1	.265	.533	1	1	OF-154
1949	Pitt	152	549	170	19	5	**54**	9.8	116	**127**	117	61	6	.310	.658	0	0	OF-152
1950	Pitt	150	547	149	21	6	**47**	8.6	112	118	122	79	2	.272	.590	0	0	OF-150
1951	Pitt	151	531	164	31	6	**42**	7.9	**124**	109	**137**	57	2	.309	.627	0	0	OF-94, 1B-58
1952	Pitt	149	516	126	17	2	**37**	7.2	90	87	110	77	3	.244	.500	0	0	OF-149
1953	2 Teams: Pitt (41 G - .270); Chi NL (117 G - .283)																	
1953	Total	158	562	157	20	3	**35**	6.2	100	116	100	88	2	.279	.512	1	0	OF-157
1954	Chi NL	147	557	159	36	5	22	3.9	88	73	76	90	2	.285	.487	0	0	OF-147
1955	Cle	113	321	78	13	0	18	5.6	56	54	65	46	0	.243	.452	28	11	OF-87
Totals		1472	5205	1451	216	39	369	7.1	971	1015	1011	749	22	.279	.548	33	12	OF-1382 1B-58

*Numbers in bold-face type indicate league leader.